THE ABYSS *or* LIFE IS SIMPLE

The Abyss
or
Life Is Simple

READING KNAUSGAARD WRITING RELIGION

Courtney Bender / Jeremy Biles / Liane Carlson
Joshua Dubler / Hannah C. Garvey / M. Cooper Harriss
Winnifred Fallers Sullivan / Erik Thorstensen

The University of Chicago Press
CHICAGO AND LONDON

The University of Chicago Press, Chicago 60637
The University of Chicago Press, Ltd., London

Published 2022
Printed in the United States of America

31 30 29 28 27 26 25 24 23 22   1 2 3 4 5

ISBN-13: 978-0-226-82132-0 (cloth)
ISBN-13: 978-0-226-82134-4 (paper)
ISBN-13: 978-0-226-82133-7 (e-book)
DOI: https://doi.org/10.7208/chicago/9780226821337.001.0001

Library of Congress Cataloging-in-Publication Data

Names: Bender, Courtney, author. | Biles, Jeremy, author. | Carlson, Liane, author. | Dubler, Joshua, author. | Garvey, Hannah C., author. | Harriss, M. Cooper, author. | Sullivan, Winnifred Fallers, 1950- author. | Thorstensen, Erik, author.
Title: The abyss or life is simple : reading Knausgaard writing religion / Courtney Bender, Jeremy Biles, Liane Carlson, Joshua Dubler, Hannah C. Garvey, M. Cooper Harriss, Winnifred Fallers Sullivan, and Erik Thorstensen.
Description: Chicago : University of Chicago Press, 2022. | Includes bibliographical references and index.
Identifiers: LCCN 2022009752 | ISBN 9780226821320 (cloth) | ISBN 9780226821344 (paperback) | ISBN 9780226821337 (e-book)
Subjects: LCSH: Knausgård, Karl Ove, 1968- Min kamp.
Classification: LCC PT8951.21.N38 M56333 2022 | DDC 839.823/74–dc23/eng/20220304
LC record available at https://lccn.loc.gov/2022009752

⊗ This paper meets the requirements of ANSI/NISO Z39.48-1992 (Permanence of Paper).

15 JANUARY 2016 NEW YORK CITY

BENDER: . . . there's . . . the language of the abyss and chaos that comes into these passages . . .

SULLIVAN: So, the face in the sea is . . . one of those?

BENDER: Yes. I think it's a minor point but a counterpoint to the repeated story of the things we've been talking about mostly.

BILES: A counterpoint or a counterpart?

BENDER: But are we thinking of these as being part of the same? Is this stuff real? If this is real? The darkness, the topsy-turvy-ness, it's not madness, but it's these other kinds of things. Then it suggests a different kind of order for the experiences that one works toward or has labor toward. This is a very theological space.

DUBLER: Does anyone doubt that the abyss is real?

Contents

Introduction / *A Knausgaard Reading and Writing Collective* / 1

1 Keeping It All at Bay / *Courtney Bender* / 23

2 Love Tears / *Erik Thorstensen* / 39

3 Aesthetics of an Abused Child / *Liane Carlson* / 57

4 The Knausgaard Swarm / *Joshua Dubler* / 77

5 Angels / *Winnifred Fallers Sullivan* / 105

6 Incidentals (When the Slugs Come) (In the Cut) / *Jeremy Biles* / 127

7 Shaping Our Ends / *M. Cooper Harriss* / 169

Outro / *Hannah C. Garvey* / 185

Acknowledgments / 191
Index / 193

Introduction

A Knausgaard Reading and Writing Collective

The first book of Karl Ove Knausgaard's six-volume novel, *My Struggle*, is bookended by deaths, each of which opens onto the abyss. At the very beginning of *Book One*, the narrator, Karl Ove, tells us of an incident in his childhood. It comes on all of a sudden after several pages of detached speculation on what death does to the body. He begins to sum up with a paragraph beginning, "It might thus appear that death is relayed through two distinct systems. One is associated with concealment and gravity, earth and darkness, the other with openness and airiness, ether and light." This observation is followed by reflection on our common indifference to TV images of death in war, on a ski slope, and elsewhere. Mid-paragraph and mid-sentence, the detached third-person voice abruptly ceases:

> A fishing smack sinks off the coast of northern Norway one night, the crew of seven drown, next morning the event is described in all the newspapers, it is a so-called mystery, the weather was calm and no mayday call was sent from the boat, it just disappeared, a fact which the TV stations underline that evening by flying over the scene of the drama in a helicopter and showing pictures of the empty sea.[1]

With "that evening" we have left the almost clichéd rehearsal of contemporary numbness to death and are in the living room of Karl Ove's childhood.

> The sky is overcast, the gray-green swell heavy but calm, as though possessing a different temperament from the choppy, white-flecked waves that

1. Karl Ove Knausgaard, *My Struggle, Book One*, trans. Don Bartlett (Brooklyn, NY: Archipelago Books, 2012), 11. Throughout this volume we use the convention of referring to the narrator as Karl Ove and the author as Knausgaard.

> burst forth here and there. I am sitting alone watching, it is some time in spring, I suppose, for my father is working in the garden. I stare at the surface of the sea without listening to what the reporter says, *and suddenly the outline of a face emerges.* I don't know how long it stays there, a few seconds perhaps, but long enough for it to have a huge impact on me.[2]

The portent is not just about the spookiness of a child having such an experience alone. It is about what follows.

He goes to find someone to tell. The only person he can find is his father in the garden, digging:

> "I've just seen a face in the sea on TV," I say, coming to a halt on the lawn above him."
>
> "A diver?" Dad says. He knows I am interested in divers, and I suppose he cannot imagine I would find anything else interesting enough to make me come out and tell him about it.
>
> I shake my head.
>
> "It wasn't a person. It was something I saw in the sea."
>
> "Something you saw, eh," he says, taking the packet of cigarettes from his breast pocket.
>
> I nod and turn to go.
>
> "Wait a minute," he says.
>
> He strikes a match and bends his head forward to light the cigarette. The flame carves out a small grotto of light in the gray dusk.
>
> "Right," he says.
>
> After taking a deep drag, he places one foot on the rock and stares in the direction of the forest on the other side of the road. Or perhaps he is staring at the sky above the trees.
>
> "Was it Jesus you saw?" he asks, looking up at me. Had it not been for the friendly voice and the long pause before the question I would have thought he was poking fun at me. He finds it rather embarrassing that I am a Christian; all he wants of me is that I do not stand out from the other kids, and of all the teeming mass of kids on the estate no one other than his youngest son calls himself a Christian.
>
> But he is really giving this some thought.
>
> I feel a rush of happiness because he actually cares, while still feeling vaguely offended that he can underestimate me in this way.
>
> I shake my head.

2. Knausgaard, *My Struggle, Book One*, 11.

> "It wasn't Jesus," I say.
> "That's nice to hear," Dad says with a smile.[3]

By the end of *Book One*, Karl Ove's father too is dead, also owing to mysterious circumstances. In the narrative that falls between the deaths, amid scenes from a childhood sometimes remarkable, sometimes banal, the reader discovers the smiling figure in the garden to be a difficult and abusive father.

Caught in the ambivalence of his own feelings of resentment and filial obligation that he cannot shake as he negotiates his new identity of "dead man's son," Karl Ove/Knausgaard's prose takes on a vertiginous quality, opening everyday life into new revelatory possibilities. As Karl Ove begins to clean his grandmother's house–the house where his father died–he describes an experience of what he names *mise en abyme*:

> . . . there was a packet of washing powder with a picture of a child holding the identical packet, and on that, of course, there was a picture of the same boy holding the same packet, and so on, and so on. Was it called Blenda? Whatever it was called, I often racked my brains over mise en abyme, which in principle of course was endless and also existed elsewhere, such as in the bathroom mirror by holding a mirror behind your head so that images of the mirrors were projected to and fro while going farther and farther back and becoming smaller and smaller as far as the eye could see. But what happened behind what the eye could see?[4]

What happened behind what the eye could see? Dwelling within a moment carved out of experience–a flash, and yet a dwelling place for development of character and personality–the paradox of *mise en abyme* corresponds to a related problem in the study of theology and religion: the boundless within the necessary boundaries of the human.

People have described the experience of reading *My Struggle* as provoking a sense of immersion; critics consistently note that the novel's verisimilitude to life results from Knausgaard's willingness to narrate the nothing of experience–its existential white noise or blank spaces. Consider the cleaning scenes, including the memorable ones at his grandmother's house in *Book One* and his own flat in *Book Six*, or the countless times a reader is brought to observe Karl Ove prepare simple meals of potatoes and sau-

3. Knausgaard, *My Struggle, Book One*, 12–13.
4. Knausgaard, *My Struggle, Book One*, 352.

sages and coffee, or the exacting accounts of his descent into inebriation, or of lighting a cigarette. Part of what readers find so compelling is his remarkable rendering of these quotidian activities in passages that occupy as much or more "time" and space than those narrating pivotal moments of life. The books reflect many facets of time—external and internal clocks; the lingering fears, anxieties, and resentments that long belie a moment's madness; the cathartic mindlessness of cleaning up, of setting the chaos of our surroundings into some semblance of order with which we can never fully imbue the world.

Knausgaard's literary renderings of *mise en abyme* rely on a similar disjuncture. They are consuming—immersive—yet fragmentary. To put a finer point on it, the abysses consume the reader *precisely because* they are and must be fragmentary. The visions we plumb, the eternities we ponder, the experiences of narrative time and real time as somehow seeming to align, are illusions—fictions and truths that require one another to lend coherence to the disjointed relationships between the experience of a life and the necessary compromises of abridgment and fragmentation that undergird our ability to relate such experience to others.

David Tracy argues,

> We must let go of the hope for any totality system whatsoever, paying attention instead to the explosive marginal saturated fragments of our heritages. . . . [W]e should try to blast the marginalized fragments of the past alive with the memories of suffering and hope: release the frag-events from their seeming coherent place in the grand narratives we have imposed upon them, learn to live joyfully, not despairingly with and in the fragments of the traditions we *do* in fact possess.[5]

Central to Knausgaard's mission across the six books of *My Struggle* is the challenge of saturated fragments and of arranging them so that they open, even within these finite limits, into glimpses of, gestures toward, the infinite. Images converge. Captivity and freedom collapse into each other. The frames that bind us are the forms by which otherness—the unthought, the unfelt, the as-yet-unlived—appears and is made accessible. This place that we can never reach, in which all things converge, Knausgaard calls *grace*.

Knausgaard's grace: open and undifferentiated, always prospective, always receding, forever drawing us toward it in our stumbling advances. "Grace is the undifferentiated, that which is without difference.

5. David Tracy, *Fragments: The Existential Situation of Our Time*, vol. 1 of *Selected Essays* (Chicago: University of Chicago Press, 2020), 31.

It cannot be grasped by language because language is in its very nature differentiating"[6]—a form of framing, the framing of form. Grace is, impossibly, where self and other dissolve, where the frames that separate appear to break down, eradicating the lines that we draw around ourselves. I am you: a "divine thought." These words appear in *Book Six* of *My Struggle*, the final volume, which concludes as *Book One* began—with death.

At the end of *Book Six*, the writing of the narrative is enfolded into the narrative—another *mise en abyme*. The writer "catches up" with the reader and the two merge. Here the retrospection that has defined *My Struggle*, the past tense that has prevailed in the preceding six volumes, switches into the present tense, the "now." This happens in the very final moments of *Book Six*—on the last page, page 1152. Here one reads, "Now it is 7:07, and the novel is finally finished." But in the very next sentence, there's another switch. The present writing becomes the future tense. "In two hours Linda will be coming here, I will hug her and tell her I've finished, and I will never do anything like this to her and our children again." Karl Ove then muses on the upcoming interview he will have to endure. He considers with admiration the arrival of Linda's own book, which "glitters and sparkles like a star-filled night." And he looks forward to riding the train home from the interview, when he "will revel in, truly revel in, the thought that I am no longer a writer."[7]

He looks forward, switching to future tense. He looks forward, in anticipation and into the future. He looks forward to no longer being a writer. The thought in which he will revel—the thought of no longer being a writer—is a thought still and forever in the future. No matter how often the reader returns to read it, it remains on a horizon that recedes with each new reading. It is forever prospective. Life and death, past and present, converge in a future that recedes before us.

In that infinite space before death, with the death of the writer and with our own deaths before us, readers of Knausgaard encounter a space. In that space we, the group who met to read his work together and whose essays and interchanges are contained in this volume, found work to do—the difficult, often painful, but potentially transporting work of reading and writing—and of religion.

It is the nexus of limitation and infinity, uncanniness and excess, boundlessness and boundary, time and narrative, fragment and illusion in *My Struggle* that is thematized in this volume and that marks Knausgaard's achievement as a religious one. Or, put somewhat more softly, as occasions the present volume: Knausgaard's writing invites a conversation about re-

6. Karl Ove Knausgaard, *My Struggle, Book Six*, trans. Don Bartlett and Martin Aitken (Brooklyn, NY: Archipelago, 2018), 373.
7. Knausgaard, *My Struggle, Book Six*, 1152.

ligion. Is he a religious thinker? Is he religious? What would it mean to say that he is? What, as scholars of religion and as people in the world, might we wish to say about what *My Struggle* means for writing and thinking religion today?

Are these questions perverse? At the very least they would seem to cut against the Karl Ove Knausgaard who was constituted in the frenzied flurry of his initial Anglophonic reception. According to now-received wisdom, Knausgaard is a secular thinker. His method? Empirical. His world? Displayed in all its quotidian expansiveness–essentially flat. As might be clear from the preceding pages, we do not see it that way. Instead we propose that Knausgaard's work be read as religious–religious in a committedly fragmentary sense, religious in a variety of modes and forms. Passages such as those examined above explode recent renderings of Knausgaard's effects and affects as interior, bounded, deflating. Such flat renderings are also endemic to much of contemporary religious-studies writing. These renderings hold their own potentials, yet they also have shown themselves to be ill-equipped to deal with the otherness–perhaps the radical otherness–of things called religious.

By "religious" we are not committed to a definition but to fragments and gaps where this term takes on different possibilities. We mean the quotidian dimensions of ethics, practice, duty, self-craft, and meaning-making–concerns with which Knausgaard is preoccupied and which his secular critics note. And to these preoccupations we add the face in the sea, the *mise en abyme*, the fact of the uncanny, the peculiar resistances of language and of writing encountered by both hero and author–in other words, those instances where the relation of life to its fragments is much more complicated, and unsteady. As a group, we have found these dimensions of the religion of Karl Ove Knausgaard to be generative of different ways of writing and thinking religion. More than some critics acknowledge, Karl Ove the character is a self-consciously ethical man. Desperately, sometimes explicitly, as a Christian, sometimes not, he struggles in earnest to be good. Whether realized or unrealized, this experience of ethical striving often arrives with alarming intensity. In this way, the religious ethics figured in the novel provide a template for thinking about other modes of religious encounter. The religion of the novels is sensate, embodied, intuitive, felt.

Reading, for Knausgaard, is not primarily a matter of (critical) thinking but a matter of *feeling*. It is "an emotion-based way" of being in the world. Writing, he says, is about "allowing something to reveal itself."[8] We ourselves, in our reading of Knausgaard, feel that we discern his religion–

8. Knausgaard, *Inadvertent* (New Haven, CT: Yale University Press, 2018), 24.

and also, perhaps, learn to write religion. Writing religion is a matter with which scholars of religion unceasingly struggle. But it is through intuition and feeling—sensible, sensate, sensational—that practices of reading and writing religion proceed. These practices take the shape of what Birgit Meyer calls "sensational forms."[9]

In *Book Three* of *My Struggle*, Karl Ove collapses on the shale while playing in the Norway Cup. Coming to the brink of consciousness, he hears Roxy Music's song "More Than This" playing in the distance and describes feeling "as happy as I had ever been for some reason I did not comprehend but acknowledged."[10] He considers a number of "empirical" reasons for his state of mind—friends and experiences in Oslo and elsewhere. Yet he recognizes that such happiness more likely derives from something nameless: "'More than This' was so captivating and so beautiful, and around me in that pale, bluish summer night lay a whole capital, not only crowded with people, of whom I knew nothing, but also record shops with hundreds, perhaps thousands, of good bands on their shelves. . . . The traffic hummed in the distance, everywhere there was the sound of voices and laughter, and Bryan Ferry singing *More than this—there is nothing. More than this—there is nothing*."[11] The heat exhaustion moves him outside of himself, where he finds ecstatic, incomprehensible happiness that provides not only a kind of perspective on the world he inhabits but also causes him to recognize all of the music out there, in shops and clubs, through which he may ritualize these feelings in his day-to-day experience.

Karl Ove's world is laden with fugitive immanence and peppered with traces of transcendence, while Knausgaard's prose is a realm of irruption, overflow, and undoing. Yes, *My Struggle* is sometimes read as nonfiction, as a documentary of the secular life—its veritable apotheosis. Certainly, such readings are not entirely incorrect. Nonetheless, as this volume argues, there is substantially "more than this."[12]

/

It's not clear, exactly, when the group really began to coalesce. It might have been the moment when we all sat down and began to read a passage

9. Birgit Meyer, "Religious Sensations: Why Media, Aesthetics and Power Matter in the Study of Contemporary Religion" (inaugural lecture, VU University, Amsterdam, October 6, 2006).
10. Karl Ove Knausgaard, *My Struggle, Book Three*, trans. Don Bartlett (Brooklyn, NY: Archipelago Books, 2014), 398.
11. Knausgaard, *My Struggle, Book Three*, 399.
12. See *Is This All There Is?* Curated by Courtney Bender and Nancy Levene. https://tif.ssrc.org/category/is-this-all-there-is/.

from the early pages of the book. *Book One* begins, as we've said, with a broad meditation on death–sociologically, biologically, culturally. Then, abruptly, it downshifts into a description of the narrator as a young boy watching a television report of a shipwreck. He sees a face in the water, runs to tell his father, and is met by the half-mocking question, "Was it Jesus?" Reading the transcripts of this meeting, you can see the conversation loosening and picking up speed. The group members begin to riff off each other. One muses on the move from light to shadow in the text when it comes to discussing the first image of the father, standing in his garden, digging. Another picks up the thought without hesitation, observing that it's as if the father is standing in a grave. Soon members of the group are continuing each other's sentences, observing shifts in the text's tenses and color continuity among the images. Slowly, without anyone planning it, a body of thought about these texts emerged. A face we all could see, yet contended with and deciphered in distinctive ways.

The group of scholars and writers who have created this volume first met in 2016. We had gathered by happenstance, on a basis of curiosity and enthusiasm, loose ties of professional friendship, and a shared commitment to reading *My Struggle*. The particularities of Knausgaard's text shaped our meetings, as did our plan, from the beginning, to resist predetermined ends for our discussions. With one exception, we could not call ourselves experts in "religion and literature." We brought other expertise–in philosophy, aesthetics, ethnography, law–and thus different approaches to reading, different ideas about the author and text. With one exception, we were all Americans, and could read the text only in English. There were aspects of the books that escaped the Americans in the group–did you know, for example, that the region where Knausgaard had grown up is known as the Norwegian Bible belt? The one member with native knowledge of Norway had to explain.

At the time of our first meeting, only four of the novel's six volumes had been translated into English. We did not know how it would end. We assigned our meeting the title "The Religion of Karl Ove Knausgaard," even though we admitted that we did not know exactly what that "religion" signified. (Did it refer to the preoccupations of the group? Of the text? Of the hero? Or to something else yet to be discovered?) The title named our interest in exploration, a staking of a question, and a raising from the beginning of the question of how best to go about exploring an answer–or answers. In the beginning the title was a wager. It could refer to any or none of these possibilities. The details would be worked out through conversation, through the development of our patterns of reading. They emerged from the ways the questions came to overlap and in the territory we claimed that others could not abide. "The Religion of Karl Ove Knausgaard" staked a hypothesis with no presuppositions about how it would play out. What brought us together was both Knausgaard and religion.

Truth be told, we were uncertain about how to begin under the conditions that had been set, not knowing the ending of the novel, not really knowing each other very well, or, for that matter, knowing what the ends of our group discussions might be. After a first day of reading and discussing passages that had caught our attention—the face in the sea, the *mise en abyme*—our transcript of the second day of our first meeting reports as follows:

Open dispute over how to begin.
One faction wanted to just get started.
One faction was afraid of setting the tone/reference point by just jumping straight in.
An alternative is posed: Open a page, see what is there, and keep going.
One person in favor of opening a page and starting.
Another suggests it's like opening the Bible and finding a passage.
A third references Toni Morrison describing naming of children by reference to open passage.

And so we opened to a page and began to read and talk together, oriented toward ways of reading and writing that featured the indeterminate and the inadvertent.

Acts of opening a book have been used in many times and places to summon other voices—other presences, forgotten or neglected—into the present world and to find unexpected meanings. Repeated over and over, conducted collectively or alone, the practice provides a virtually inexhaustible font of possible beginnings. The act might provide an opening to a new course of writing or speaking. Or it might merely provide to the reader the necessary portion of courage to say what is already known and merely needs to be said. Or the act of opening the page might insist on the visibility of things that have been overlooked or neglected and that are only possible to consider when the reader's subject position is displaced. It draws on happenstance and contingency. In all of these ways, the practice of opening the book to a random page invited us to do something different, unexpected, and new.

Over six years we continued to meet together to try out different ways of reading and writing religion, which we debated. And continue to debate—we are still debating. The number of books and marked pages amassed over time on the tables between us, among the coffee cups and orange rinds, candy wrappers and laptops. We engaged a rapporteur, and our transcripts joined pages of metacommentary, our full digest of discussions, our essays, our rejoinders, our responses soon rivaling the heft of the novels. Within the context of these meetings, and without worrying about publication or "product," we eventually found some freedom to think and write without performing expertise. We found community and trust.

It is not incidental that our practices of reading and writing together and the games of inadvertency that we played have also occasionally been put to divinatory and religious uses. To open a book–a particular book–also means to commit to beginning "in the midst" of things and words. Such an act builds from what is present, even if that present is read in a different or unexpected way. In this way, hewing to the text was always critical to our operations. Remaining close to Knausgaard's novels and other writings was a process committed to finding common ground for addressing the religion of Karl Ove Knausgaard as a hypothesis.

We were not alone, of course, in reading these books. In his contribution to this volume, Joshua Dubler proposes the concept of the "swarm" as a way of understanding the attention to *My Struggle*. The swarm of critical attention surrounding the content of the novels and the persona of the author raised questions about our attention to an author who was regularly described by others as egotistical. There were, certainly, more than enough reasons on the surface to turn away from these books: the title, the subject(s), the author's apparent betrayal of friends, foes, and family alike. One way we dealt with this was to focus on the texts instead of the author. Indeed, a running joke among the group considered whether we ought to inform Knausgaard of our meetings or invite him to respond to our efforts. In the end we decided not to pursue such efforts–and in so doing, found a boundary that we needed to set. Although we the authors might be a part of the swarm struggling to distinguish ourselves, Dubler suggests that Knausgaard is properly thought of as "the man who would not swarm."

Placing boundaries around authorship also became an important recurring theme in our discussions. Karl Ove, the protagonist across *My Struggle*, shares a name and other attributes with Knausgaard, the author. But they cannot be the same. Were there other (implicit, or not-so-implicit) characters with these names? And other authors? Consider again the figure of the writer who effectively resigns near the end of *Book Six* ("I am no longer a writer."). Like the occasionally violent fracturing of time and space constantly recurring in these books, there seemed to be multiple "I"s. Noting this fragmentation and working together through the frames of attention and commitment that they necessitate, we found our way into otherness.

And into the monstrous. In these ways we felt the stirrings of validation for our wager on the religion of Karl Ove Knausgaard.

/

When asked "Why do I write?" Knausgaard begins where all writing, all writing of value, really begins—with nothing. No ideas, no path forward, because there is no groove to follow into the unknown. The ruts, furrows, lines of thought, and trajectories of attention that have served past pursuits must be avoided if one is to open the world, or open oneself to the world—to allow *something*—something as yet unknown, something *more* than what is already captured in our concepts, our ideas, our habits—to appear, to become "accessible."[13] Inadvertent writing of the sort Knausgaard propounds is writing that makes contact with a world as yet unburdened by "criticism and self-criticism," by "reflection and judgment," by concern for "how our thoughts and feelings will seem to others, how it will look." And yet such open writing is necessarily bounded by form, without which the unknown *something* (the more, the other, the new) will remain inaccessible. "Forms of writing" must "lead the way" in accessing the something, the more that lies within, before, and beyond the writer.[14] This is difficult work. It entails, inevitably, tripping, stumbling, struggling. It's dangerous.

"The question of why I write sounds simple, but simplicity is treacherous," Knausgaard observes in the first sentence of *Inadvertent*, "for now I have been sitting here in front of my desk in southern Sweden for three days without making any headway."[15] He's blocked up. The world he wishes to access feels closed off. Strangely, then, the birth of writing—the particular act of writing the lecture, but also writing more generally—coincides with a failure to write. In fact, the failure, the stumbling block, the blockage, stimulates the writing. Inadvertently, in *Inadvertent,* failure itself—writing about this failure to write, writing about the block—opens the way forward, past the block. It is the means of accessing the peculiar power, the flow, the energies of writing itself. Once Knausgaard finally begins writing, the pathway is marked out—"the material [takes] a certain direction, excluding all other possible paths"—even if he "still [doesn't] know what lies ahead."[16] The end remains obscure, the conclusion imminent but unforetold—as inevitable but unpredictable as the formation of clouds.[17] Failure to write is

13. Knausgaard, *Inadvertent*, 40.
14. Knausgaard, *Inadvertent*, 39.
15. Knausgaard, *Inadvertent*, 1.
16. Knausgaard, *Inadvertent*, 39-40.
17. See Knausgaard, *My Struggle, Book One*, 388, 419.

the starting point for at once accessing and capitulating to the excessive forces and flow of writing itself. Blockage presages the flow; the tide must first be stemmed so that its energies may accrue and be released in the form of text.

One is reminded of the short passage in *Book Three* of *My Struggle* that finds a preteen Karl Ove in the forest with his friend Geir. They clamber up onto "a tall pine tree on its side," where, balancing on the trunk of the fallen tree, they pull down their pants, squat with asses out, and defecate onto the ground below. Dropping turds like "bombs" produces a "wonderful feeling" in the boys: exuberant release, cathartic freedom.

What is remarkable here is not the fact that these boys take delight in shitting in the woods–the pleasurable thrill of transgression that comes from doing outdoors what we are taught must be done inside, behind closed doors. Rather, what makes the scene salient, and what makes it something of an allegory for both writing and religion–for Knausgaard's writerly and religious *experience*–is the further dynamic of boundary transgression that Karl Ove concocts around his defecation: a doubled transgression to redouble his pleasure. Knausgaard describes the ritual that forms on the basis of a yearning for an ever more excessive delight. It is a ritual arrived at inadvertently, emerging from an intuition that it might lead to greater ecstasies. An experiment, one might say, in rapturous discharge. Driven by something beyond the pleasure principle, by the desire to produce an exceedingly pleasurable–indeed ecstatic–defecatory experience, Karl Ove stumbles upon a gesture, soon formalized, by which he withholds his stool, "sometimes . . . for days," such that the painful accumulation of excrement promises a more pleasurable catharsis.

> When I really did have to shit, so much that I could barely stand upright but had to bend forward, I had such a fantastic feeling in my body if I didn't let nature take its course, if I squeezed the muscles in my butt together as hard as I could and, as it were, *forced* the shit back to where it came from. But this was a dangerous game, because if you did it too many times the turd ultimately grew so big it was impossible to shit it out. Oh Christ, how it hurt when such an enormous turd had to come out! It was truly unbearable, I was convulsed with pain, it was as if my body were exploding with pain, AAAAAAGGGHHH!! I screamed OOOOOHHH, and then, just as it was at its very worst, suddenly it was out.
>
> Oh, how good that was!
>
> What a wonderful feeling it was!
>
> The pain was over.
>
> The shit was in the pan.

> Everything was peace and light throughout my body. Indeed, almost so peaceful that I didn't feel like getting up and wiping my bum. I just wanted to sit there.
>
> But was it worth it?[18]

Sometimes, he tells us, the impacted shit is of such quantity and firmness that it requires delving into his ass with his finger in an endeavor to bring forth the stool. With great pain, in a playful but laborious act of anal masturbation, he "maneuver[s] the shit" and "widen[s] the passage," allowing for evacuation.

But is it worth it? Is the ecstasy of release, the rapturous and literal disclosure of what was within him, worth the "pain," the "dread," and indeed the "terror" that Karl Ove goes on to describe in this passage?

Writing–which, by this allegorical reading of Knausgaard's ritual, is revealed to be more like shitting than some among us may like to admit–is a painful game. But without this pain of accumulation and the struggle for release, there is no pleasure; without the work of playing at boundaries, the excessive, violent pleasure of being opened up to the beyond–of accessing the "illimitable that dwells within us," the otherness that is the inner self–the bringing into contact, the convergence, of the inner with the outer world is impossible.[19] This is the necessary matter (literally and in every sense) of boundary play. Knausgaard's defecatory ritual is also a writerly method for encountering the excessive otherness within the self and bringing it into contact with the otherness of the outside world.

And "what a method it was!" exclaims Karl Ove. It is a ritual method born in the wilds of the woods but brought home, to the bathroom. Much as Karl Ove glimpses the divine in the everyday, the other within the b/anal, so too does this act of transgressing boundaries (shitting outdoors, in the openness of the forest) come home, to the domestic toilet. But for Knausgaard, it is even and especially in the home, within the everydayness of the everyday, that passages are opened, widened. Contraction and dilation, withholding and release: these are the dynamics of the writer seated at a desk, or on the pot.

Knausgaard's method, this inadvertent work-play that finds form in the ritual transgression of boundaries, moves against simply "letting nature take its course."[20] This is to recognize that it takes labor to give birth to what is given–the givenness of reality itself. That the ritual is punctuated by a

18. Knausgaard, *My Struggle, Book Three*, 105.
19. Knausgaard, *Inadvertent*, 43.
20. "In nature there are no frames." Knausgaard, "Frames," in *Autumn* (New York: Penguin Press, 2017), 45.

religious (blasphemous?) ejaculation—"Oh Christ!"—may seem incidental, but surely Knausgaard teaches us that attention to the incidental can reveal hints of the infinite, the sublime, the "illimitable."[21]

/

As we read, talked, and wrote together, we sometimes found that the texts struck us uncannily as falling directly within our ambit of disciplinary discussions about religion. Indeed, our sense was that the aspects of excess, odd and strange boundaries, fragments, enthusiasm/swarm, *mise en abyme*, and so forth, that we found in the books sounded all too familiar. At first, we thought that the sense that Knausgaard was speaking our language—that he had read what we read, and knew what we knew—might be the result of our having lived in the same times, or perhaps produced by our imaginations. With Knausgaard's novels, we not only discovered but, sometimes in the same moment, actively created from these texts religious ideas, associations, and concerns—concerns that might have been miles away from the thoughts of other readers or even (and especially) of the author himself. Yet, wasn't that his point?

As additional volumes of *My Struggle* were published (and sometimes delayed), our reading expanded. Following our discussion of *Book Five*, publication of the English translation of *Book Six* was postponed, leading us—again, inadvertently—to focus instead on Knausgaard's second novel, *A Time for Everything*. We were stunned to observe it conclude with an episode that might as well have been included in *My Struggle*—almost as if *My Struggle* might be imagined as having emerged as a new world from Knausgaard's biblical meditations in *A Time for Everything*.

In reading *A Time for Everything* we also came to see that our uncanny sense of familiarity was not entirely of our own creation. We found Knausgaard again engaging with our bibliographies, and then in *Book Six* as well—familiar images and themes broke in upon us. We were not under a collective hallucination. The space between us and our texts and those of the author was collapsing. This collapse suggested another way in which we might understand Knausgaard to be a religious writer and his work (*My Struggle* in particular, but other work such as *A Time for Everything* as well) to be religious writing. Time will tell, but if, according to one well-worn notion, a classic is a text that furnishes the occasion for limitless discussion and interpretation, our years of joyful toil would suggest *My Struggle* to be a worthy candidate for the designation.

21. Knausgaard, *Inadvertent*, 43.

Somewhat closer to home, we might consider *My Struggle*'s candidacy as a *religious* classic. In *The Analogical Imagination*, David Tracy describes a classic as effecting "nothing less than the disclosure of a reality we cannot but name truth."[22] He proceeds to describe the experience of both the permanence and excess of meaning of a classic as one of both participation and distanciation, the interpretation of which is necessarily public. In this way we might understand the relationship between Knausgaard and Karl Ove, or the "I" of *My Struggle* viz. the "I" spoken (even if silently) by the reader in the phenomenon of reading. Furthermore, we begin to see ways that the novel facilitates the collapsing of experience–the illusion of immersion in the narrative experience of cleaning house, or cooking meatballs, or mowing the yard–with the knowledge that such immersion can never be total. It must always remain fragmented. The religious classic, Tracy argues, involves radical participation in a whole that is not one's self. And yet, he insists, the whole should never be mistaken for something stable and known.

In 1981, the religious classic was, for Tracy, already a capacious category, and the border between classic and might-be classic, as well as between the plain old classic and the religious classic, was fuzzy and porous. Forty years later, having apparently abandoned his often-announced project to write a book on God, Tracy has published a two-volume series of essays entitled *Fragments* and *Filaments*. Like the classics of his earlier work, the fragments he touts also possess the potential "to transport," as Erik Thorstensen said in his description of the invitation of Knausgaard's work.[23] These frag-events "negatively shatter or fragment all totalities, even as they are positively open to Infinity."[24] They point readers toward a kind of immersive totality that remains necessarily contained–particular and yet universal. Readers recognize Karl Ove's experiences as their own. They see in his descriptions of the phenomenology of mundane life something familiar, haunting, uncanny. They find a sense of common ground with the truth of an invented other. Knausgaard's religiousness, along with that of *My Struggle*, emerges from the unlikely, unexpected imbrication of author and reader with a text as a point of convergence. To call this perception an illusion, a fiction, does not mean that it is not also real.

One thing that makes these books so compelling–jarring, even–is Knausgaard's boundary-work: that is, the way he constructs and plays across frames and boundaries between narrator and reader; Karl Ove and

22. David Tracy, *The Analogical Imagination: Christian Theology and the Culture of Pluralism* (New York: Crossroad, 1981), 108.
23. See Thorstensen's chapter in this volume.
24. Tracy, *Fragments*, 1.

Knausgaard (and I); narrative and real life; narrative and time; reading and experience; artifice and reality. For the most part, they retain recognizable distance (even as we sometimes marvel at their proximity in Knausgaard's hands)—until the end, that is. Until *Book Six*. Early on in *Book Six* the narrator enters the narrative in a more proximate way. It is arguably always there. The ordeal with his uncle Gunnar, the ramifications of fame and publicity, the malign effect this has on Karl Ove's family—especially through his wife Linda's mental collapse. There are other fleeting moments as well. In earlier instances there's a conscious sense of writing, of invention, as when Karl Ove goes to the office apartment, lights a cigarette, writes, and observes. This moment and these observations nevertheless take place in the past tense. As readers, we encounter them in a kind of present, but they are rendered as *fait accompli*. In *Book Six* Karl Ove sits down at the computer, short on available time, and types. The effect here becomes something like autoscription—the self-aware, self-generating text that doesn't just produce the illusion of firsthand experience but, theoretically at least, puts us on the front lines of creation.

The gradual erosion of boundaries and boundary-work renders for the reader a kind of glimpse into a more eternal present. It provides an arcing glimpse into (and out of) the possibility of limitlessness, hewing creation with creation. There is a kind of oscillation: everything blurs together—the times he writes about and recounts, his moods of wonder and loss, himself as author and as character—and then there are breaks and blank spaces. A section of narrative might go on for hundreds of pages then stop, bookended by empty lines, only for the narrator to pick up on another topic or in another decade. There are interruptions in moods and modes of thinking that are never integrated into his more familiar attitudes of philosophical reflection, absorption in sensory detail, transcendent rapture, or melancholic memory.

One such break that moved us as a collective comes in *Book Four*, which is largely devoted to a more-or-less chronological account of his year as a student teacher in the far north of Norway. The narrator recounts an encounter with a snowplow one night while walking. The passage itself is surrounded by two hard returns. Nothing connects it to what went before; nothing connects it to what comes after. "One night I was out walking, on my way to the school, when a bulldozer drove up behind me," the passage begins.

> It had a snowplow mounted on the front, the snow flew alongside into mounds by the road, an orange light flashed from the roof, thick black smoke belched from an exhaust pipe at the front. The man driving didn't

> look at me as he passed. Some way up the hill he stopped, with the engine still running. As I came alongside he set off again. He drove at the same speed as I walked. I watched him, he was staring straight ahead, and I shivered with unease, the vibrating, roaring, scraping, flashing vehicle shook my soul. I walked faster. He drove faster. I turned right, he turned right. I turned round, he drove straight on, then bugger me if he didn't turn round as well, and as I reached the hill leading to the school he was right behind me again. I set off at a run, this was scary, because around us everything was lifeless and black, the village was asleep, it was just us two outside, me and some mad snowplow man chasing me. I ran, but I was no match for him, he accelerated and followed me right into the school playground. I unlocked the door, my heart pounding in my chest, would he follow me in here as well?
>
> From the staffroom I watched him steadily and methodically clearing the playground of snow, it took him perhaps a quarter of an hour, before he turned and drove back down to the village.[25]

The passage is a classic example of the uncanny. What could be more homely and familiar in Norway than a snowplow in the familiar environs of school? And here it is, rendered strange in the cold of the polar night—but even then the passage is also in some ways a defiance of expectations. It *ought* to be a comic piece; that would be in some ways the logical move of a narrator looking back on all six-foot-three inches of his nineteen-year-old self, sprinting through a playground, convinced that the snowplow has become a monster. Certainly, Knausgaard is painfully aware of how ridiculous Karl Ove's younger self can be. But the laughter never comes and is never even implied. The narrator is utterly straight-faced in his terror. He never admits to embarrassment, he never admits to shame, he just stands at the window for far longer than is necessary to realize his mistake, watching the man placidly scrape the playground clean. The piece remains firmly in one time period, with none of the chiasmatic twining of different narrative temporalities. Then it ends and is never commented on again.

In a written response to the passage, which was pre-circulated with others prior to our first meeting, Courtney Bender singled out this passage as an example of ethnographic surplus. "It doesn't appear to fit in with anything, it appears to be part of the book's surplus. I am thinking of Bakhtin's notion of surplus—to quote his interpreter, Gary Saul Morson, 'real life, true historicity, and genuine individuality are to be found in what is left over . . . after all rules are applied and all generalizations are exhausted.'

25. Karl Ove Knausgaard, *My Struggle, Book Four,* trans. Don Bartlett (Brooklyn, NY: Archipelago Books, 2015), 419.

In that surplus we find 'the singular world in which we create, become aware, contemplate, in which we live and in which we die.'" Surplus has a meaning beyond just "more stuff"—it makes available to the author/reader/hero "sides of a human being not previously assimilable from monological positions, including a real sense of eventness and freedom." It indicates or leaves open other events; it brings an indeterminacy to the work. The effects of these passages—how are they meant to mean something? do they? might they resonate or mean in many ways?—is a compositional question that is left open.

/

It is somewhat paradoxical for a group of scholars to spend many pages of writing and long days of discussing the writings on a novel that ends up with the narrator/protagonist proudly—even exuberantly—declaring that he is no longer a writer/author. Is not-writing the end of writing?

The rather coincidental nature of early choices of orientating ourselves toward different freely chosen formats, places, and media are now felt by us as deeply affecting our freedom of choosing the place and the format for the last encounters and discussions over Knausgaard. Freely exploring a theme through attention to how texts produce lives and life produces texts has in time become *the way we do things*.[26] Writing religion or writing on religion is fundamentally challenging as we, critically speaking, create the phenomenon that we analyze. In the context of *My Struggle* and/or Knausgaard, we have transformed these texts into religious concerns.

We must write. That is a Knausgaardian imperative. We must write, we must *give in* to writing, acceding to what Knausgaard describes as the "blind" force and "merciless" flow of writing. Whether one waits for a subject to announce itself, to emerge into one's perceptual field, or whether one "stumble[s] over" it "in the dark," writing "comes along inadvertently"—as a matter of a chance encounter in the writer's field of attention.[27] It happens—must happen, Knausgaard tells us—without calculation and without critical intention.

There is a religious dimension at the heart of literary expression: we are only for a while; it's all so much, yet we can imagine so much more, and what our imaginations conjure is but a speck as compared to those things

26. As Jonathan Z. Smith showed in "The Bare Facts of Ritual," ritual and routinization follow each other closely—regardless of how one values change or routine, permanence or randomness. See "The Bare Facts of Ritual," *History of Religions* 20, nos. 1/2 (1980): 112-27, https://doi.org/10.1086/462864.
27. Knausgaard, *Inadvertent*, 28.

not yet dreamed of in our shared philosophical lore. Our project here has been to build community around these limits, to combine our efforts, and to embrace the possibility for new dreams beyond the assumptions we brought individually to Knausgaard's writing. In short, we sought to think together in excess of our philosophy, to allow these novels—fragmentary though they must be—to gesture toward a more infinite universe that emerges from the conversation and friendship of our common endeavor.

What did we do? We read (a lot). We talked (a lot), and laughed quite a bit. We ate and drank, we traveled, we walked (together and in solitude), and some of us swam. We played with ideas, with interpretations. . . . We played across boundaries of all sorts. We gave ourselves permission. We risked things (ideas, interpretations . . .). We thought freely. We trusted each other with our thoughts. We disagreed. We got contentious sometimes. We carried on. We thought ourselves into confusion and sometimes into something approaching clarity. We disclosed (the texts, ourselves). We shared memories, stories (we shared the stories Knausgaard has written, we shared stories from our own lives). We wrote a great deal (about the texts, about ourselves, about ourselves in relation to the texts). We developed friendships. We read together such that reading alone became reading-alongside. We have been critical (of Knausgaard, of his work, of each other's work) but not condemning. We have been enthusiasts whose enthusiasms have intensified with the analysis of the texts that generated those enthusiasms. We discovered? invented? many Knausgaards. We have not even begun to comprehend "the religion/s of Karl Ove Knausgaard." We have all, it may rightly be said, experienced *gratitude*—for Knausgaard, for each other, for the time-space in which we could share the gift of reading-writing-thinking together. We delighted in the sense of being *up to something*. We cultivated fascination. We became, in ways, more attentive—to the texts, the worlds of the text, and the worlds beyond the text. We opened worlds. We became worlds. We explored those worlds. We entered each other's worlds. We discussed and, though without always saying so, we variously defined, deformed, dismissed, and displayed "religion/s"—of Knausgaard, beyond Knausgaard. We bonded along elective affinities. We rejuvenated (our) pleasure in (academic) collegiality. We became—may we say the word?—a kind of *community*.

With this volume we invite our readers to read and write with us. About Knausgaard and Karl Ove—and also about religion.

15 JANUARY 2016 NEW YORK CITY

THORSTENSEN: What I would like to hear more on from you, Josh, is strangely similar to what you asked of me. It is connected to the issue of Dostoevsky and significance versus meaning. You're right about what's important: it is not meaning but the feeling of meaning. . . . What is this feeling of meaning? . .

I would also mention that you write: "the highest goods are found not in transcendence but in immanence. Not in truth and meaning but in forgetting and fucking around." I was thinking about this . . . and also about another thing that Knausgaard immerses himself in: writing. So, is writing an immanent activity? Can it be classified among those activities? . . .

DUBLER: I think I'm wrong about that . . . the fucking around issue . . . writing is something higher . . . when it is good, it's immanent . . . when it's bad, it is transcendent . . .

In the final analysis, I think that Knausgaard's philosophy is anti-meaning. What do we make of that? On the one hand, there is a kind of naturalism, or realism, or I would say ethnographic fidelity. He's trying to get the world right. There is a kind of ethnographic fidelity. Then I take him to be like, again and again, like Heidegger, not Descartes. . . . Intentionality, meanings that are attached to things, this is not actually . . . Yes, we do these things in practice, but they need not be privileged. This practice of talking about these books, given the nature of this practice, is going to tip the scales in the direction of those kinds of meanings. Interpretation takes a surface and extracts a depth. But there is another side. What I'm using as shorthand with Heidegger—this ethnographic fidelity—could also be a form of bad faith. The book could be a confession of bad faith. I mean that the disavowal, the other side of the prelapsarian condition whether it was childhood or premodernity, when the world was full and enchanted. We see that the world is still saturated, the world is not so shitty now, yet the narrator insists that it is. The narrator gets it wrong–that is the bad faith. This could tack back to the ethnographic fidelity. He's fucking up. His insistence that the world is not full of meaning . . .

SULLIVAN: He's not always insisting that the present is without meaning. Sometimes he tries that on and sometimes he takes it off. I think that view is voiced at various points, at different levels, but I would resist the notion that this is somehow the attitude of these books or the attitude of what we can discern of the author of these books.

DUBLER: That is absolutely right. I'm speaking out of the Dostoevsky passage in particular . . . in which he seems to resign not only existentialism to childhood, but also resigns the kind of cultural criticism that he's doing in those passages.

SULLIVAN: Isn't that one of the problems of picking out these paragraphs? *Then there are all the other paragraphs.*

/ 1 /

Keeping It All at Bay

Courtney Bender

When I was twelve or thirteen, my mother's father pulled out an old movie projector and my uncles Randy and Dick sorted through the shoeboxes filled with film. As I recall, the purpose of this was to prove to my sisters and me, and all assembled cousins, that in the summer of 1958 a juvenile black bear had wandered through their vacation cabin in Banff "while the men were out golfing" and that my sixteen-year-old mother had grabbed the movie camera in time to film its ambling through the hallway. They found the reel, and we laughed with surprise when the bear came into focus.

Of course, now that the projector was all set up on the piano bench, we had to see more. The movies were all black-and-white, all shot in the late 1950s. The cousins sat in rapt attention: Here was my grandfather, graceful and tall, figure skating on a pond in the cattle field. And here was my mother and her brothers sledding down the big hill by great-uncle Howard's, with a bunch of their first cousins. Here was a summer birthday and my wiry, fearsome great-grandfather eating an ice cream cone.

Then here was another one, the subject of which appeared to be a half dozen especially handsome Angus cattle. A group of men, one of whom was my grandfather, were sizing them up. A few dogs ambled and sniffed in the foreground. "And there's Al," said Randy. The camera had caught a man standing alone in its frame. He was smiling and then waving at the camera. We could see that his smile was a bit skewed, and that his posture was also. In fact everything about Al was aslant, a point that became even more clear as the camera pulled back and we could see him standing along with the other men. He had taken up their pose, with hips slightly forward and arms crossed, his head gently nodding. But his stance wasn't quite right, he kept twisting his torso—much as children do when waiting impatiently or inattentively. We saw a dog run up to Al and lick his hand, and then watched as Al bent over to pet it, and one of the men snuck up behind him and tipped his hat off his head. Al immediately snapped upright, his face suddenly pinched, and hands and fists went whirling. To us children watching it appeared that an inhuman power had erupted into the frame. The camera stepped quickly away from Al's swinging arms just as the film ended, abruptly spooling out, leaving the white screen. My cousins and I looked around at the others. Randy set to work rewinding the film without commentary. The grown-ups didn't seem to have been much bothered by what we had all just witnessed, but they didn't have anything funny to say either. Mimie said, "They always did pick on him like that."

None of us cousins were brave enough to ask aloud who Al was, but we pieced it together later that afternoon. It came to us as we talked that this man was our great-grandmother's brother, our grandmother's uncle. He must have been at least seventy years old in the film, though he had appeared much younger. None of us had ever seen a picture of him before, and I don't think any of us knew much about him. So during the long car trip home, my sister worked up the courage to ask my mother what had happened to Al. "He died about ten years before you were born," Mom said. No, my sister persisted, what happened to him? Why was he like that? He had been kicked by a horse as a child, she said, though she wasn't really sure and perhaps he had had his problems from birth. Mom remembered that he was mostly very sweet, and was good with the animals on the farm. But she and her brothers were regularly reminded never to tease him.

/

In *Book Five* of *My Struggle*, our hero finds work for a summer on a ward of an institute where adult men with severe mental impairments live. It is the young Karl Ove's job to help the full-time staff on the ward to take care of the men: to make sure they get dressed and wash, to give them breakfast, to clean up after and around them, to take them to the "work" and all of the various activities that surround the residents with a "semblance of the meaning lives outside had." On weekends he spends time with his girlfriend, who lives nearby with her family. In the middle of the summer the institute holds a disco in its gymnasium, and Karl Ove works through the party, keeping tabs on the residents from his ward while music plays and snacks and sodas are served, and observing the residents' actions. These actions seem to his seventeen-year-old self to be wrong in every respect.[1]

The disco is not a failed ritual. Failure does not begin to account for what Karl Ove sees. The happenings at the disco reside outside of the frame where we can speak of ritual failure. In the disco and in the institution, we gain an image, a sliver image, of an entire world of people for whom rituals as we understand them do not take, where routines and other words like that have no meaning. That is, a world where our vision of a ritual's constitutive work, the separation and reorganization of inside and outside, exterior and interior, meaning and action, has no traction. Yet the teenaged Karl Ove sees the disco only as a simulated ritual, and these passages set forth at the beginning the anxieties and anger elicited by this mismatch, returning him and the reader to the topic, broadly, of the relation of the interior and exterior, the need for such distinctions and the trouble at both maintaining them and arriving at the right relation between them. This topic is recurrently complicated by the blurring of author and hero. Here in the faux-discotheque, then, Karl Ove finds himself confronting a world that is alien and disturbing precisely because the very ground of this expected separation is absent, and its familiar (if hardly comforting) complications that make up a life have no value at all.

Everything about the disco is wrong according to the hero—and in several competing ways. At first Karl Ove doesn't seem quite sure what most aptly indexes the wrongness. We see him working this through. But the sense grows for the hero that nothing that happens in the darkened room has the capacity to transform the people into the youthful souls for which the ritual is meant. There is no way for the people in the room to be carried by the ritual of dance and snacks toward an understanding of the disco's given purpose, message, meaning, affect. Or even to be carried to a sense that there is a meaning or a proper affect. The simulated disco cannot perform this ritual transformation, any more than the institute's efforts to offer daily work to these same residents will transform them into bankers or teachers.

This isn't the fault of the ritual. There is no fault. This is the fact of the residents' being. Why should he feel bad about this?

But he does. The immediate objection to this abnegation of meaning on their behalf goes like this: Really, now, how can Karl Ove know what another person can or cannot find pleasurable, what they can and cannot

1. Karl Ove Knausgaard, *My Struggle, Book Five*, trans. Don Bartlett (Brooklyn, NY: Archipelago Books, 2016). Passages quoted in this section are from pages 344–48.

experience? How can he even presume to know? How does he know what a person like Hans Olav does or does not find important, much less presume that he finds nothing important in the way that he does? Especially a person whose life experience is (we might put it kindly) radically different? How can he be so callow as to think this? And, with the Beach Boys' "Good Vibrations" playing in the background, no less? It seems like a failure of his own imaginative possibility to say that the only real value of a disco was what the youth of Bergen imagined for it: "dreams of romantic love, charged with the future and potential." Given that it is none other than Karl Ove handing down this pronouncement–the man who has throughout this novel encountered a recurrent, maybe inevitable failure of ritual praxis to live up to its *doxa*–isn't it all a bit rich?

Knausgaard invites this volley of objections to his observations, but he does not bend. In the suspended time of the disco, Karl Ove looks around and is startled by Alf "staring into his eyes." He experiences a fleeting, spine-tingling sense that Alf had second sight and that Alf could see directly into his "innermost thoughts and hated [him] from the bottom of his heart." But then Alf drops his eyes, and he–and Karl Ove–return to their rightful places: Alf to a churn of bodies and actions that have absolutely no communicative value, and Karl Ove to his anxiously protective observations. There is no "otherworldliness" in Alf's vision, redemptive or otherwise. It would be a further embarrassment on Karl Ove's part to cling to this idea. No matter what else it might be, this world of Alf and Hans Olav is outside of the quotidian. The particular kind of failure that Karl Ove encounters in the residents is their incapacity to join in the frisson of the mismatched interior and exterior (the struggle of *doxa* and praxis)–that is, that thing that establishes Knausgaard's quotidian.

Does the novelist's (and hero's) decision to present the residents' lives as entirely outside this project of meaning-making open up a new angle on the question of what it means to be good? At the end of this passage the hero reflects, "I wanted to be a good person, full of empathy for those worse off from me, but if they came too close, what I felt for them was contempt or anger, as if their deficiencies touched something deeper inside me." What is that something deeper inside that provokes contempt? Maybe it is empathy itself, its hope of connection, that protects oneself from that something deeper inside–a different sense of the self, or sense of the good–something unknown to and radically different from the self that our hero cultivates. A different self or part of the self that can only be identified and built by an abandonment of the normal life of meaning. A different good that is built on a sense that for some, or maybe many others, life's meaning does not depend upon or even acknowledge the existence of Karl Ove's world. In which case, it is necessary to reject the work of translating freakish and grotesque bodies into normal human life.

MANY THINGS HAD HAPPENED

The disco is over, and Karl Ove stands in the dark, misty parking lot waiting for his girlfriend to arrive in her car. "I wanted to be a good person."[2]

The refrain repeats and reverberates with the scenes in *Book Two*, where Karl Ove and his family are in a church celebrating the christening of his eldest daughter, and where he has, to the surprise of all, stood up with his cousin Jan Olav and walked to the communion bar.[3] Why had he done it? It was "for some reason."

> For some reason I got up and followed suit. Knelt before the altar, had a wafer placed on my tongue, drank the communion wine, was given the blessing, got up, and went back, with Mom's Kjartan's, Yngve's, and Geir's eyes on me, disbelieving to varying degrees.
>
> Why had I done it?
>
> Had I become a Christian?

For some reason Karl Ove got up. The passage offers many explanations—the first suggests that it was a compulsion act, following his cousin, Jan Olav, wanting to participate in his goodness, and all of the actions that were part of that goodness. Jan Olav "was a whole person, a good person, and in some way it also drew me up the aisle as well and down on my knees: I so much wanted to be whole. I so much wanted to be good."[4] These simple sentences ("I so much wanted . . .") are the culmination of a desire that has been parceled out in half-hour intervals of the preceding forty pages as the hero finds himself in a state of ongoing movement, travel, conversations, schedules, and interactions that are orchestrated into this event of the christening. The pressure breaks with the communion service and christening. The ritual does its work. But it also seems that this coming together is not just made real in the text in these admissions of desire ("I so much wanted. . . .") but in the hierophanic announcement embedded within six very brief lines that punctuate the longer passages. Extracted from the longer narrative in which they appear, they can be read as follows:

2. Knausgaard, *My Struggle, Book Five*, 348.
3. Karl Ove Knausgaard, *My Struggle, Book Two*, trans. Don Bartlett (Brooklyn, NY: Archipelago Books, 2013). Passages quoted in this section are from pages 438–41.
4. Knausgaard, *My Struggle, Book Two*, 441.

Why had I done it?

Had I become a Christian?

Many things had happened.

However, the sacred.

Flesh and blood.

Everything that changes and is the same.

Read together, these lines dissolve Karl Ove's desire for goodness into something else, and another world surfaces. Such dissolution turns our attention from the alignments of praxis and *doxa* shaped in this church ritual and toward something else that has pulsed through the pages and stories that lead up to the christening. "Many things had happened. However, the sacred. Flesh and blood." We find ourselves not in the world of the church but back in the disco again—where the ritual has not repaired the mismatch of belief and practice, inside and outside, and so appears to touch something outside or beyond the world of ritual normalcy and its complications, a place where there is still flesh and blood, still the sacred, and where time stretches in a different way.

"I had thought a lot about this," Karl Ove says. "It was about flesh and blood, it was about birth and death, and we were linked to it through our bodies and our blood, those we beget and those we bury, constantly, continually, a storm blew through our world and it always had. . . ." But still the storm in the world is constant and continuous, and in this long time, where "everything . . . changes and is the same," nothing—nothing at all—can be truly catastrophic.

How different is the sacred that opens up here, in these spaces and lines, from other kinds of sacred time more familiar and prosaic—for example, a calendar that is marked by auspicious moments or days when there is an expectation of a disturbance or change from the routine of "bodies and blood," begetting and burying. How different is this sacred from the kinds of time marked by cataclysm or apocalypse, or even a belief in the sacred's numinous otherness. And how different is this from the quotidian events of any daily life, including that of the institute where Alf lives, and where a flat and secular time and its rituals makes sure that the unpredictability of its daily violence and trauma are never misrecognized as otherworldly, sacred, or meaningful.

Karl Ove then turns to reflect on his father's funeral. "The funeral, the ritual itself, was almost physical, something to hold on to for me. It turned Dad's life, so miserable and destructive toward the end, into a life." The funeral (and the ritual of communion that summoned his reflection upon it) pulls Karl Ove's father back into time and out of the mismatched world. That is what Karl Ove at seventeen expects rituals to do, and that is what makes the disco so horrible. This is also what Karl Ove in his early thirties hopes a ritual can do: in this case to translate his father's "life into a life," replacing if not excising memories where he was outside of the order of things, only monstrous surface and meaningless gaze. But in the process of accepting this kind of ritual world, Karl Ove has sacrificed other worlds that this monstrousness might have opened (even if their possibilities would have remained entirely otherwise to Karl Ove). And here, it seems, we see the very outlines take shape for the novel's hero: Where being good has any meaning at all, for the author and for the hero, and wherein he comes—as a secular person—to know the good in, among other things, the obliquely framed contrast he offers between the old and new testaments. The Old and New Testaments. A variety of arcane "sacrificial practices" are cast aside, and the wildness of the Hebrew scripture turned into the "newer" temporality. What remains is "just a swirl of dust, [that] brought us to what was always there and never changed."

RETURNING TO THE DISCO

In the corner of the gymnasium, one of the residents named Hans Olav screws and unscrews a wall lamp. Karl Ove observes "This is deeply disturbing. Disturbing because . . ." A reader may expect this to be disturbing because we know that Hans Olav is unpredictably violent. There has been so much foreboding in earlier scenes that we anticipate that screwing and unscrewing a lamp will lead to a next moment where the bulb is smashed on the ground, flung across the room, or where Hans Olav shorts a fuse or electrocutes himself. But these dangers are not what disturb Karl Ove. Instead Knausgaard veers, and the line reads "This is deeply disturbing. Disturbing because all these misshapen bodies and crippled souls who had been trundled into the discotheque . . . didn't experience any dreams, any yearnings, any electric charges."[5] We are back on firm, familiar ground of disturbance. But where has the danger of unpredictable outside violence gone?

Of course, it hasn't gone anywhere. It is still there. Knausgaard has

5. Knausgaard, *My Struggle, Book Five*, 345.

turned us only slightly away from it. Real rupture, mayhem, violence remain; the jagged edge continues to appear.

I think back to the unspoken question that sat alongside my sister's query to my mother. "What happened to Al?" was an effort to search out how my mother and her siblings had lived alongside the grotesque. Such a question had never occurred to us. It had certainly not occurred to me that such a figure as this had marked my mother's childhood. What did the silence of my uncles and grandmother on this matter say? Was this silence embarrassment, or was this diffidence a trace of a strategy, a collective unspoken that resisted an effort to recuperate such a life through quotidian strategies? Or was it merely the world that they accepted as real and given, to be suffered, flesh and blood? Or was it something else that my sisters could not fathom? Certainly my mother could not answer this question with a story about how Al came to be Al.

A TIME FOR EVERYTHING

In January 2018 Joshua Dubler wrote pages on how he read and thought about Knausgaard's *A Time for Everything*, which begin like this:

> I can't be the only one here for whom the sheer mass of unvarnished *religion* in *A Time for Everything* was grounds for some uneasiness. Angels, biblical archetypes, a remote scriptural tone that feels at times like a cruel theological argument: it was a challenge for me to find a home in these pages.
>
> Because of what precisely does one fail to connect to a work of literature? With the language of "failure" I tip my hand. The problem is me of course: the failure to pay proper attention, the failure, one might say, of insufficient devotion (or, somewhat more mystically and less judgmentally, the failure to properly intersect with a propitious reading moment). But my experience of failure in this case might also signal something about the aesthetics of the secular.
>
> Like God to Moses on Sinai, religion, I think—and I think Knausgaard would agree—is something best approached obliquely. For when the stuff of religion is thematically centered and one is forced to confront it head-on, a secular reader such as myself is set up for failure much in the way that church or synagogue sets one up for failure. Where the promise of the divine is ostentatiously intimated, one can bet on bumping up against a wall of boredom, alienation, and distraction.

Dubler ends with this paragraph:

At risk of writing myself onto our author, I think I am ready to argue that part of Knausgaard's process of preparing himself to write *My Struggle* was to get all the explicitly religious stuff out of his system. Only by getting angels and the Bible and a low-hanging, hidden God out of the way could he come to fully understand his own devotional practices: ironically, his Wittgensteinian restraint; and his will to exhaustively mine the world–the past, his past–for the moments of hierophany in which the materiality of an unyieldingly immanent divinity is made once again manifest in a world that is revealed, and proclaimed to be, holy, holy, holy.

THE SNOWPLOW

Karl Ove's run-in with the snowplowing bulldozer in *Book Four* stands on its own, bracketed by several hard returns.[6] The paragraphs bear no evident connection to the other events in these passages. It's one of the many passages in the novel that appears immediately to my ethnographic mind as surplus (or maybe it is all surplus). Surplus in a sense of material that makes available to the author/reader/hero "sides of a human being not previously assimilable from monological positions, including a real sense of eventness and freedom."[7] Ethnographically (or literarily), surplus indicates or leaves open other events; it brings an indeterminacy to the work. The effects of these passages–how are they meant to mean something? Do they? might they resonate or mean in many ways?–is a compositional question that is left open.

The snowplow event appears in the midst of a volume that, structurally speaking, hews closely to the unfolding of time, a year in the life of Karl Ove. The discipline of the calendar imposes an episodic unfolding, but it also makes it even less clear that any of the events or episodes matter (to the reader, to Karl Ove, and even possibly to Knausgaard). Likewise the snowplow, an event that just happens, that has no evident connection to whatever has happened or will happen, except that it happens during the period when Karl Ove is wandering around at night in the fishing village. It is a pleasure to read in such a way that allows for the things that happen not

6. Knausgaard, *My Struggle, Book Four*. The passages referred to in this section are on pages 418–21.

7. Or as Gary Saul Morson writes of Mikhail Bakhtin's theories of surplus, "real life, true historicity, and genuine individuality are to be found in what is left over . . . after all rules are applied and all generalizations are exhausted. In that surplus we find 'the singular world in which we create, become aware, contemplate, in which we live and in which we die.'" See his "Bakhtin and the Present Moment," *American Scholar* 60, no. 2 (1991): 206.

to have any direction (they are not emplotted) even though of course–of course!–some person has added it to the book, and put it here, and could have left it out, or could have put it in another place. This short section's lack of sentimentality is nonetheless invigorating. It is not tied to anything, it is not thus made precious, its presence is not given to identify the specialness of any other thing. Rather than the world being contained in these events, the events indicate the opposite. That the whole world is not in the book. This volume presses against the notion that events are about the world, or that the volume or the novel is faithful to the world. That we know that there are many other nights, which may or may not be like the one that we know about. There could be any number of episodes that could have started out similarly: "One night I was out walking. . . ." And, we know not only that there could have been other episodes, but that there were other episodes, moments forgotten or remembered by the narrator or hero, and which have not slipped into the story.

It is necessary however to contradict this thought that the snowplow scene is an easy surplus, or that its presence is extra to narrative. And in that way, we might consider it as one of those moments in the book that addresses the uncanny.

There is not too much in this volume (there is some in others) that comes close to the uncanny. There are many instances of a rapturous or quasi-transcendent sensibility that confront Karl Ove. He drinks and he works and he swims. He works, he reads, . . . he stops this normal life to "wander . . . listen to the roar of the waves. . . . gaze up at the mountainsides. . . ." He occasionally drinks to the point of self-erasure or does himself harm. But these are all acts that trace back to the hero–we see that he has set them in motion. The snowplow event in contrast happens to him. First the machine passes him, but then it seems to wait for him. But the man driving does not look at him or acknowledge him. It just stalks him–(the machine, the man)–Karl Ove "shivered with unease" . . ."this was scary" . . ."heart pounding" he races away, "would he follow me in here too?"

The experience of being followed (or stalked or, maybe relatedly, haunted) is not an immediately self-evident one. It requires an effort of interpretation, an awareness. Being followed is different from someone jumping out from the bushes to scare you. Being followed unfolds in time, and that time is composed of a shift in interpretation. Recall, if you've ever felt like you've been followed by some unknown party (when you're driving home alone, or walking alone on a street, or returning very late to an old, creaky inn) how much convincing you need to do to convince yourself that this isn't your imagination. Or to in fact convince yourself that you had reason to trust your imagination. To discover with relief your embarrassment that you've acted on your imagination and find there is nothing there.

Knausgaard's text is spare, but the question that looms in the rendering is indeed there. Is it true, is a "mad snowplow man chasing me"—or is it he, himself, imagining that he is being followed, finding in these arbitrary actions of another some malevolent intent of an inscrutable other? The question is not really answered, we see. Rather, the transformation of a moment's terror into a banal scene (clearing off the playground) offers two further questions. The first is about the boundaries of the hero's experience.

The second question returns (recursively) to this issue of whether the author is in control of the meaning of the events that take place. Are we (is Karl Ove, is Knausgaard) going to make this a meaningful event—or do we merely find it to be so. That is, are there given relations among these events to be discovered in the world, or is it all purely what we do, what we make of things. If it is the latter, what will save Karl Ove from that "feeling of chaos . . . a feeling of not having anything under control . . ." that arises when his co-worker Richard walks in to the school staff room where Karl Ove had inadvertently fallen asleep after one of his late night peregrinations.

The snowplow episode takes place during the long northern Norwegian winter, when it is dark twenty-four hours a day. Karl Ove has chosen to use this darkness to his advantage, and "To ensure I had more time to write." The lack of sunlight cues and the distinctions of night and day no longer have a hold on him, allowing the young man to radically secularize his life, hour by hour. He observes it made "no difference when you slept and when you were awake, morning and evening, night and day, in practice everything was the same." So, he would make his night day, and his day night. This experiment was made possible by his tenuous relationship to anyone in this small town.

Among other things, the volume had started out with a promise that the young hero would spend his year working in the north in order to embark on a trip the following year, to go south, write, and return to Norway with a novel. But as his world turns dark, Karl Ove's fantasy of an author's life written through geographical expansion, where he endeavored to place himself in a story shared by Kerouac and Orwell, has been replaced by the experience of being in a space of vast temporal expansion. He has become a reader of Hamsun. He has replaced the future imagined as a place unfettered by norms of home and geography with a future imagined as being unfettered by normal time. A weirder and unexpected unsettling. What happens in this shift from place to time, from movement around a person to movement through a person? How can we read this uncanny moment of the snowplow as a moment when things are now moving through the hero rather than his moving through them?

A NEW EVERYDAY

The father is undone. In the funeral, his monstrosity is overcome. It is possible, it seems, to contain–and thereby to remember and summon a life–a life within a ritual. It is likewise possible for the atheist son, at his daughter's christening, to be summoned to the communion rail and to be likewise pulled back into the family web and their associations and notions of wholeness. These are the expectations, these are the activities.

But neither of these rituals works this way, despite Karl Ove's expectation and even hope–his own hope for repair and wholeness, and even goodness. Rather, the many rituals of *My Struggle*–discos, funerals, christenings–have a tendency to call attention to their unraveling, and to point not to the anticipated world of ritual containment, and the quotidian, profane realms to which they relate, but to the world outside and uncontained–the world of monsters, a world where communication falls away. Uncanny moments and the rituals that point beyond their failure are nonetheless doing their work to touch something different. In the world of Karl Ove, both mark the presence of something deeper, enduring, ever-present: recognizable yet unspeakable, immanent to the quotidian, marking the quotidian as the product of our work to keep it a bay. As old as the fjords and the ladybugs, as autochthonous as the face in the water. Present with us, yet beyond us, and existing unaware of–and uncontained by–the languages that we have given ourselves to mark the wild.

Is this what happens when a person in the twenty-first century writes a novel from within the everyday? Or we should say, Yes, this is what happens when Knausgaard writes. Rather than gathering everything in to an expansive embrace, the everyday shows its startling narrowness. Even the recognizable space of modern sublimity cannot contain what is happening, what happens, what this life is. We can read Knausgaard and see what we should have always known (we did, didn't we?): that our belief that the everyday is continuous and everywhere, and containing everything, is a story itself. And it is an unreliable narrator. It is less Knausgaard than the everyday itself–our everyday too–which has become unreliable. And, perhaps, the unreliability is becoming more and more clear to us too. What then comes next in this history of the everyday?

I do not want to suggest that Knausgaard intends *My Struggle* as a meditation on these limits. But I have been drawn in reading the novel to consider just how gossamer-thin our everyday has become. We all receive the forms and the language of the everyday with gratitude and curiosity, and find it generative of thinking. It is familiar–and it is also threadbare. Oh, how much it can do! It can still do so much! But we are also becoming more familiar with the sight of things that appear through the tiny tears and frayed edges of its thinning frame. Not the hierophanic, not the mystical. These are still terms that can reside within the world of our everyday. But the other things, the monstrous father, the wife nearly dying in a closed bedroom while the children play in the yard, the seagull-angel. . . . They can be told through the old quotidian, but do they not also announce, in concert, that it is time for a new one? A version emerging that is not yet settled in its relationship to all those things that the old ritual powers of language, writing, and devotion sought to contain and even at times to redeem.

15 JANUARY 2017 NEW YORK CITY

DUBLER: Why repeat? Why repeat the life?

THORSTENSEN: I was just thinking, maybe *exegesis* could be a term to think about? That you try to deliver an interpretation according to your current standpoint, and it's a bit beyond hermeneutics because you have sort of devotional practice in mind. . . . That he could see one of the many Knausgaards as the exegete for the other Knausgaards. That he's mapping out some kind of doctrinal . . . and I was thinking about the different meanings that you can attach to scripture. Moral meanings, metaphysical . . . and you can think of the different Knausgaards in a setting, one as a metaphysician and one who is an ethicist.

HARRISS: I see it almost entirely opposite. Not exegesis but stylization. To sort of trace some of this, we live in the midst of everything. We don't know where we came from or where were going. The only way we can experience a life is to engage with and develop a novel that gives a form of shape. And then offers a kind of ethics . . . but it does so in a stylized way. So why go back to life? To stylize it.

/ 2 /

Love Tears

Erik Thorstensen

For the heart, life is simple: it beats for as long as it can. Then it stops. This is the first line of *Book One* of *My Struggle*. The authors of these essays have discussed the deaths and the hearts–and the life and the beats–concretely, metaphorically, criminally, metonymically, rhetorically, and personally throughout our years. Furthermore, these discussions have been connected to art, writing, figures, sociology, ethnography, Hitler, Kai Åge, etc. One central feature that we've always returned to in reading *My Struggle* is family. This topic is central to Sullivan's, Carlson's and Bender's chapters. Closely connected to family is the everyday–or the quotidian. Biles writes concerning everyday life in this volume, "Details–incidents accruing in increments–falling to pieces, leaving deposits, depositing traces–parts and particles and particulars: this is nothing other than *everyday life* itself." In this essay I explore a specific element of Knausgaard's writing, namely inversion in daily life as a narrative trope that connects his (or Karl Ove's) love for his family to the books' overarching project of truthfulness and goodness.

That inversions display a form of truth is elaborated by Bakhtin in literature and van Gennep in the study of religion.[1] Bakhtin saw the alterity of the carnival as providing an element of contingency as well necessity to the existing culture, structures, and powers. The contingency is expressed

1. Mikhail Bakhtin, *Rabelais and His World*, trans. Helene Iswolsky (Bloomington: Indiana University Press, 2009); Arnold van Gennep, *The Rites of Passage*, trans. Monika B. Yizedom and Gabrielle L. Caffee (Chicago: University of Chicago Press, 1960). Other approaches to inversion, such as that of survival of pagan traditions (even though Bakhtin also refers to the survival theory) as cultural devices for letting off steam or as an alternative perspective on life are not discussed directly here. See Harvey Cox, *The Feast of Fools: A Theological Essay on Festivity and Fantasy* (Cambridge, MA: Harvard University Press, 1969); Anton C. Zijderveld, *Reality in a Looking Glass: Rationality Through an Analysis of Traditional Folly* (London: Routledge & Kegan Paul, 1982).

by the otherness of symbols and placing the social structures upside-down, whereas the necessity comes from the structure of the symbols' relation to those of the everyday life. Van Gennep theorized that rites had a liminal phase where the time, persons, or places are (or become) taboo through their association with elements considered impure, through suspension of power, or through specific licenses. Such inversions take place at several levels in *My Struggle*. We find inversions on a structural level of composition, in scenes and in sentences. I inquire into whether it is through paying attention to these inversions that some of the more mystical claims in *My Struggle* might become more accessible.

FAIRYTALE LAND

Book Two of *My Struggle–A Man in Love*–starts in the archipelago off the western coast of Sweden. More precisely *A Man in Love* starts in Tjörn. In this book we meet the complete Knausgaard family and the summer cabin visit ends prematurely after three days rather than the envisaged full week. The perfect childless couple they visit, Mikaela and Erik, seem to Karl Ove to be carefree and careless of children and minding more to the façade of their lives than the play of Vanja, Heidi, and John.

The Knausgaards then start their odyssey back to Malmö by car. The story drifts off in a reflection on the children and children in general, but this trip is revisited toward the end of the book.[2]

This journey is filled with basic contrasts or opposites that would arouse anyone with a structuralist leaning, but here I will use some opposites and in addition investigate some of the stories that are told. One example can be found already in the visit with Mikela and Erik, who have regular jobs and are without children as opposed to the freelancing and royalty-based couple with three toddlers. An example at the very start of the journey is how the Knausgaards are prevented from eating at a restaurant reserved for yacht club members, and in their quest to find an alternative, they cross a long bridge in the summer heat, while Linda *hissed*,

> [W]e were useless, now we should be eating, the whole family, we could have been really enjoying ourselves, instead we were out here in a gale-force wind with cars whizzing by, suffocating from exhaust fumes on this bloody bridge. Had I ever seen any other families with three children outside in situations like this?[3]

2. Knausgaard, *My Struggle, Book Two*, 527.
3. Knausgaard, *My Struggle, Book Two*, 10.

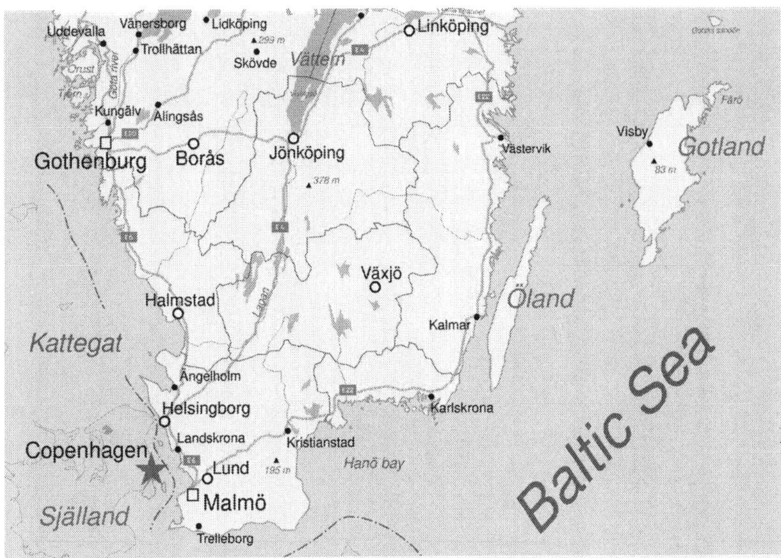

FIGURE 1: Map of southern Sweden with cities and country borders. Online at https://commons.wikimedia.org/wiki/File:Map_of_Sweden_Cities_(polar_stereographic).svg.

And our narrator then tells us that "The road we followed ended at a metal gate emblazoned with the logo of a security firm." This hopeless adventure ends up at a McDonald's on the outskirts of Gothenburg next to a petrol station.

The episodes of the failed visit and the unsatisfactory meal are prequels to the next adventure. Even this adventure is marked by contrasts, opposites, the high and the low, and serves as a point of departure into Karl Ove's childhood as well as introducing his new life in Sweden.

The Fairytale Land episode starts when the narrator tells us that the Knausgaards "scrapped the planned trip to Liseberg Amusement Park, it would only make things worse given the atmosphere between us now; instead, a few hours later, we stopped on impulse at a shoddy so-called 'Fairytale Land,' where everything was of the poorest quality."[4] Liseberg rates among the best amusement parks in the world. Rather than opting for the well-organized, high-quality Liseberg in a large city, they stop somewhere by the road at a random park called Fairytale Land, attracted by its two carved gnomes.

What I find striking in this description is, on one level, the deep contrast with the socio-philosophical treatise at the start of *Book One*, but, even

4. Knausgaard, *My Struggle, Book Two*, 11.

FIGURE 2: "Kiviks marknad" (Kivik's fair). Photo by Bo Seinknecht. Bohusläns Museum.

more so, how it tells a story of baseness, cheapness, and lowness in a tender and caring way that connects the reader to both Linda's and Karl Ove's pasts. The whole Fairytale Land scene invites a reading based on Bakhtin, since it constitutes an inversion of the quotidian on the one side and of the mainstream divertissements on the other side.[5]

Our narrator emphasizes the inverted aspects and the low quality of the amusement park, "a stout manly-looking lady, probably from somewhere in eastern Europe; the low ceiling; pathetic wooden façade; all sorts of shrill, plinging sounds; coffee tasted bitter and was almost undrinkable; three newly built sheds,"[6] in a setting with scorching heat infested with wasps and horseflies. Karl Ove and Linda cope with the practical challenges of parenting in the park through feeding and nurturing, but mainly they seem to participate fully and engage in their children's experiences of the fairy tale. The whole family takes part, for example, in the sad and sore donkey riding, where Linda manages to get the stubborn animal to move. (Vanja does not want to ride because she used to ride horses, but quit.) Karl Ove buys lottery tickets for a far larger amount of money than the two doll mice are worth; they buy candy floss and play around in the cheap cowboy village. Karl Ove looks across at Linda, who has Heidi on her lap, and sees that she has tears in her eyes.

5. Bakhtin, *Rabelais and His World.*
6. Knausgaard, *My Struggle, Book Two*, 11.

The Fairytale Land donkey ride scene recalls the flight of Mary, Joseph, and Jesus into Egypt, and Linda's tears, the weeping virgins of Christianity. *Virtus Asinaria*—the virtue of the donkey—the animal's closeness to Jesus and saints such as Francis and Martin was a theme in medieval Christian writing.[7] In the Feast of the Ass the metonymical identification was ritualized through a set of inversions where the lower clergy some place celebrated an ass (*festum asinorum*) or a member of the lower clergy (*festum stultorum*) as the center of liturgy during the Christmas cycle. "The elevation of the Ass implies a temporary change in the ideology and therefore a temporary change in the reality dependent on that ideology."[8] In an inverted ritual praising of the ass, normal day-to-day hierarchies were simultaneously confirmed and put into play. In the hymn of the Donkey, *Orientis partibus*, the ass was given the role of one of the Magi who recognized Jesus as Lord in the Christian tradition. Jacobus de Voragine (1230-1298), the compiler of the vita of the saints, wrote in *The Birth of our Lord Jesus Christ*, "The ox and the ass, miraculously recognizing the Lord, went to their knees and worshiped him."[9] The effect of placing Linda on a donkey closes the story, which began with tears; both are scenes of inversion.

Victor Turner distinguished between the liminal and the liminoid, both modes distinct from daily life. But the liminal takes place in seasonal rhythms in agrarian cultures, where an individual or society changes through the rite,[10] whereas the liminoid is a reversal that is optional and without specific transformative characteristics. Fairytale Land is an adventure inserted into a holiday and thus doubly liminoid for Karl Ove and Linda. They both nurture the children's stories and move along with them in order to strengthen the reality effect of the Fairytale Land experience. The transformative and liminal in this scene is the continued existence of a different or parallel world where other families tour the Swedish countryside's third- or fourth-rate amusement installations.

Linda is moved by her children's immediate and rapt response to what

7. Erik Thorstensen, "'Og du, gamle pave, hvordan kan selv du forsvare å tilbe et esel som gud?': En lesning av dårefestens eselliturgi [And thou thyself, thou old pope, how is it in accordance with thee, to adore an ass in such a manner as God? Reading the Feast of Fools as liturgy]" (MA thesis, Universitetet i Oslo, 1999).

8. Ingvild Sælid Gilhus, *Laughing Gods, Weeping Virgins: Laughter in the History of Religion* (London; New York: Routledge, 1997), 85.

9. Jacobus de Voragine, *The Golden Legend: Readings on the Saints*, trans. William Granger Ryan (Princeton, NJ: Princeton University Press, 2012), 41. The donkey as especially truthful is further an element in novels such as George Orwell's *Animal Farm*, where Benjamin is sardonic and loyal, and he gets to read the remaining commandment at the end of the book, "Some animals are more equal than others."

10. Victor W. Turner, *From Ritual to Theatre: The Human Seriousness of Play* (New York: Performing Arts Journal Publications, 1982).

she perceives to be sad and cheap. An expected reaction would be disdain. Instead, Karl Ove observes, "and then I looked across at Linda. She was sitting with Heidi on her lap and had tears in her eyes," since circuses have always moved her, due to that "it's so sad, so small and so cheap. And at the same time so beautiful."[11] They are fundamentally engaged in their children, and this engagement is in a sense a poetical one as it is expressed through Linda's tears. As readers, we are not given any explicit or immediate report of Karl Ove's reaction to Linda's tears except that Vanja was not as seduced as the others were. Vanja's position in this scene functions as an extra-inversion, where she takes on the role of an "adult." This lack of reaction is untypical of *My Struggle*; where Karl Ove is usually prone to write inner monologues or comments regarding his thoughts and become stressed based on Linda's reactions. In this case his lack of reaction, I would suggest, signals sympathy or compassion with Linda's feelings–and maybe also identification. Linda's reaction to the lowness, the sadness and cheapness is what I would call an aesthetic reaction to what I would have reflected upon in sociological terms. Aesthetic reactions seem fitting for these couples who initially met through literature.

When the narrator picks up the Fairytale Land story again later in the book, the Knausgaard family is in the car returning to Stockholm. Karl Ove drives, and the rest of the family falls asleep. Looking out on the landscape, and looking back on his family, "Happiness exploded inside me,"[12] Karl Ove writes and relates this feeling to the music, to the sleeping family members, and the flatness of the landscape mirroring Nykøbing in northern Denmark. What distinguishes this explosion of happiness is the thorough exhaustion of the Knausgaard family after their Fairytale Land experiences. As we recall, the first instance of complete happiness in *My Struggle* is also associated with Linda and Karl Ove telling her how much she meant to him, and they kiss–after which Karl Ove fainted and woke up feeling "completely happy."

I venture that it is Linda's tears over her children's seduction by the gnomes, the low ceilings, and the newly built sheds that transport Karl Ove into happiness. As the eminent historian of religions at the University of Bergen, Ingvild Gilhus, has pointed out, the connection between women and weeping has a long and profound theological and historical connection in Christianity.[13] Tears are a sign of a truthful and loving character. Laughter and weeping are opposites, and the female tears could be the sole permitted bodily expression of connection with the divine in Christianity.

11. Knausgaard, *My Struggle, Book Two*, 11.
12. Knausgaard, *My Struggle, Book Two*, 528.
13. Gilhus, *Laughing Gods, Weeping Virgins*.

The crying mother is a forceful image in Christianity, from Mary with the dying Jesus in the *Pietà* to popular references of crying Madonna statues, expressing both divine truth and maternal goodness and care. Linda's emotions are not caused by grief over the poverty and the poor conditions but by the beauty in the eyes of the children.

Chaos and unforeseen events are a recurring theme for the Knausgaards. The flat is messy, laundry heaps up, and the trips to and from the kindergarten can be a logistical nightmare. A different holiday scene, the trip to the Canary Islands, which is also their honeymoon, works as a contrast to Fairytale Land. At the Canary Islands, we learn that the kids' enthusiasm is not in itself something that moves Linda. We travel with the Knausgaards to the Canary Islands in *Book Six, The End*. Here, the kids thrive while the parents suffer the conformism and commercialism in the resort hotel:

> Rows of two-story concrete blocks, a parched lawn, tarmac and two big hotels, all inside high fences, next to a pile of rocks, full of Scandinavians and Brits, this was the location for our honeymoon. I was so wound up with frustration and Linda was so exhausted that she began to cry when I growled at her for not being able to find the key when we were standing outside the door. . . . When I returned Heidi and Vanja were in their swimming costumes. For them this was a fairy tale come true, so, I realized, if I pulled myself together, they would be happy.
>
> For us it was anything but a fairy tale. In fact, the very antithesis. There was nothing enchanting about it, there was no magic, not so much as a hint of allure. We fell into a rhythm.[14]

The kids' happiness is consequently not all that matters for them, and Linda's tears are not always the source of warm feelings. The rhythm there is not the rhythm of music but the rhythm of socially imposed structures, the opposite of the unstructured Fairytale Land. Understanding gestures, bodily movements, or corporal interaction depends on the social structuration or social control of space.[15] The "two-story concrete blocks, a parched lawn, tarmac and two big hotels, all inside high fences," as described by Knausgaard, give a highly structured space where every action, gesture, and thought becomes tainted with external order. Here, the kids adapt to the setting, but rather than offering beauty, the resort hotel life becomes a farce over their quotidian life where swimsuits replace snowsuits.

14. Knausgaard, *My Struggle, Book Six*, 893.
15. Mary Douglas, *Natural Symbols: Explorations in Cosmology* (London: Routledge, 1996).

STYLE

Karl Ove wants to be good. In addition, Knausgaard wants to be true. This movement between being truthful and being good is an underlying aporia in *My Struggle*, as Courtney Bender addresses in her essay in this volume. Knausgaard addresses this aporia through stylistic inversions. He reflects upon why he hasn't been able to write about his father earlier, and he relates that to the change of form between the lived experience and converting that experience into writing. He concludes:

> That is its [literature's] sole law: everything has to submit to form. If any of literature's other elements are stronger than form, such as style, plot, theme, if any of these overtake form, the result suffers. That is why writers with a strong style often write bad books. That is also why writers with strong themes so often write bad books.[16]

Looking at the opening in *Book One*, we encounter Karl Ove as an adolescent with a strict–or abusive–father and a mother who throughout the books becomes his closest family member–except for Linda. In marked contrast to the beginning of *Book Two*, the first pages of *Book One* revolve around death and thus allude to his father's death. The transition from death as a cultural phenomenon to a specific experience with death happens through a change in perspective, where the narrator first describes what is shown on the televised news and then turns the gaze away from the screen to the viewer:

> A fishing smack sinks off the coast of northern Norway one night, the crew of seven drown, next morning the event is described in all the newspapers, it is a so-called mystery, the weather was calm and no mayday call was sent from the boat, it just disappeared, a fact which the TV stations underline that evening by flying over the scene of the drama in a helicopter and showing pictures of the empty sea. The sky is overcast, the gray-green swell heavy but calm, as though possessing a different temperament from the choppy, white-flecked waves that burst forth here and there. I am sitting alone watching, it is some time in spring, I suppose, for my father is working in the garden.[17]

Immediately after, Karl Ove sees what the readers learn almost 150 pages later, at the start of *Part 2* of *Book One*: the face of Jesus in the sea. This

16. Knausgaard, *My Struggle, Book One*, 195.
17. Knausgaard, *My Struggle, Book One*, 11.

180-degree shift in perspective– from the viewed to the viewer– exemplifies a key aspect of the narrative craftmanship in *My Struggle*.

Craft is one element of *style*. Another element of style can be found in the difference in the ways of telling the introduction stories in *Book One* and *Book Two*, and the way in which these are told might provide insight on how inversions work at the level of *My Struggle*. As Cooper Harriss shows in this volume, the ending in *Book Two* echoes the Fairytale Land scene, where Karl Ove's mother talks about the father, saying, "We were so young, you know. . . . Yes, it was an adventure. The beginning of an adventure. That was how it felt."[18] Fairy tale–adventure. The start and the end are symmetrical. Likewise, death is the beginning and the end of *Book One*. Furthermore, the last scene in *Book Two*, which is a conversation between Karl Ove and his mother, starts with, "Later that spring, when I was nearing the end of the story about dad's death, the terrible days spent at the house in Kristiansand, mum came to visit me." Thus, the two books are, narratively speaking, complete stories in which the beginnings and the endings meet. The third and the fourth books are of a different character: the third book treats Karl Ove's childhood and adolescence, while the fourth concerns his stay in Northern Norway. However, as *Book One* and *Book Two* constitute parts of a larger total, the difference in style between the sociocultural essay on death in *Book One* and the attentive and emotional narrator in *Book Two* is meaningful.

In *Book Six*, Knausgaard presents the reader with what I would call a tension between style and the written text, on the one side, and morality and behavior, on the other:

> Style is little more than self-awareness, not in the singular I, but in the I of the text, arising in assumptions about the receiver of the communicative act. These assumptions exist as a kind of horizon of expectation against which the I defines and molds itself. Style is to the written text as morality is to behavior, setting the boundaries of what may and must be said or done, and how.[19]

By "style is to the written text as morality is to behavior," Knausgaard asserts a correspondence between these two disparate phenomena.

We see Knausgaard working through the tension between style and morality in the beginning of *The End* where Karl Ove cheers on the three-and-a-half-year-old Vanja so that she wins over her nameless friend who injured

18. Knausgaard, *My Struggle, Book Two*, 576.
19. Knausgaard, *My Struggle, Book Six*, 757.

herself during the race in a fun run. Her friend had a clear lead, but as she turned to wait for the much slower Vanja, she fell:

> Come on, Vanja! I said. You're almost at the finish! Run as fast as you can! And Vanja heard me and ran as fast as she could, past her friend, whose knee was grazed and bleeding, with me alongside her, past child after child she ran, as fast as the wind and over the finishing line![20]

For Karl Ove–and Linda–this victory is also a moral victory, however counter-intuitive that might seem, based on this brief quotation. Here, good morals come out of seemingly bad behavior. The fun run scene is the end of a reflection starting in an associative manner that reflects the role of the quotidian (as well as the Norwegians' perspective on Swedes),

> I piled up a plate with macaroni and meatballs, Sweden's national dish, cut a tomato into bite-sized wedges, squirted some ketchup over it all and sat down. The first year we lived in Malmö I talked about it with one of the other dads from the nursery. How did they cope at mealtimes?[21]

In his naïveté, it is as if meals were only a question of logistics and practicalities. Karl Ove asks one of the other fathers how they arranged the meals. The father answers, "She knows she's got no choice. . . . How does she know that? I asked. We broke her will, he said." In Karl Ove's eyes, this father is a typical, modern, enlightened, alternative, soft, BabyBjörn-carrying, and active Swedish father. He understands why their daughter is always obedient and seemingly independent, whereas Vanja is the opposite.

As Liane Carlson shows in her essay in this volume, the nameless father's methods correspond to what Yngve and Karl Ove experienced in their childhood. Their own outward conformity was a result of having had an abusive father. That Karl Ove makes this association in the text further supports Carlson's thesis concerning the aesthetic of the abused child. Karl Ove seems to believe the other father. Could this nameless father be joking? How can the reader know that he is not playing Karl Ove? Regardless, being a good Scandinavian, Karl Ove does not confront the other father but rather reflects "Did he realize what he was telling me about himself, I wondered, but said nothing."

The trigger event for Karl Ove's behavior in the fun run can be found when Vanja eats dinner with the nameless Swedish family.

20. Knausgaard, *My Struggle, Book Six*, 31.
21. Knausgaard, *My Struggle, Book Six*, 28.

> There had been a minor episode, he said, but we sorted it out no trouble, didn't we, Vanja? What happened, I asked. Well, she asked for more dinner, but then after we'd given her some she wouldn't eat it. So she had to sit there until she did.[22]

Karl Ove contains himself. Even though he is close to exploding on the inside, he does not confront the father directly. When he gets home, Karl Ove has told himself that it is good that Vanja experiences that families are different from her own. Linda, on the other hand, reads the scene as a criticism of their family and of them as parents. Vanja becomes the Knausgaards through metonymy.

During the dinner, Vanja had been invited to join her friend in a fun run. In the fun run, a crowd of children with numbers pinned to their jackets or sweaters starts simultaneously with an accompanying parent. Vanja is not a strong runner, but her friend runs "like the wind." When Vanja needs to pause, her friend stops and waits, it is clear that her friend would have crossed the finish line long before Vanja had she not waited. At the last stretch, the friend stumbles, and we're back to the quote that started this section. Karl Ove violates all common morality and cheers on Vanja to beat her friend. The Swedish family assumes that Vanja was the one who made the decision to run ahead:

> They could understand a four-year-old not being able to show empathy with a friend her own age. But the idea of a nearly forty-year-old man being equally incapable was naturally beyond their imagination.
>
> I burned with shame as I laughed politely.
>
> On the way home I told Linda what had happened. She laughed like she hadn't laughed for months.
>
> "We won, that's the main thing!" I said.[23]

The outburst of laughter might be read as (comic) relief. We do not learn whether Linda shares Karl Ove's conclusion—and it is unclear what they won; was it the competition to be the best family or the fun run? What seems inescapable from this scene is that Karl Ove takes revenge on the other family. A cruel, but unnoticed revenge. There is a morality behind the revenge in a double sense. First, Karl Ove has observed that the behind the behavior of Vanja's friend lies "uncompromisingly Victorian parenting methods" while Vanja behaves as she does because Karl Ove avoids being

22. Knausgaard, *My Struggle, Book Six*, 29.
23. Knausgaard, *My Struggle, Book Six*, 29.

like his own dad. Second, the unnoticed nature of the revenge suggests that Karl Ove's internal need for restitution is the predominant factor behind it. Karl Ove's embarrassment over his out-of-character behavior seems quelled by the higher morality. There are then two intertwined elements in this scene, one cultural and the second moral.

Seen from the cultural or ritual perspective, the fun run mixes adults and children and fun and competition. Central to rituals is the transition from one social status to another with a middle or liminal phase that "may also include subversive and ludic (or playful) events."[24] Turner directly connects the liminoid to play or collective games. In Swedish and Norwegian, the word used for "competition" is "konkurrans(e)," coming from the French "concurrence" which means "running together."[25] The fun run is a collective event, where the subversive act is Karl Ove cheering on Vanja to run past her suffering friend and using Vanja to exert revenge on what he identifies as the parents' Victorian morality.[26]

Morally speaking, the wrong behavior can consequently be justified by a right morality, which then makes the behavior right. But what kind of morality are we then talking about? Later in *The End*, morality seems to be related to the individual's ability to distance itself from nations or other collectives in a manner inspired by Hannah Arendt's understanding of Adolf Eichmann:

> A morality that proceeds from the community of an all, that proceeds from we, is dangerous, perhaps more dangerous than anything else, because committing to an all is to commit to an abstraction, something existing in the language or the world of ideas, but not in reality, where people exist only as separate individuals. In this sense, Knut Hamsun and Peter Handke's morality is utterly superior to that of their critics.[27]

In both his understanding of participation in collective events and his understanding of morality, the narrator takes the ideal of an individual opposed to the collective as the source for good or proper morality. A key to

24. Turner, *From Ritual to Theatre*, 27.
25. A large amount of Swedish (and Norwegian but mostly Swedish) words have their origin in French. The reason is–beyond the usual loans between languages–that the state of Sweden-Norway (1814-1905) imported Napoleon Bonaparte's general Jean-Baptiste Bernadotte as King Karl Johan in 1818. See also Erik Thorstensen, "Ostendit populo–Å vise fram for folket [Displaying to the people]," *Arr. Idéhistorisk tidsskrift*, no. 4 (2002).
26. In Scandinavia, organized competitions for children are increasingly moving away from selecting a winner toward an emphasis on participation. This is nothing new. We (Scandinavians) also have competitions where the winner is the one who has the finishing time closest to the mean time of all the competitors; what we call "ideal time." The most well-known literary description is in Roy Jacobsen, *Seierherrene (The Conquerors)* (Oslo: Cappelen, 1991).
27. Knausgaard, *My Struggle, Book Six*, 238.

FIGURE 3: "Trollgagene. Tivoli" (Troll days. Tivoli), Tynset, Norway. Photo by Thomas Jergell. Used with permission from Anno Musea i Nord-Østerdalen.

the scene is the identification between Knausgaard and Vanja. This identification is pronounced metonymically in passages leading up to the fun run. In the form for moral nominalism expressed above, one might find a commitment to acting for restoring the Knausgaards through a violation of the norms and the rules of a fun run, a collective event. If I then return to Knausgaard's formula, and replace style with morality and text with behavior, it reads "Morality is little more than self-awareness, not in the singular I, but in the I of the behavior." If Karl Ove and Vanja are one "I" in the fun-run scene, then it would be that it is their understanding of themselves as norm violators that constitutes the morality of "We won, that's the main thing!"

As Turner writes, "Re-membering is not merely the restoration of some past intact, but setting it in living relationship to the present."[28] The scene might be read as a prelude to Karl Ove's ceaseless discussions with himself and others over the morality of his project with *My Struggle* and his correspondence with his uncle about the morality in and of the writing project.

LOVE IS A FAIRY TALE

One of the central elements in the fairy tale, according to the founding father of fairy-tale studies, Vladimir Propp, is the transfiguration of the

28. Turner, *From Ritual to Theatre*, 86.

hero.[29] "Happiness exploded inside me,"[30] is Karl Ove's sensation after having visited Fairytale Land. The first time we encounter an explosion of happiness in *My Struggle* is the first time Karl Ove gets drunk in *Book One*. Knausgaard emphasizes just this transformative aspect of the fairy tale,

> For me the fairy tale was a kind of literary archetype, or rather a primordial force of literature itself, since on the surface everything was about transformation, including the world's own transformation into fairy tale, and at the same time this transformation involved a kind of simplification, reality contracting into a small number of figures that were so precise and so perfectly honed after having been through so many differently shaped experiences that their truth surpassed any individual experience of the circumstances, this was the same for everyone, and when these different figures were set into motion, the depths in each and every listener opened, and those depths were bottomless. For many years I'd thought of having a novel take place in that domain . . .[31]

I have proposed that the two first books might be read as complementary to each other. Their openings and endings with death in the one and adventure and fairy tale in the other prepare the reader for the coming pages and close the stories. Death is the ultimate transfiguration but also a central element in the fairy tale, in Propp's account of them. This element, called "the punishment of the villain," follows the transfiguration of the hero in Propp's sequence, where "he is killed in battle or perishes during the pursuit (a witch bursts in an attempt to drink up the sea, etc.)."[32] As discussed above, the time of the story and the time of the narration differ in *My Struggle*, and this is a question of form. Here, *My Struggle* obviously differs from the traditional folk tale with its strict chronology. The different episodes are, formally speaking, distributed narratively in *My Struggle* (and this theme is given a very insightful discussion by Cooper Harriss later in this book).

The question then is, Why are we given the background for the transformation (the explosion of happiness) at the outset and the conclusion at the end? Look at the title of the book, *A Man in Love*. How to tell the/a story of love? In our modern and romantic times, love is the ultimate fairy tale. If one can infer anything about Knausgaard, the author, from Karl Ove, the

29. Vladimir Propp, *Morphology of the Folktale*, ed. Louis A. Wagner, trans. Laurence Scott (Austin: University of Texas Press, 1968).
30. Knausgaard, *My Struggle, Book Two*, 528.
31. Knausgaard, *My Struggle, Book Six*, 126.
32. Propp, *Morphology of the Folktale*, 42.

character, it is that he finds it awkward to say, "I love you." In *Inadvertent*, Knausgaard writes,

> Whom is one addressing when one writes? Who am I in my writing, when form makes it seem foreign to me? How is it that all thoughts seem to vanish when one writes, even during the most intense and cerebral reflections? What are feelings in a text that consists of letters, black marks on a page?
>
> On the other hand, I know–the way you just know something, for example roughly how much a stone will weigh in your hand (a certainty you become aware of if the stone turns out to be surprisingly light and made of papier-mâché) or that you love someone (in which case the answers to the question of why can never be as persuasive as the feeling)–both why I write and what writing is.[33]

What happens if we think of Fairytale Land as a declaration of love through the inversions? The feeling, I think, is expressed by narration of the observation of Linda's tears over the joy the children find in the unfancy, run-down amusements. It is a specific and distinct kind of love, beautifully written but with a seemingly chaotic and unstructured interior. Maybe Stendhal's theory of love might illuminate us. As we remember, he compares love to the process of the crystallization that happens to a bough in the salt mines in Salzburg.[34] Love is a process where the mind of the lover increasingly sees new qualities of the loved one: "What I have called crystallization is a mental process which draws from everything that happens new proofs of the perfection of the loved one."[35] Knausgaard consequently portrays Karl Ove's love for Linda through a new proof of perfection. This proof of perfection, in Karl Ove's eyes, is the kids' love for a "pirate ship, a pathetic wooden façade with gangways behind, . . . the llama and ostrich enclosures, . . . a stand with a bungee trampoline and a donkey-riding ring."[36]

33. Knausgaard, *Inadvertent*, 43-44.
34. Stendhal, *Love* (Harmondsworth: Penguin, 1975).
35. Stendhal, *Love*, 59.
36. Knausgaard, *My Struggle, Book Two*, 19.

13 JANUARY 2018 BLOOMINGTON, INDIANA

CARLSON: So, what I wrote was pretty fragmentary. I was trying to figure out why I find the father the most compelling part of *My Struggle* and why I was so irritated with the treatment of the father in the Coda of this book [*A Time for Everything*] and it has something to do with catastrophe–that it is the violent death of the father that recasts the past. Whereas I think the thing I get out of *My Struggle* is that there is no sensible ending that would allow the father to be done and past. The fact that he dies in this way that may or may not be bloody is in some sense irrelevant. The thing that makes him impossible to get beyond is the struggle to be good–the realization of the inability to . . . the feeling that you ought to be able to mourn your father and then the building of all of these structures, the mask . . . the conjuring of these memories, like when he is on the plane and [the memory of] his father trying to ski really awkwardly down the slope summons forth these feelings that he thinks he ought to be having. And the fact that the death is bloody is beside the point. The father will always be there because the father was not what he ought to have been. If we are talking about *our* Knausgaard, the father's death is peripheral to *my* Knausgaard.

SULLIVAN: So, if *My Struggle* is, in some sense . . . a care for the ancestors . . . then actually the Coda [in *A Time for Everything*] *is* underdeveloped in that way? . . . It is a bit crude, even, and still colored by his emotions about [his father's] death and that the ambivalence he has about his father and his desire to be good and to do the right thing for his father is evident in *My Struggle*. And is embryonic and maybe not quite there in the Coda [in *A Time for Everything*].

CARLSON: I think that's right. And it could just be a fantasy element—had he died in a car crash, then everything would be fine, and we'd move on. It's him trying out the alternative world. I think it is the care for the ancestor thing that interests me. And also, I guess I assume that we are not going to find out how the father died in the end?

SULLIVAN: Well, it is also the problem of what Henrik Vankel did that made him go into this self-imposed exile and what that might mean. That is a much stronger self-condemnation than what we see in *My Struggle*. Knausgaard takes much better care for himself in *My Struggle*.

/ 3 /

Aesthetics of an Abused Child

Liane Carlson

From the very first glimpse of Karl Ove's father, we know it will not end well for him.[1] The narrator has opened the novel with a long, winding meditation on death. It is a biological account of how the heart beats as long as it can, then stops; it is a social account of the norms of privacy that prevent us from leaving the young dead girl smashed on the pavement for her parents to find; it is an anthropological account, musing on why we feel compelled to keep corpses low to the ground, even when a refrigerated morgue could just as easily exist on the sixteenth floor. It is shades of Rilke, who lamented the removal of the dying to sterile hospitals when death had so recently ripened inside us like a fruit;[2] and shrouds of Vico, who thought that one of the three distinctive traits of humanity was the desire to bury the dead, imagining that we are *homo humandi* because we inter the human in the *humus,* the earth.[3] It is a scattershot list of deaths seen and forgotten on TV (always catastrophes for someone else), culminating in Karl Ove's vision of the face in the sea. It is, in short, everything but personal.

And then we see Kai Åge.

> He is standing at the rear of the house, down in what will be the vegetable plot, lunging at a boulder with a sledgehammer. Even though the hollow is only a few meters deep, the black soil he has dug up and is standing on together with the dense clump of rowan trees growing beyond the fence

1. Throughout this chapter, I follow our group's convention of referring to the narrator as Karl Ove and the author as Knausgaard.
2. Rainer Maria Rilke, *The Notebooks of Malte Laurids Brigge* (New York: Vintage, 1990), 16.
3. Robert Pogue Harrison, *The Dominion of the Dead* (Chicago: University of Chicago Press, 2003), 34. The other two traits were marriage and religion.

> behind him cause the twilight to deepen. As he straightens up to turn to me, his face is almost completely shrouded in darkness.[4]

He is powerful. He is primal. He is standing in a grave. But he is also something else—an object to be read:

> Nevertheless, I have more than enough information to know his mood. That is apparent not from his facial expressions but his physical posture, and you do not read it with your mind but with your intuition.[5]

This is only the first passage where Karl Ove mentions reading his father's mood. As he leaves his father, not quite sure if he is being mocked when his father asks if he saw Jesus's face in the water, his father tells him not to run. Karl Ove retreats to his room, troubled.

> I knew his moods and had learned how to predict them long ago, by means of a subconscious categorization system, I have later come to realize, whereby the relationship between a few constants was enough to determine what was in store for me, allowing me to make my own preparations. A kind of meteorology of the mind. . . . The speed of the car up the gentle gradient to the house, the time it took him to switch off the engine, grab his things, and step out, the way he looked around as he locked the car, the subtle nuances of the various sounds that rose from the hall as he removed his coat—everything was a sign, everything could be interpreted. [. . .] So, what frightened me most was when he turned up without warning, . . . when for some reason I had been inattentive.
>
> How on earth did he know I had been running?[6]

His brother Yngve, too, it transpires, shares in Karl Ove's wariness. As he arrives just in time for dinner, he hurries down the hall in "the familiar, slightly jerky, almost duck-like gait we had developed so as to be able to walk fast inside the house without making a sound."[7] Neither remarks on Yngve's strange walk. On the contrary, Karl Ove anticipates his worry that he will be in trouble for being late and soothes him. Yngve, in turn, has so deeply normalized the efforts to evade surveillance that he doesn't pause to thank him but, rather, proceeds to give the young Karl Ove shit in the way that older siblings do. That, more than anything, sums up the house.

4. Knausgaard, *My Struggle, Book One*, 12.
5. Knausgaard, *My Struggle, Book One*, 12.
6. Knausgaard, *My Struggle, Book One*, 17.
7. Knausgaard, *My Struggle, Book One*, 18.

Fear is the backdrop, and like any backdrop, it is tacitly taken for granted, even as it is navigated around.

Karl Ove's troubled surveillance doesn't stop at his father. His mother, too, is an object of his silent observation, if only because her actions help him read his father by proxy. He sits up past his bedtime reading until he hears her car coming up the hill.

> I put the book on the floor, switched off the light, and lay in the dark listening for her: the car door slamming, the crunch across the gravel, the front door opening, her coat and scarf being removed, the footsteps up the stairs. . . . The house seemed different then, when she was in it, and the strange thing was that I could *feel* it; if, for example, I had gone to sleep before she returned and I awoke in the middle of the night, I could sense that she was there, something in the atmosphere changed without my being able to put a finger on what it was, except to say that it had a reassuring effect."[8]

Karl Ove sneaks to the living room, where he silently watches the evening news from a crack in the door, waiting to see how his parents will react to the face in the sea, waiting to see if they can even see it. The nightly news shows a different clip, interviewing the drowned men's families. Karl Ove retreats, suffused with shame.

The overture is an amazing piece of writing and a rebuke to those who insist Knausgaard writes automatically, without craft. All of his major themes and modes of writing are woven together. The surveillance of the father, the protection of the mother, the solidarity with the brother, the image of the face that will return so many times (as Jesus in the floor of a later apartment; as his own, slashed with razors when his future wife Linda rejects him). The poetic mode, the philosophical mode, the ambiguous relationship with religion, the obsession with meaning and the constriction of meaning in adulthood, the tacking between the first-person immediacy and the abstraction of philosophical reverie. Shame.

Yet what I take to be the single most distinctively Knausgaardian trait—the obsessive attention paid to the sight, sound, and feel of the quotidian things that surround him, whether the logo on laundry detergent or the dull jolt of a stroller as it navigates a curb—emerges here as something decidedly more (and less) complicated than a mere aesthetic choice.

That surveillance of the things that surround him is a learned coping strategy for child abuse.

8. Knausgaard, *My Struggle, Book One*, 25.

A CONFESSION, AN ADDENDUM, A WAGER

I have to confess, it had never occurred to me until I presented this paper in an earlier workshop in Bergen that there was anything to be debated about the presence of child abuse in these books. Kai Åge was not the very worst father imaginable, of course. He never burns Karl Ove with cigarette butts, or molests him, or breaks his arms. He is sometimes kind, in a fumbling way, even though Karl Ove fears and loathes him. Kai Åge is, on the whole, less Sade than sad.

What he does do is hit Karl Ove for forgetting a sock at the pool, belittle him for showing surprise or emotion, mock him for a speech impediment until he cries, and so thoroughly dominate his thoughts and body that Karl Ove cannot walk in his own house for fear of triggering some whim. At one point in *Book Four*, Karl Ove and Yngve discuss their childhood.

> Yngve began to talk about himself, and it wasn't long before we were going through one incident after the other. Yngve told us about the time the B-Max supermarket opened and he was sent off with a shopping list and some money, under strict instructions to bring back a receipt. He had done that, but the sum in his hand hadn't tallied with the till receipt and dad had marched him into the cellar and given him a beating. He told us about the time his bike had had a puncture and dad had walloped him. I, for my part, had never been beaten; for some reason dad had always treated Yngve worse. But I talked about the times he had slapped me and the times he had locked me in the cellar, and the point of these stories was always the same: his fury was always triggered by some petty detail, some utter triviality, and as such was actually comical. At any rate we laughed when we told the stories. Once I had left a pair of gloves on the bus and he slapped me in the face when he found out. I had leaned against the wobbly table in the hall and sent it flying and he came over and hit me. It was absolutely absurd! I lived in fear of him, I said, and Yngve said dad controlled him and his thoughts, even now.
>
> Mom said nothing. She sat listening, looking at me then Yngve. Sometimes her eyes seemed to go blank. She had heard about most of these incidents before, but now there was such a plethora of them she might well have been overwhelmed.[9]

I fail to see why we should be more defensive of Kai Åge than his former wife is.

That said, I do not believe in monocausal explanations. I do not think

9. Knausgaard, *My Struggle, Book Four*, 146–47.

there's a straight line from the tyrannical father to the sensitive, observant, artistic son–Yngve, after all, never wrote any novels. I do not think the style of the book is solely explicable through Knausgaard's childhood, and I do not think the development of the artist's style is the only theme. I am not even particularly interested in whether Karl Ove Knausgaard, the person, sees a line between his early abuse and the idiosyncrasy of his style in this novel cycle. He had already written two novels, and *A Time for Everything* subordinates his eye for detail much more strictly to narrative demand.

All of this hedging is tedious, though. What I want to hazard for this piece is this: One of the struggles in this book is Karl Ove's effort to transmute his titanic attention to detail, first introduced in this book as a survival tool for managing his father's anger, into art. Or stronger, but vaguer still: The attention to detail is an inheritance from the father, much like the alcoholism, the rage, and the shame. This style is not the only way he could have written this book, but there is an affinity between the style and subject matter, between an artistic eye born out of anxiety and self-surveillance, and the subject matter of the all-seeing father. He learns to observe–not just in the ordinary way, but as a way of reading mood and location into the most innocuous cadence of a step, the tenor of a door shutting, the sound of keys splaying on the counter–in order to live around his father and then must learn what to do with that skill.

To wit, some examples.

Food

The very first moment Karl Ove mentions food occurs the same day he sees the face in the sea. His father has set the table, which Karl Ove knows means that the bread will be cold, and there will be no choice of toppings. That night, his father serves one of Karl Ove's least favorites, sardines.

> With sardines it wasn't the taste that was the worst part–I could swallow the tomato sauce by imagining it was ketchup–it was the consistency, and above all the small, slippery tails. They were disgusting. To minimize contact with them, I generally bit them off, put them to the side of the plate, nudged some sauce toward the crust and buried the tails in the middle, then folded the bread over. In this way I was able to chew a couple of times without coming into contact with the tails, and then wash the whole thing down with milk. If Dad was not there, as was the case this evening, it was possible of course to stuff the tiny tails in my pockets.[10]

10. Knausgaard, *My Struggle, Book One*, 21-22.

The first thing to note about this passage is that it doesn't register as remarkable in any way in the context of the surrounding pages. Which is not to say it is mediocre–it is an excellent description of the tricks and tactics children in strict houses use to game their parent's rules around "clearing their plates." (For me, the equivalent was the fatty bits around beef. The same day my fourth-grade teacher told us about parasites, my mother served roast beef, riven with little white lines of fat. I decided to become a vegetarian that day, though it took another twelve years to enact. In the intervening years, my dogs were surreptitiously fed a lot of meat scraps.) But it is not an obviously stylized decision or something that stands out as particularly strange for a child to notice. While reading it you think, "Yes, a child *would* notice the texture of food he finds revolting and is forced to eat." And, maybe more importantly, there aren't any extraneous details that might interrupt the idea that this passage is being narrated by a young boy. There are no clever metaphors, no exacting observations of color, no self-reflection bound up in the description. It is the texture that matters to young Karl Ove, so it is the texture he describes. The disgusting food is one more obstacle placed by the father and is treated as such. He has to eat it to appease him; the tactic of burying fish tails in bread is the best solution Karl Ove has.

Likewise, it is not even particularly strange when he starts focusing on food later in the same book when cleaning his grandmother's house. He's in a decaying hellhole, filled with filth, grime, and shit, where his father died. The normalcy, the cleanliness of outside food would have been a relief. Karl Ove even says as much.

> I switched on the stove, took a frying pan from the cupboard under the counter and some margarine from the fridge, cut off a slice and scraped it into the pan, filled a large saucepan with water and placed it on the rear burner, opened the bag of potatoes, spilled them into the sink, turned on the tap and started washing them as the dollop of margarine slowly slid across the black frying pan. Again it struck me how clean and, for that reason, heartening the presence of these purchases was, with their bright colors, the green and white of the frozen beans bag, its red writing and red logo, or the white paper around most of the loaf, though not all, the dark, rounded, crusty end peeped out like a snail from its shell, or as it appeared to me, like a monk from his cowl."[11]

Here, the description has grown a little more elaborate, fitting the fact that Karl Ove is now thirty and an author. He notices colors, he pays attention

11. Knausgaard, *My Struggle, Book One*, 365.

to the movement of the margarine. "Or as it appeared to me, like a monk from his cowl" is a delightful flourish—as if the whole description did not take place from his viewpoint or as if everyone else would obviously see a snail and he alone saw a monk. But the whole description is, again, primarily psychologically motivated in this passage, rather than aesthetically. (By that I mean in the eyes of the narrator—obviously the author Knausgaard crafted it with care.) It is incredibly psychologically plausible for anyone, not just an artist. Matter out of place is disturbing; it *would* be a relief to focus on the normalcy of supermarket produce in such a situation.

By *Book Two* it has become obvious that Karl Ove's attention to food is no longer a coincidental plot contrivance or a way of underscoring the unreality of the situation (the controlling father, the decaying house); it is a central feature of his artistic practice in these books. The scene where this becomes most obvious to me is the extended New Year's party in *Book Two*. Karl Ove has just brought out lobster for his friends Geir, Christina, Helena, and Anders, and his wife Linda. The conversation has not yet taken off in the way it will later in the evening. Still reticent, he focuses on food. "Cracked the large claw with the pliers from the seafood set I was given as a present by Gunnar and Tove some time ago. The meat that grew in such tasty profusion around the tiny flat white cartilage, or whatever it was. The space between the flesh and the outer shell where there was often water: What kind of feeling would *that* have been when the lobster was walking around on the seabed?"[12] Then again, a few pages later, "I looked down, forked out the soft content of a mussel, it was dark brown with an orange stripe along the top, and when I bit, it crunched like sand between your teeth."[13]

By this point the attention paid to food has become something quite different. His gaze is not directed at dinner in the spirit of a young boy who sees his food as an obstacle to overcome or as a man in desperate need of distraction and normalcy. It might, perhaps, be a momentary distraction from his discomfort in society, but he is focused on the food as an aesthetic object because that is what this iteration of Karl Ove does. He observes the colors (white, then brown and orange), he still notices the texture. Only this time he adds the whimsical moment of empathy for the lobster walking on the seabed.

With each iteration of these early food scenes, he piles on more detail. By the final book, I expected food descriptions reflexively, right alongside descriptions of drinking inexplicably terrible coffee and smoking cigarettes.

12. Knausgaard, *My Struggle, Book Two,* 282.
13. Knausgaard, *My Struggle, Book Two,* 287.

What started out as one more form of control by his father becomes an aesthetic reverie and then, perhaps, a habit.

Cleaning

Cleaning is the other obvious activity that is gradually transformed as the novels progress. A few pages after the face in the sea scene, Knausgaard introduces the theme of cleaning. (It is remarkable, rereading these books, how early and subtly he introduces his preoccupations.) Karl Ove is now a teenager. His mother is out of town, and he is living alone with his father, though they barely see each other. For the first time, his father begins to unravel.

The first sign is the house. His father is barely there; ditto Karl Ove.

> This left its mark on the aura of the house, which, as Christmas was approaching, had taken on an air of abandonment. Tiny, desiccated lumps of cat shit littered the sofa in front of the TV on the first floor, old unwashed dishes on the kitchen drainer, all the radiators, apart from an electric heater which he moved to the room where he was living, were turned off. As for him, his soul was in torment.[14]

Drinking soon follows.

Cleaning, by contrast, is associated with his mother and a return to at least the semblance of normalcy. "Going into the house, I knew at once he had been cleaning. It smelled of green soap, the rooms were tidy, the floors were shiny. And the dried up cat shit on the sofa, that was gone."[15]

The cat shit foreshadows the human shit that Karl Ove will find on his grandmother's sofa at the end of the book, but what really interests me is the way he yet again uses the presence and absence of particular things (sights, sounds, smells) as proxy for the presence of a person. It is no longer the jangling keys and the whisper of his mother's scarf as she takes off her coat in the hallway that alerts Karl Ove to her presence; it is the return to order, the scent of soap, the gleam of the wooden floors. I imagine Karl Ove in these scenes almost as a spider, spinning out threads of awareness to the surrounding objects in order to capture a sign of his mother's presence.

Karl Ove's search for signs in these early childhood scenes is clearly defensive; his motive becomes more complicated in later scenes with Linda. Early in *Book Two*, after returning with their daughter Vanja from a birth-

14. Knausgaard, *My Struggle, Book One*, 43.
15. Knausgaard, *My Struggle, Book One*, 54.

day party, he stops outside the door to their apartment. "A faint odor of putrescence and something worse rose from the large bag of rubbish and the two small diaper bags in the corner by the folded double stroller. Heidi's shoes and jacket were on the floor next to it. Why the *hell* hadn't she put them in the wardrobe?"[16]

It is not the content of the scene, a married couple's resentment over housework, that is interesting; it is the way it mirrors the scene in the first book where the scent of soap signals his mother's presence. It is the same gesture, reading signs of order and disorder to capture the mood and presence of the other, but the smells associated with Linda (shit) literally invert those associated with his mother, Sissel (soap). If anything, the disorder, disrepair, and—why not?—defecation tie Linda to Karl Ove's father, and his compulsive cleaning around the flat is a repetition of his earlier efforts to manage the destruction Kai Åge leaves in his wake. (I genuinely wonder sometimes if the pair would have stayed married if Linda had been better at cleaning.)[17]

The clever repetition of motifs, the immediacy of the sensory input, and the sheer wash of detail make it easy to miss how much Knausgaard withholds in describing his surroundings. There are, in fact, whole categories of surroundings that Knausgaard essentially never touches on, despite his lapidary eye for detail, or certainly doesn't treat with anything like the same degree of scrutiny. After all the meals we have watched Karl Ove prepare, can anyone describe his plates or silverware? Can anyone reading this describe what color paint his home in Malmö is or what style his couch is? I can imagine the table Linda stabbed in Stockholm, and my mind fills in the rest of the apartment with broad, stereotyped details of high ceilings and elaborate crown molding, which might not even be correct. Mostly, though, I remember the mayonnaise he smears on lobster, the fatty chunks in his unpasteurized milk, and the *mise en abyme* printed on the box's logo.

But why would it occur to you to notice that he never tells us the color of his walls during the New Year's Eve party in *Book Two* when he wonders what it would feel like to be a lobster walking on the ocean floor with water in his claws? The abundance of detail overwhelms you.

Still, it is a puzzle why Knausgaard chooses to focus so very much atten-

16. Knausgaard, *My Struggle, Book Two*, 65.

17. An entire essay could be written about the gender dynamics of relationships throughout the books. His relationship to his mother, as one reviewer pointed out, could be read as Freudian. Linda assumes the role of the volatile, loved-feared-hated object after his father dies, and, in many ways, his long phone calls with his friend Geir echo the type of conversations he reported having with his mother when young. Unfortunately, I think a greater discussion here would take the piece too far off topic.

tion on the types of categories he does (food, disorder, cleaning supplies, clothes in his youth) and not on others. A lobster is not inherently more interesting than a table, but it is the lobster that gets the extended description, while the table is just described as "expensive." It is no use to say that he notices food because he cares about it more; he's quite clear throughout the books that he's anything but a foodie.

For this question, too, I have a guess. It has to do with his depiction of space.

Space

Roughly halfway through *The Phenomenology of Perception,* Maurice Merleau-Ponty suggests a rough schema for understanding the different experiences of space that I think is helpful for interpreting Knausgaard. First, there is what he calls "clear space," a type of public, impartial space, "in which all objects are equally important and enjoy the same right to existence." This is something like space understood as a map, or a description of a room compiled by a sufficient aggregate of strangers, or, better still, space as it exists apart from human perception. No one really lives in clear space; we are too embodied, too subject to cultural assumptions about the significance of certain objects and directions, too idiosyncratic in our personal relationships to objects.

In addition to clear space, Merleau-Ponty believes there are widespread social attitudes toward space. Sounding like Durkheim in the early parts of *Elementary Forms* that people seldom read, Merleau-Ponty traces the emergence of social space back to "primitive man," for whom, he writes, "There is a mythical space in which directions and positions are determined by the residence in it of great affective entities."[18] Contemporary cultures still imbue space and direction with significance, he argues. We can see the traces of these attitudes in language, as in the tendency when he wrote to describe morals (or art) as "high" or "low." Alternately, think of the prohibition against placing the Qur'an on the floor. There are also public sites that are charged with broad, social significance, like monuments or Wall Street. (This is surely correct. The World Trade Center, for example, is not primarily a site of *personal* significance for Americans, even if a given individual might happen to have personal feelings about it.)[19]

18. Maurice Merleau-Ponty, *The Phenomenology of Perception*, trans. Colin Smith (New York: Routledge Classics, 2002), 229.

19. Though Merleau-Ponty writes decades before affect theory, I nonetheless think Eve Sedgwick's discussion of affect as a type of emotional charge that can take any object is helpful here (and roughly correct). Sedgwick, following and quoting Silvan Tompkins, differentiates affects

Finally, there is the personal dimension of space that makes certain objects or areas recede or advance in significance, based on the feelings attached to them. These affective reactions can be either positive or negative or something else altogether. The corner where I was dumped leaps out when I pass it, just as surely as the café where I met my husband does. Even in my house, there are relatively neutral objects that my eyes gloss over as insignificant, like the spare kitchen stools tucked out of the way until guests arrive, while there are others that my eye lingers on without fail, like the mirror I inherited from my grandmother. Objectively, they are all just things, stuff. A chair is arguably more useful than a mirror and might even have a greater claim on my attention, in the abstract. Subjectively, though, the mirror draws me to it because of the memories and feelings attached to it, while the chair fades into the background.[20]

For Merleau-Ponty, this mixture of clear space, cultural maps, and affective charges simply is how humans perceive space. It is not a question of an individual's greater or lesser sensitivity; stripping out any one of these components would be, in fact, a symptom of some form of psychosis.[21]

To bring this back to Knausgaard, one way of making sense of Knausgaard's compulsive readability is through Merleau-Ponty's discussion of space. Though not psychotic (most of the time), he, the artist, cares about the objects that are emotionally near, about things that belong, overwhelmingly, to that third sphere of Merleau-Ponty's. Setting qua setting–which is to say, clear, public space, distinct from his emotional connection to it–holds relatively little interest for him. Even when he is walking through a city, his descriptions have very little of the panoramic in them. He is interested in people, he is interested in the odd architectural detail that catches his eye, but not usually buildings or spaces in relation to each other. He is interested in objects in relation to him. He is not particularly interested in

from drives. A drive, they argue, is instrumental and oriented toward a particular aim, such as sexuality. "Affects have far greater freedom than drives with respect to, for example, time (anger can evaporate in seconds but can also motivate a decades-long career of revenge) and aim (my pleasure in hearing a piece of music can make me want to hear it repeatedly, listen to other music, or study to become a composer myself). Especially, however, affects have greater freedom with respect to object. . . . Affects can be, and are, attached to things, people, ideas, sensations, relations, activities, ambitions, institutions, and any number of other things, including other affects. Thus, one can be excited by anger, disgusted by shame, or surprised by joy." Eve Kosofsky Sedgwick, *Touching Feeling: Affect, Pedagogy, Performativity* (Durham, NC: Duke University Press, 2006), 19.

20. Note: Merleau-Ponty never claims these relationships are fixed. What draws your attention changes as you pass through space.

21. Though it is not relevant to Knausgaard, it's worth noting that Merleau-Ponty does dwell at some length on what a world would look like without clear space. He believes it is the experience of a schizophrenic.

places of social significance like monuments or post offices. (Though he does, of course, care about socially significant *events*.) Nor is he interested in the things that are physically closest to him, necessarily. (Think again of all the things we do not see. What color are his plates?) No, he cares about things as they elicit a charge, a response in him and more or less ignores them otherwise.

Look again at the early passage where he waits for his mother to return as an example. "I put the book on the floor, switched off the light, and lay in the dark listening for her: the car door slamming, the crunch across the gravel, the front door opening, her coat and scarf being removed, the footsteps up the stairs. . . . The house seemed different then, when she was in it, and the strange thing was that I could *feel* it."[22] He does not attend to what is physically close—walls, stairs, furniture, distance all recede—rather, he attends to what is emotionally close. It is his mother he cares about and describes, even though she is on a different floor and only exists for him through a few routine jangles and crunches. All of this is another way of saying that space in Knausgaard is not primarily concerned with physics or objective distance. Rather, it is all measured in affective proximity.

Of course, sometimes affective and physical proximity can overlap, as when he is cracking a lobster claw. And sometimes he can give quite a good overview of a space, like the moment he first walks into his northern home in *Book Four*. But the uniting theme is what he cares about.

This is not an obvious artistic choice, even though I understand the impulse to shrug and say that all novels filter scenery through emotional pull in one way or another. That is true, to an extent. Where Knausgaard differs from many is in his resolute unwillingness to break from that phenomenological perspective, particularly in the narrative mode, as opposed to, say, the philosophical mode. His focus on the affectively near denies the reader any glimpse of his surroundings as they exist independently of his awareness. You might, by chance, see enough to piece together a mental map of the landscape but that is a result of your interest, not the flashlight's.

Knausgaard's refusal to grant the reader a glimpse of his surroundings apart from his perspective is part of what makes his voice so compelling, I think. He captures the extent to which we navigate our habitats by physical habit without really ever thinking about them. It would be unnatural to describe the layout of your apartment when walking through it in the morning or think about your neighborhood in terms of left-right or north-south, even if that would help the reader orient herself. In fact, unless I am making a deliberate effort to think about it, nearly the only time I think about a place in

22. Knausgaard, *My Struggle, Book One*, 25.

terms of its immensity or location on a north-south grid is when I am lost or giving directions to someone who is lost. Deliberately or intuitively, Knausgaard grasps that. Even when Karl Ove describes his neighbors in those early pages of *Book One*, he always does so in terms of "the neighbor who lived on the other side of the wall" or "Fru Gruber," never "the neighbor to our left." The topography makes perfect sense to him and, after a while, as the reader I forget that I do not really know what he is describing.

Another way of putting this last paragraph is to say that Knausgaard is a great artist of habitus. He has an excellent sense of what recedes to background bodily habit and what intrudes on conscious awareness. That is part of what makes it feel like you are in his head–he notices exactly what a person would notice when navigating a familiar space and nothing more.

This perspective is not an accident or a freak bit of luck on Karl Ove, the narrator's, part. There are hints of his interest in spatial perspective extraordinarily early on, as when the narrator in philosophical mode remarks,

> As your perspective of the world increases, not only is the pain it inflicts on you less but also its meaning. Things that are too small to see with the naked eye, such as molecules and atoms, we magnify. Things that are too large, such as cloud formations, river deltas, constellations, we reduce [. . .]. Throughout our childhood and teenage years, we strive to attain the correct distance to objects and phenomena. We read, we learn, we experience, we make adjustments. Then one day we reach the point where all the necessary distances have been set, all the necessary systems have been set in place. That is when [. . .] everything is set, time races through our lives, the days pass by in a flash and before we know what is happening we are forty, fifty, sixty. . . . Meaning requires content, content requires time, time requires resistance. Knowledge is distance, knowledge is stasis and the enemy of meaning.[23]

Time dilates in Knausgaard's novels. Sometimes it is tethered to the narrative present, sometimes it zooms all the way out and looks at individual experience in the fullness of historical or even biblical time. A wonderful passage, as Karl Ove watches the crowds in the airport concourse:

> In twenty-five years a third of them would be dead, in fifty years two-thirds, in a hundred all of them. And what would they leave behind, what had their lives been worth? Gaping jaws, empty eye sockets, somewhere beneath the earth. Perhaps the day of Judgment really would come? All these bones

23. Knausgaard, *My Struggle, Book One*, 11.

> and skulls that had been buried for thousands of years would gather themselves up with a rattle, and stand grinning under the sun, and God, the almighty, the all-powerful, would, with a wall of angels above and below Him, judge them from his heavenly throne. . . . Also those walking around here, with their roller suitcases and tax-free bags, their wallets and their bank cards, their perfumed armpits and their dark glasses, their dyed hair and their walking frames, would be awakened, impossible to discern any difference between them and those who died in the Middle Ages.[24]

But space is typically tethered to Karl Ove's perspective. It is not static—he notices new and different things at different moments—but it is usually tied to his gaze, to his sense of what is worth noticing. Perhaps this is a choice to capture the sense of suffocation he feels in his viewpoint as he writes. The few times he is surprised by the landscape, as when he stumbles on a cruise ship in *Book Six*, he experiences the view as sublime.[25]

To bring this back to my opening thesis, the categories of things Knausgaard the artist cares about are established fairly early on in his surveillance of his father. Food is a site of contention in those early pages, as are objects that signify the presence or absence of people, and postures that express moods. Disorder, dirt, and shit also enter in early on, as signs of his father's decline. Does Knausgaard the author mean to draw a line from those early pages to his later outlook? Does he mean there to be a psychological link between the sardine scene and the later scenes eating lobster, or simply a thematic link? I do not know, but I do not think the intent matters.

TO REGROUP

There is another way to tell the story I have been trying to put together. It would go something like this: Young Karl Ove grew up in a home of constant surveillance. Or, much like the prisoners within Jeremy Bentham's panopticon, he grew up with the fear of constant surveillance. As adults reading his novels, we know that his father could not possibly be omni-

24. Knausgaard, *My Struggle, Book One*, 233.
25. "The same day I saw something utterly sublime and quite different to anything else on that trip. I was out with John in the area surrounding the apartment, walking through the narrow, dark and damp passages where little bags of rubbish with knots tied in their tops had been left outside every door and clothes had been hung out to dry on washing lines that ran up above between houses, it was late afternoon and we were approaching the square facing the lagoon where the vaporetos came in, when an enormous ship suddenly appeared above the rooftops, gliding slowly away. We emerged on to the square and that very special light that is always in Venice, under cloud or sun, in autumn as well as in spring and summer, made everything, the walls and roofs of the building, shimmer." Knausgaard, *My Struggle, Book Six*, 636.

scient, that the times he happened to discover Karl Ove breaking the rules could mostly be explained by other means. In *Book One*, Karl Ove eventually realizes his father knew he was running in the garden because he heard his footsteps pounding on the flagstones. He likewise would have figured out that Karl Ove was hiding candy under his bedcover in *Book Three* by fairly pragmatic means–either seeing the lump in the bed or reading Karl Ove's guilty face.

(I am reminded, as an aside, of a story George Orwell tells in "Such, Such Were the Joys" about smuggling candy back to the private school where he went as a child. He was convinced that the school had enlisted every adult in town to report any infractions to the superintendent. As an adult, he calls it, I believe, "one of those lunatic misunderstandings of childhood." For Karl Ove, the idea that everything he did could potentially be seen and condemned was no misunderstanding. But, to resume–)

There was no point in reasoning with the tyrannical father, no point in arguing with the capriciousness of his law. So Karl Ove and Yngve did the only thing that made sense: they began surveilling their father in turn. And not just their father–themselves. Every petty thing that might set him off, they tried to anticipate and hide. They learned Yngve's soundless duck walk to hide their footsteps from their father. Karl Ove discovered how to wrap sardine tails in bread to hide the texture, rather than refuse to eat them. Karl Ove learned to read his father's mood in his footsteps, the speed of his car, the strength with which he slammed the door, the presence or absence of a wine bottle left on the counter.

In short, he internalized the disciplinary regime of surveillance and some thirty years later began to write a book that plucked out exactly the sort of details he learned to pick out to avoid enraging his father–the texture of his food, the ambient sounds of his car, the presence or absence of clutter in the house.

And perhaps as he turned the surveillance inward, he also turned some of his father's immeasurable cruelty inward as well. In describing the evolution of the bad conscience in the human animal, Nietzsche offers a theory. Humans originally delighted in cruelty and had even an instinct to discharge it. Eventually, though, one portion of the population was conquered by another, more brutal, domineering population. The weaker portion had no way to fight back against the aggressors, who thoughtlessly inflicted cruelty on them. Worse still, the subordinate population was now left with anger against the aggressors they could not express and their own, unsatisfied instinct for cruelty. "All instincts which do not discharge themselves outward will receive an inward direction," Nietzsche concludes. "The entire inner world of man, originally as thin as if it were stretched between two membranes, expanded as outward discharge was *inhibited* and extended itself, acquired depth, breadth, and height, in the same measure . . . . *Man* . . . impatiently lacerated, persecuted, gnawed at, maltreated himself."[26] The result was the creation of previously unimaginable interiority, filled with self-reproach and guilt as the weak took mistakes that previously would have been paid for in money or suffering and made them occasions to berate themselves.[27]

Is there an instinct for cruelty? Is Nietzsche's story right? Who knows, who cares? But does it sound plausible that a child (Jane Eyre, Karl Ove, whoever), living under capricious, excessive violence, subordinate, unable to fight back, unable to make sense of the situation, trained to think that he must trust, respect, or even love said capricious authority might turn his thoroughly understandable rage and disappointment inward, for lack of a better way to express it? And does it seem plausible that, in addition to deeply damaging him, that long, confused masochistic childhood might also have a role in carving out that tremendous sense of interiority, which so fills the books? Oh my, yes.

There's more than one way to understand Knausgaard's remark that a troubled childhood made him a writer.[28]

THE STAKES, THE FUTURE

All that being said, what are the stakes? How does this change the books or how we read them?

26. Friedrich Nietzsche, *On the Genealogy of Morals and Ecce Homo* (New York: Macmillan, 1897), 84–85.

27. I am often reminded in reading these books of a revelation I had midway through graduate school about the great nineteenth-century female novelists. I had never put much thought into the great classics written by women. Austen, Eliot, and the Brontës didn't exactly bore me, but seemed much less interesting to me than, say, Kafka or Nabokov. But at some moment when studying for exams, I picked *Jane Eyre* and discovered a particular passage. Jane Eyre has started to suspect she loves Mr. Rochester; Mr. Rochester has gone to a neighboring house, where he will socialize with the impossibly beautiful Blanche Ingram. Disgusted with herself for losing sight of propriety and her own best interest, Jane sentences herself to make two drawings. The first, done in chalk, would be her own. It would be as harshly honest as possible, omitting no asymmetry, no wrinkle, no unflattering angle. Underneath, she vowed to write, "Portrait of a Governess, disconnected, poor, and plain." The second, done on ivory in oil paintings, would depict the most beautiful woman she could imagine, complete with lustrous curls, glowing skin, luxurious clothing, and dazzling diamonds. Underneath that image, she vowed to write "Blanche, an accomplished lady of rank." The masochism of this whole scene is breathtaking, and it also made me viscerally grasp Nietzsche's point in *Genealogy of Morals* about the instinct for cruelty turning inward, creating interiority.

28. Ben Walsh, "Karl Ove Knausgaard: 'I'd Rather Shoot Myself than Be in Therapy,'" inews.co.uk, July 17, 2020, https://inews.co.uk/essentials/karl-ove-knausgaard-troubled-childhood-can-good-made-writer-102677.

In one sense, it doesn't. It has never been subtext that Karl Ove's father has deeply damaged him at the same time he inspired these books. You do not need Foucault to get from, "Shut your maw. You look like an idiot . . ." in Karl Ove's first conversation with his father to the scene when he first arrives in Stockholm and cringes while walking down the street.[29] "All the faces I saw were of strangers and would continue to be so for weeks and months as I didn't know a soul here, but that didn't prevent me from feeling that I was being watched. . . . Was there something wrong with my coat? My collar, shouldn't it be turned up like that? My shoes, did they look the way shoes should? Was I walking a bit oddly, leaning forward too much? Oh, I was an idiot, what an idiot. What a stupid, idiotic fucking idiot. My shoes. My coat. Stupid. Stupid. Stupid."[30] We know these books are acts of masochism and aggression, bent on transforming trauma into art.

I do think there's some worth and interest in figuring out how these books work. Knausgaard remarks that art requires that life and subject submit to form.[31] A book can fail if it has too strong of a subject or too strong of a style and not enough formal discipline. I do not think these books fail, mostly. Maybe *Book Four* fails for me. I think it is worth figuring out what some of the formal constraints are. I, at least, enjoy the books more after thinking through how he gets his effect of immediacy.

But mostly, I think it helps make sense of a particular ethical position Karl Ove takes toward his children. I am thinking of the passage in *Book Three*. The narrator is looking back on the brief time when they had a kitten. They only have two pictures of the kitten. In one, he has a paw raised to catch a swimmer on TV. In the other, he is reclined between Karl Ove and Yngve, wearing a blue bow tie.

The passage is worth quoting, if not in full, then at length.

> Who put the bow tie on?
>
> It must have been Mom. That was the sort of thing she would do. I know that, but during the months I have been writing this, in the spate of memories and events and people who have been roused to life, she is almost completely absent, it is as if she hadn't been there, indeed, as if she were one of the false memories you have, not one you have experienced.
>
> How can this be?
>
> For if there was someone there at the bottom of the well that is my childhood, it was her, my mother, Mom. She was the one who made all our meals and gathered her around us in the kitchen every evening. She was the one

29. Knausgaard, *My Struggle, Book One*, 16.
30. Knausgaard, *My Struggle, Book Two*, 132.
31. Knausgaard, *Inadvertent*, 29.

> who went shopping, knitted or sewed our clothes; she was the one who repaired them when they fell apart. She was the one who supplied the bandage when we had fallen and grazed our knees. [. . .]
>
> All the things mothers do for their sons, she did for us. [. . .]
>
> She was always there, I know it, but I just can't remember it. [. . .]
>
> She saved me because if she hadn't been there I would have grown up alone with Dad and sooner or later I would have taken my life, one way or another. But she was there, dad's darkness has a counterbalance, I am alive and the fact that I do not live my life to the full has nothing to do with the balance of my childhood. I am alive, I have my own children and with them I have tried to achieve only one aim: that they shouldn't be afraid of their father.
>
> They aren't, I know that.
>
> When I enter a room, they don't cringe, they don't look down at the floor, they don't dart off as soon as they glimpse an opportunity, no, if they look at me it is not a look of indifference, and if there is anyone I am happy to be ignored by, it is them. And should they have completely forgotten I was there when they turn forty themselves, I will thank them and take a bow and accept the bouquets.[32]

This is a passage about returning the parent-child gaze to a healthy state of asymmetry. Karl Ove, Knausgaard—whoever you want to call the speaker—can't or won't escape the intensity of his compulsion to observe. It is part of his craft, it is beaten into him and, in the case of his children, it is (perhaps?) a less sinister by-product of being a parent. (Here I speculate as a non-parent.) That is what parenting is in large part in these books and in the quartet that follows—it is watching, observing, interpreting, mourning.

But parenting, or at least successful parenting, for Knausgaard, is also shielding your child from developing that same compulsive attention to you in turn.

32. Knausgaard, *My Struggle, Book Three,* 247–48.

12 JANUARY 2018 BLOOMINGTON, INDIANA

BILES: Earlier Josh and Erik were talking about consuming as a way of destroying. I think he is consuming the Bible and excreting his own version of it as a way to displace it. I think he has ambitions on that level.

DUBLER: But the Bible has been displaced in the world. If anything, it is a reactionary move.

SULLIVAN: How do you know that the Bible's been displaced?

CARLSON: Because he grew up in New York.

/ 4 /

The Knausgaard Swarm

Joshua Dubler

I have never had particularly good taste. When, in my life, I've forged connections to cool things, it's generally been because I've been downwind from somebody with better aesthetic judgment. When it comes for me, a connection to an artist or artwork tends to happen later. Before the lightning of cathexis comes the flypaper of mimesis.

One of the things that has interested me, therefore, in reading and thinking about *My Struggle* has been the question of what bound me to these texts. This is not the same question as what I like about them. That latter question pertains to matters of form, content, and the experience of reading them. The former touches on these aesthetic concerns, but it also opens up space to think about sociology, history, and how as a reader and writer I continue to be shaped by these forces. It is within these overlapping spheres, which are at once textual and extratextual, that *the swarm* has emerged for me as a driving analytic for thinking about these novels, their reception, and about the men—Karl Ove the character and Knausgaard the narrator—at their center.

THE COMPULSION TO PARTICIPATE

Kathleen Stewart writes of the swarm.[1]

> We will follow any hint of energy, at least for a little while. When something happens, we swarm toward it, gaze at it, sniff it, absorb its force, pour over its details, make fun of it, hide from it, spit it out, or develop a taste for it. We complain about the compulsion to participate. We deny its pull. We blame

1. Kathleen Stewart, *Ordinary Affects* (Durham, NC: Duke, 2007), 70.

FIGURE 4: Still from Black Mirror, season 3, episode 6, "Hated in the Nation." Directed by James Hawes. October 21, 2016. Netflix.

it on the suburbs and TV and ourselves. But we desire it too, and the cure is usually another kind of swarming, this time under the sign of redemption: a mobilization for justice, a neighborhood watch committee, some way of keeping our collective eyes open. Something to do.

The swarm is the murmuration of popular enthusiasm. Spectacles of horror are reliable provocations; beauty and craft pull and push more haphazardly. A murder swarms frictionlessly; a work of literature swarms with greater resistance.

The swarm is not new *per se*, but it is a quintessential species of the digital age. Though it promises moments of heightened significance and meaning, the swarm as a formal matter is recreational and stupid. Just as a mathematical mind can identify patterns in the seemingly random, a finely tuned sensibility versed in its chaos might well call the swarm form beautiful. But to the common eye, the swarm is ugly. The faint whiff of Arendt's Eichmann hovers around the swarm, and I am susceptible to the suggestion that an ethically serious person ought to refuse to swarm on principle.

The internet did not invent the swarm, but inasmuch as its structured flow of capital, images, and feelings makes swarming ever easier and more intense, it makes good sense that it is in the internet age that the swarm emerges as an object for discourse. In the digital era still dawning, celebrity deaths become civic holidays, killings caught on cellphones furnish rituals of civic witness, and a Twitter feed becomes a mode and mood of governance. The affects come fast and cut deep. These swarms stir us to move, sometimes as one, or at least what *feels* like as one.

The Knausgaard swarm took me up during the summer of 2015, which coincided with the publication of the American paperback of *Book Three*. The object itself attests to just how dense the Anglophonic enthusiasm for *My Struggle* was at that time. In addition to five superlative blurbs on the back—"most anticipated," "most memorable," "biblical," "brilliant,"—the front matter includes five plus pages of testimony assembled from the receptions of the preceding volumes. In all, outside and in, there are forty blurbs, many from other top-tier novelists: Rachel Cusk, Ben Lerner, Zadie Smith. It feels tautological to write, but more than anything, in its heyday the Knausgaard swarm was a *literary* swarm.

Across the sea of blurbs one finds expression of the many intrinsic qualities that make *My Struggle* catnip for those who love it: the thinking, the detail, the truth-telling, the profundity of the mundane that captures (in Knausgaard's own words) the "inner core of human existence," the dense description, the way the book "transforms the personal and mundane into the universal and perennially significant," how the prose "achieves an aching intimacy," producing "a memoir that burns with the heat of life," an unexpectedly entrancing combination of detail and intimacy that is visceral and immersive, powerfully alive, ceaselessly compelling."[2]

The compulsive pleasure of *My Struggle's* "I can't stop, I want to stop, I can't stop, just one more page" reading experience is another common theme: how "it immerses you totally" and kept the reviewer "up till two almost every morning for a week." That the subsequent novels would also prove "fit for devouring" was the seeming consensus: "Why would you read a six-volume, 3,600 page Norwegian novel about a man writing a six-volume 3,600 page Norwegian novel? The short answer is that it is breathtakingly good, and so you cannot stop yourself, and would not want to."

As a party to this swarm, I cosign many of these judgments. But as a student of the swarm form, it is hard not to observe a certain kind of *swarm recursion*. Echoing in the key of hyperbole, swarm recursion is the psycho-epidemiological phenomenon where the swarm swarms in response to its own swarming. By the publication of *Book Three*, the literary event of the

2. All critical praise quoted from the front matter of Karl Ove Knausgaard, *My Struggle, Book Three* (New York: Farrar, Straus & Giroux, 2015).

Knausgaard swarm was in part a celebration of the Knausgaard swarm's profound literary *eventness*: "the most significant literary enterprise of our time;" "a literary project that flies in the face of every known commercial principle;" "a revolutionary novel;" "a masterpiece;" "an early twenty-first century masterpiece;" "a masterpiece of staggering originality;" "a remarkable work of art," "a work of genius;" crafted by a "rock star;" "a writer strong enough to survive the hype." In sum, *My Struggle* was "the literary event of the century;" "a literary event the likes of which we will not see again in our lifetimes." Consumed with the thrill of having been there when, the literary class found in the *My Struggle* swarm an opportunity to celebrate the fact that, even at this late hour, a daring, formally experimental novel can remain an occasion for widespread cultural celebration.

Literature is literature, and publicity is publicity, but for present purposes I am reluctant to fully disaggregate the two. That is to say: Why *this* swarm here and now?

With certain swarms, sociological interpretations are irresistible. This would seem especially true for the swarms in which one's own participation takes the form of refusal. Ergo, in its moment, it was impossible not to notice how the Bush-era Lincoln Center revival of Wagner's *Ring* Cycle betrayed a variety of cultural truths ranging from the hegemony of the war machine to the full assimilation of Upper West Side Jews into whiteness. Similarly, the cult of *Hamilton* was a jewel in the crown of the willful disaggregation, during the era of finance capital and under Obama, of liberal race politics from class politics. Less stirring cases are more opaque. Was there something particularly 2010s-ish about *Game of Thrones* that it would behoove us to critically attend to? Was there something inescapably 2019 about the Lil Nas X "Old Town Road" phenomenon? Not that I've had occasion to consider. No doubt others have. Under communicative capitalism, we have a name—"the take economy"—for the internet's reflex of attributing outsize momentousness to what invariably prove to be fleeting occasions of collective swarming.

Perhaps the question I am asking about *My Struggle* merely reflects that for a historical materialist with a hammer, everything looks like a nail. Or maybe some works of literature are especially hammerable. Between the rigors of qualitative methods and the pacing of the publication process, ethnographies are invariably time-lapse portraits of a present already past. The swarm-scape Stewart's *Ordinary Affects* explores is that of TV news, local newspapers, and water-cooler gossip; the internet is a decidedly marginal character. But this world was already on its way out, to be supplanted by a landscape ever more saturated by the digital. The year 2007, when *Ordinary*

Affects was published, was the year that Apple released the iPhone, Facebook launched its public platform, and Google introduced Street View—a string of pivotal moments in a rush of territorial expansion that Shoshana Zuboff would liken to the Spanish conquest of the Americas.[3] Digital media no more invented the swarm than they invented narcissism or consumerism, but the encroachment of digital modes of engagement into domestic space that made the impulse to swarm ever readier to hand also rendered the swarm newly visible—an object to be named, criticized, theorized.

As an organizing category, the swarm has numerous antecedents. As "culture," as "ideology," as "*habitus*," modern social thought has given us a variety of names for the structures and processes by which the forces of history and society fill the world of everyday experiences with a particular spirit and invest individuals and collectives with capacities to move in this way or that. The swarm's coordinates belong on this map, but the magic and intensities of the swarm are also made of newer stuff. Whereas in the era that preceded ours, participation in a rally, revival, or concert required a person to leave home, the saturation of media into every space of life has had effects not merely quantitative in kind.

To make sense of this newness, Byung-Chul Han contrasts the digital swarm to the analog crowd.

> Occasionally, digital individuals come together in gatherings—in smart mobs for instance. However, their *collective patterns of movement* are like the swarms that animals form—fleeting and unstable. Their hallmark is volatility. Furthermore, these groupings commonly seem carnivalesque—ludic and nonbinding. Herein lies the difference between the digital swarm and the classic crowd, which—as in the case of workers assembling in mass—is not volatile but voluntative. Organized labor is not a matter of fleeting patterns: it consists of enduring *formations*. With a single spirit, unified by an ideology, it *marches in one direction*. On the basis of will and resolve, it has the capacity for *collective action* and takes standing relations of domination head on. Only when a crowd is resolute about shared action does power arise. *The mass is power*. In contrast, digital swarms lack such resolve. They do not *march*. Because of their fleeting nature, no political energy wells up. By the same token, online shitstorms prove unable to call dominant *power relations* into question. Instead, they strike individual persons, whom they unmask or make an item of scandal.[4]

3. Shoshana Zuboff, *The Age of Surveillance Capitalism: The Fight for a Human Future at the New Frontier of Power* (New York: Public Affairs, 2019), 176-80 especially.
4. Byung-Chul Han, *In the Swarm* (Cambridge, MA: MIT Press, 2017), 11-12.

To treat the workers' strike as paradigmatic for the crowd is perhaps a bit nostalgic. If the crowd was the historical form for the building of labor power, it was also the form for Beatlemania and book burnings. But the contrast does call attention to the swarm's dominant features: its spontaneity, fleetingness, and capriciousness; its nonbindingness and playfulness; how it's not built to *go* anywhere, and how all of these factors in combination have a funny way of directing its fury onto the relatively powerless.

Famously and not entirely unfairly, Twitter has come to represent the worst of this impulse. I'm thinking of Jon Ronson's *So You've Been Publicly Shamed*, #HasJustineLandedYet, and the notion of the "milkshake duck"—the newly adored entity, which, on a dime becomes an object for contempt.[5] Like the man said: "Each day on Twitter there is one main character. The goal is to never be it."[6]

For some time now, therefore, the rapturous swarm of Knausgaard's Anglophonic reception has felt as though it belonged to an earlier, simpler moment. In 2015 it was possible for a cultural object to garner unadulterated acclaim. This simply doesn't happen anymore. I do not like *Book Six* all that much. However, not only due to its shortcomings as a novel did its reception pale compared to that of its predecessors. A cultural shift has taken place. Knausgaard's star has waned amid the ascendency of a new critical mood—which is itself a swarm engine—that is quicker to condemn than to extol.[7] People are furious for good reason, and our pettier hatreds are far too pleasurable—and monetizable—to be left unindulged.

It doesn't require one to be a scholar of religion to observe in the digital swarm the logic of sacrifice. Solidarity engendered at the expense of an arbitrary victim made deserving through ritual: this is the stuff of Marcel Mauss, George Bataille, and, more than anyone, René Girard—a figure to whom we will later return. As a digital form and mood, the swarm is fickle and recreationally cruel. Frequently mobilized in some circles under the guise of the political, the swarm, in Han's telling, in fact represents the foreclosure of the possibility of the political. In sum, in these over-stimulating and harrowing days, the swarm would seem an apt social form for those digital souls who would rather will nothingness than not will.

5. See Jon Ronson, *So You've Been Publicly Shamed* (New York: Riverhead Books, 2016). See also Richard Seymour, *The Twittering Machine* (Brooklyn, NY: Verso, 2020). For the milkshake duck, see https://twitter.com/pixelatedboat/status/741904787361300481?lang=en.

6. https://twitter.com/maplecocaine/status/1080665226410889217?lang=en.

7. Knausgaard being a white male novelist who takes undo interest in his own interiority makes him an easy target. As Patricia Lockwood opened her *LRB* essay on John Updike: "I was hired as an assassin. You don't bring in a 37-year-old woman to review John Updike in the year of our Lord 2019 unless you're hoping to see blood on the ceiling." See "Malfunctioning Sex Robot," *London Review of Books* (10 October 2019).

MY STRUGGLE AS CHRONICLE OF DIGITAL CREEP

With uneven force, contexts shape meanings. When our collective assembled in Bloomington in January 2019 in the days following the release of a highly discouraging UN climate report, it was the "intense and wild" thunderstorms, the likes of which Knausgaard couldn't remember from his youth–*Surely thunderstorms couldn't be increasing in frequency and intensity with every year that passes, could they?*[8]–which temporally for me colored over everything. In sum, the extrinsic force that has most shaped my reading of these novels has been the internet. On this point *My Struggle* has met me halfway.

On the last page of *Book Three,* Knausgaard, the narrator, offers a final backward salutation to Tromøya, the lost world of his childhood, a place and its people vanished (from him), and therefore eternally coherent, untrammeled, and pure of key.

> I haven't seen any of them since that summer, and if I search for them on the Net to see what they look like or how life has treated them, there are no hits. They don't belong to that class there, they belong to the class of blue- or white-collar parents who grew up outside the center and who have presumably remained outside the center of everything but their own lives.[9]

It is the *lack* of any trace of these people on "the Net," the global portal that belongs to and increasingly shapes Knausgaard's cosmopolitan world that ratifies for Knausgaard his presumption that the simplicity he once enjoyed with these people of Tromøya remains theirs to this day. That these remote, digitally uncaptured lives these left-behind northerners lead are located phenomenologically at the "center . . . of their own lives" should be irresistibly resonant to scholars of religion: the contented primitive as mirror image of the rootless modern. As a thinker, Knausgaard is sometimes hampered by a weakness for this kind of projection, but as a landscape for staging childhood innocence, Tromøya's pristine sacrality is glorious.

Book Three tracks young Karl Ove's passage from the Neverland of early childhood into a world shaped by formative encounters with popular music. This has been the structure of Western adolescence since World War II, when teenagers became a market demographic. Karl Ove's specific experience, however, as he himself names it in *Book Five,* was specifically that of "an '80s person."

8. Knausgaard, *My Struggle, Book Six,* 969-70.
9. Knausgaard, *My Struggle, Book Three,* 427.

> It was August 1988. I was an '80s person, contemporaneous with Duran Duran and the Cure, not that fiddle and accordion music that Grandpa listened to in the days when he trudged up the hill in the dusk with a friend to court Grandma and her sisters. I didn't belong here, with all of my heart I felt that. It actually didn't help that I knew the forest was actually an '80s forest and the mountains actually '80s mountains.[10]

Karl Ove's sense of generational differentiation is at once vanity, but not wrong for that. Radio and television had infused *his* small-town Norwegian life with a dose of MTV-era glitz. The juxtaposition of these unlike elements illustrates a more general point about comparatively enduring earthly landscapes and the historical spirits that haunt them, flittingly, but in their time, fully.

Book Five also documents Karl Ove's haphazard first movements into the digital world. If, in the former shift, Karl Ove moves from an experience of unselfconscious immanence–a world in which friends shit from trees and poke their shit with a stick–into a world saturated with cultural meanings and presences, his encounters with the emergent digital world pitch him into new kinds of magic and new kinds of alienation.

Karl Ove buys a secondhand computer: "And for the first time in my life I wrote letters on a screen and not on a sheet of paper," letters that were stored on floppy disks, "and could be summoned up whenever I wished."[11] That which makes writing and editing infinitely easier, however, also makes writing and editing impossible. For, with the computer, Karl Ove also acquires a game of computer Yahtzee, which he plays for hours on end, sometimes starting the day with these abject marathons.

Soon thereafter, Knausgaard ironizes his prior self's sense of wonder before his dot matrix printer, the kind that's loaded with contiguous paper perforated at the edges.

> What the connection between the floppy disk and the screen was I had no idea; something had to "tell" the machine that an "n" on the keyboard would become an "n" on the screen, but how do you get dead matter to "tell" anything? Not to mention what went on when the same letters on the screen were saved onto the thin little disk and could be brought back to life with one tap of the finger, like the seeds that had been trapped in ice for hundreds of years and then, under certain conditions, could suddenly reveal what they had contained all this time, and germinate and blossom.

10. Knausgaard, *My Struggle, Book Five*, 24.
11. Knausgaard, *My Struggle, Book Five*, 358.

> Surely the letters I saved now would be reawakened as easily in a hundred years' time as they could be now.[12]

Not all was so gloriously if foolishly divine. At long last, spurred by a looming deadline, Karl Ove is finally compelled to write lucidly. His focus is sharpened, and the prose flows. All is good until, inevitably, the new worst thing in the world befalls him: "I touched a key by mistake and everything I had written was gone."[13]

Karl Ove's induction into the digital world accelerates shortly thereafter when he takes a job at the student radio station. The year is probably 1992.[14] In the thousand words that follow, a number of things happen. Showing him around the studio, Gaute, the station manager says,

> "That's where you'll be most of the time. Your main task is to put the record archives onto the computer."
>
> "Really?" I said.
>
> He laughed.[15]

Gaute details the sundry obligations over which, in addition to digitizing the archive, Karl Ove will be responsible: a number of things having to do with coffee, mail, cleaning, copying, and documentation. These are generic office jobs, tasks similar to those that any entry-level office worker might have done since 1960, when Xerox introduced the copier. As with the task of digitizing the archive, however, the culture of this office is, in another digital respect, radically new:

> When the coffee was ready I poured two cups and put one on his desk.
>
> "Thanks," he said.
>
> "What are you working on?" I said.
>
> "*Wolfenstein*," he said.
>
> "*Wolfenstein*?"[16]

What Gaute is "working" on is *Wolfenstein*, one of the very first first-person shooter games. In *Wolfenstein*, as Gaute explains, the player finds himself in Hitler's bunker and shoots his way through ascending floors.

12. Knausgaard, *My Struggle, Book Five*, 375.
13. Knausgaard, *My Struggle, Book Five*, 413.
14. It is in the days prior to New Year's Day of 1992 that he first meets the Student Radio program manager. *Wolfenstein 3D* was first released in 1992.
15. Knausgaard, *My Struggle, Book Five*, 455.
16. Knausgaard, *My Struggle, Book Five*, 455.

Playing for only his third or fourth time, Gaute isn't very good yet, and he dies quickly. His digital avatar–also named "Gaute"–is hit, and the screen fills up with blood. Gaute says that it's time for them to leave the office. "They're very strict about that," he says.[17] "They," one can surmise, are the local university officials bound by a social democratic provision that protects workers' time from their bosses' demands. Would it be wrong to assume that these labor regulations date from an earlier era, an era in which it was imagined that with automation, working hours would soon decrease?[18] It's all gone the other way, of course. Though workers have become more productive, and though, in aggregate, there are fewer widgets to make and move, working hours have only lengthened. As celebrated in shows like *The Office*, workplace sociality in what David Graeber calls "bullshit jobs" largely entails finding ever more alienating means–often digital means–for wasting time.[19]

After sixteen months of work, "everything was digital." *Wolfenstein* was relegated to after hours but no less contained for that. Karl Ove "became obsessed, often leaving the office at two in the morning, having played nonstop from four in the afternoon, sometimes I was still playing when the others came in to do the morning program."[20] In the emerging digital world, the space for life and leisure that regulators had sheltered off from the coercions of work life is freely surrendered in exchange for compulsive, unmanageably pleasurable pleasures. A computer soccer game proves more addictive still, and Karl Ove proceeds to lose weeks at a time building a team into a European Cup winner.

But most addictive of all, with its immersive wash of everything–pornography, too, but primarily *everything*–is the goddamn internet. Karl Ove describes his first experiences of the internet as follows:

> Something else at Student Radio, which I hadn't seen before, was the Internet. This was also addictive. Moving from one page to the next, reading Canadian newspapers, looking at traffic reports in Los Angeles or centerfold models on *Playboy*, which were so endlessly slow to appear, first the lower part of the picture, which could be anything at all, then it rose gradually, the picture filled the frame like water in a glass, there were the thighs, there, oh,

17. Knausgaard, *My Struggle, Book Five*, 456.
18. See Carl Cederstrom and Peter Fleming, *Dead Man Working* (Hants, UK: Zero Books, 2012); https://www.jacobinmag.com/2015/03/automation-frase-robots/.
19. David Graeber, *Bullshit Jobs* (London: Allen Lane, 2018). Indeed, season 2 of the American version of *The Office* features a workplace in which everyone is addicted to some first-person shooter game.
20. Knausgaard, *My Struggle, Book Five*, 456.

> there was . . . shit, was she wearing *panties*? . . . before the breasts, shoulders, neck, and face appeared on the computer screen in the empty Student Radio office at midnight. Rachel and me. Toni and me. Susy and me. *Hustler*, did they have their own website as well? Rilke, had anyone written about his *Duino Elegies?* Were there any pictures of Tromøya?[21]

This would have been the first time that Karl Ove searched the internet for evidence of the semi-mythical place of his childhood pastoral, but as we already know, it would not be the last.

Book Five is not the first time in *My Struggle* the magical, horrible, world-compressing, time-devouring thing that is the internet invades Karl Ove's heretofore analog world. In *Book Two*—the most profane of the six books and the penultimate book chronologically—the word *e-mail* appears on thirteen pages, and *internet* appears twice. Of what do these moments of emailing consist? Without any curation they entail a note of congratulations on good fortune that sends Karl Ove into a mildly neurotic rumination; the means for Karl Ove's reconnection with Geir, his once and future best friend, which, though propitious, produces a vague sense of foreboding; as a site that illustrates to Karl Ove his own utter lack of retention of previous conversations; as one in a series of quotidian practices; once again as a depthless quotidian practice; the same, once more, but this time, when email delivers no thrill or stimulation, Karl Ove Googles himself and masochistically peruses blog posts about himself, one of which declares that his novels aren't even good enough to wipe your ass with; again as a quotidian practice, this time aborted; and, lastly, as a work activity to be juggled with child rearing.

With the exception of a flashback to 1999, when he first meets his future wife, Linda, and a flash-forward to the summer of 2008, when he finishes the novel, the Karl Ove of *Book Two* lives between the years of 2002 and 2005. By the period chronicled in *Book Six*, a new dispensation was dawning:

> My eyes found the steps leading down to the internet café. A new rush of anxiety surged inside me. For a month now I had been receiving the most abhorrent e-mails because of the novel I had written, and I knew there would be more, though not where they would be coming from. It was the same with the phone; every time it rang I froze.[22]

You may well remember this world of the not too distant past, but let's recall its digital infrastructure and attendant rituals: A phone rings, and the

21. Knausgaard, *My Struggle, Book Five*, 457.
22. Knausgaard, *My Struggle, Book Six*, 45.

expectation is that you answer it. This being September 2009, the iPhone had been out for two years already, but at least from the evidence on hand, it had not yet made meaningful inroads into Karl Ove's neck of the Swedish woods. Texting is now commonplace, but Karl Ove is still resistant, and checking his phone for messages is little more than an occasional ruse deployed as an ad-hoc evasion of other people.[23] With little exception, "text" in *Book Six* still stubbornly marks the term's user as a twentieth-century student of literary criticism. As compared to today, the internet remains relatively sequestered. It lives in computer terminals, and internet cafés remain a viable business for people whose homes have yet to be wired, or whose wiring is tenuous enough to merit an external backup for those durations when one's home internet is out.[24]

By the end, social media too has come into Karl Ove's world, albeit not pervasively. In 2009, media men in New York and DC, peering east through the periscope of their desktops would triumphantly name the uprising taking place in Iran the "Twitter Revolution," but in the world of *Book Six*, "twitter" remains bird speech. Facebook has arrived, but it is only a bit player in Karl Ove's social landscape. Karl Ove is predictably contemptuous of Facebook, which he sees as a vehicle for a newly prevalent mode of self-performance, where people broadcast their names and images "as an advertisement of their own idea of who they are."[25] As a thing that people in Karl Ove's immediate world actually use, aptly, Facebook is where, in the most acute stages of her mania, Linda goes to escape her anguished inability to engage her children.

If the foundational insight of the novel is that interpersonal relationships and the interior lives of ordinary people could, if presented with requisite care and craft, yield sentiments and insights akin to those fostered by tragedy and epic, the narrative portions of *Book Six* furnish a claustrophobic window into the pathological condition of the complexified human animal that the novel wrought. Digital communication for this animal is a mirror in which one may masochistically view the reflection of his swollen interiority, social anxiety, and propensity for shame. The phone rings and Karl Ove freezes. At the thought of what's in (or what's not in) his in-box, Karl Ove is physically sickened.

I once heard a prosperity preacher say that worrying is like praying for something you *don't* want to happen. Maybe it's an obvious riff on Weber, but might not the ritualized anxieties of the era of digital communication be read as a perverse form of capitalist pietism? Karl Ove's anxiety vigil in

23. Knausgaard, *My Struggle, Book Six*, 859.
24. Knausgaard, *My Struggle, Book Six*, 42.
25. Knausgaard, *My Struggle, Book Six*, 412.

Book Six over the coming reception of his novel is both the generic condition of looping narcissistic injury and also something far worse. As the English reader knows by this point, the Norwegian reception of *My Struggle* will furnish a condition substantially more acute than the general one. Rather, if some freedom may be found in the sober recognition that no one really gives a shit about your successes or failures, by becoming the smashing literary success he dreamed of being, Karl Ove will be denied the partial break from oneself that the social world makes available to all but the most acutely malignant or celebrated narcissists. In a textbook instance of Oscar Wilde's only-thing-worse-than-not-getting-what-you-want-is-getting-it, the incipient public reception of *My Struggle* proves, for Karl Ove, to be a psychic catastrophe. Karl Ove flails for the assurance of the reality principle, but digital technology makes the horror impossible to escape.

> I knew that; everything I had ever done could be used against me. As long as it was private, as long as it stayed between them and me, I could handle it. But this was terrible, I was crippled with fear every time I checked my e-mail, every time the phone rang, so much so that I could hardly move, would sit paralyzed in a chair or lie paralyzed in bed for hours at a time, and yet I knew it would pass, sooner or later I would have battled my way through it and would be able to see things in their true proportions."[26]

The three days recounted in the first section of *Book Six* are painfully familiar: Karl Ove checks his email "about twice every hour" even on the weekend, and when nothing presents itself as a viable object for externalizing his bad feelings, he resorts to googling himself.[27] A painstaking account of ritualized digital self-abuse is not something I soon need to read again. The neurotic cathexis to one's email, the familiar claustrophobia of a closed loop of shame punctuated by moments of terror—these are things I can ably perform without Knausgaard's assistance. Indeed, one might reasonably say the experience is joyless enough to make the arrival of a book-length excursus on the life of Adolf Hitler feel like a welcome reprieve.

INTERLUDE: ON THE POSSIBLE MERITS OF THINKING THE SWARM INTO THE STUDY OF RELIGION

There may be grounds for thinking about the swarm as the ur-form for the study of religion. Here's what I mean: in its genealogy from Protestant

26. Knausgaard, *My Struggle, Book Six*, 46.
27. Knausgaard, *My Struggle, Book Six*, 57.

theology—one could take William James as paradigmatic—the study of religion privileges interiority and individual experience at the direct expense of social structures. If in "religion" one pinpoints the feelings, acts, and experiences of individual men in their solitude in relation to what they consider the divine, one naturalizes the American tradition of individualist, nature religion as religion *per se*. Every other social form in and through which religion is practiced and transmitted is rendered epiphenomenal *at best*. In this tradition, the truth of God (Nature, Self, etc.) is what matters. By contrast, the social realm in which this Truth arrives pre-embedded is a minefield of wrong turns: of ritualism, of dilutions and delusions, of superstition and enthusiasm. Trace this tradition of polemics against bad religion back to Luther and one word for this noxious stuff is *schwärmerei*.[28] In other words, in all but its exceptional expression, religion is the swarm.

Non-pejorative regard for the social enters the study of religion from the field's other genealogical wellspring: the secular, anthropological tradition for which Émile Durkheim can be made an able stand-in. As per the definition, the name for the social form that unites a community around a system of beliefs and practices relative to sacred things is a "Church." But that is only partially correct. The churches of Europe that furnish the category are historically late-arriving and complex. The so called primitive religions that furnish the anthropology of religion with its ethnological prototypes are thought to be atavistic. But the elementary is not necessarily originary. In Freud's mythic telling in *Totem and Taboo*, it is indeed the primordial stuff of religion by which the horde becomes tribe. But of what stuff is this? Read from the inside out, it's about the enthusiasms of generative tribal solidarity—collective effervescence—but read from the outside in, it's about the spilling of blood, and lots of it. If in the second stage of development, priesthoods will manage and regulate sacrificial systems in which the blood of beasts ordinarily taboo is spilled for social solidarity's sake, in its untamed, primordial iteration, the bacchanal is *swarming with riotous bands*.[29] With routinization, with the curdling of charisma into tradition, the stuff of religion will become the sacrificial system, the priesthood, the church, but in its imagined beginnings, religion is the *swarm*.

Locating the swarm at the submerged center of the study of religion

28. Anthony J. La Vopa, "The Philosopher and the 'Schwärmer': On the Career of a German Epithet from Luther to Kant," in "Enthusiasm and Enlightenment in Europe, 1650-1850," special issue of *Huntington Library Quarterly* 60, nos. 1/2 (1997): 85-115. Special thanks to Courtney Bender for this insight.

29. "When the god with ecstatic shout / Leads his companies out / To the mountain's mounting height / Swarming with riotous bands / Of Theban women leaving / Their spinning and their weaving / Stung with the maddening trance / Of Dionysus" (Euripides, *The Bacchae and Other Plays* [New York: Penguin Books, 1973], 195).

demonstrates the weird role assigned to "religion" in modernity, in its so-called primitive expressions paradigmatically, as the bridge that dis/connects nature to culture. *Book Six* sheds useful light on this point. The word *swarm* appears eight times in the book. Five refer to insects (insects, lady bugs, mosquitoes, insects or animals, grasshoppers). The other three refer to people swarming on the beach, to bicycles in the city center, and, in direct quotation, to industrialized Londoners; as described by Jack London in *The People of the Abyss*, East London is a place "of remarkable meanness and vastness . . . where two million workers swarm, procreate, and die."[30] The *abyss* indeed.

As metaphor, "the swarm" animalizes humans. This is true of poor and working people living bare lives, and it becomes especially true when, with the scaling up of industry, markets, and nation states, this human swarm becomes "a mass." In anticipation of the slaughter to come, Knausgaard notes:

> A recurring motif in the literature of the Weimar Republic was the human mass, and a frequently employed perspective was that of remoteness, in which the human world seemed to consist of busy swarms of insects or great flocks of teeming animals. The reduction of the human that such a perspective entailed was not unambiguous, since at this time, perhaps more than any other, the power of the masses and the potential they held for change began to be understood.[31]

As metaphor then, "the swarm" rewrites sovereign, human individuality as something substantially more antlike. Therein, in a paradoxical way, the swarm represents the consolidation of human agency into a collective with a mass capable of finally actualizing Rousseau's general will. Never was the rural peasant as abject, as *dirty*, as the urban poor of the industrialized city. And yet, with the birth of the mass, this animalized human acquires the capacity to move worlds. In this older iteration the swarm does *not* foreclose the possibility for politics; rather, it engenders it, albeit darkly. Contrary to Byung-Chul Han, then, who pits the swarm *against* the mass, in this telling the swarm is the mass's beating heart. The swarm is the inchoate power of

30. Knausgaard, *My Struggle, Book Six*, 579. For London, workers are Europe's new Jews: "At one time the nations of Europe confined the undesirable Jews in city ghettos. But to-day the dominant economic class, by less arbitrary but none the less rigorous methods, has confined the undesirable yet necessary workers into ghettos of remarkable meanness and vastness. East London is such a ghetto, where the rich and the powerful do not dwell, and the traveller cometh not, and where two million workers swarm, procreate, and die" (Jack London, *The People of the Abyss* [Scotts Valley, CA: CreateSpace, 2008], 97).
31. Knausgaard, *My Struggle, Book Six*, 591–92.

plotting anarchist cells, workers shutting down factories, and the first, violent stirrings of revolutionary vanguards. Where there is world-historical work to be done, the task is one for the swarm.

To paint the swarm as a candidate ur-form for the study of religion is a self-consciously historical claim. It is to pinpoint the swarm as a potentially anchoring object for the study of religion for *us* thinking about imagined religious beginnings and about observable religion *now*. To honor the chaotic yet simultaneously structured circulation of affect as emblematic of the form of religion today is to call into relief and dislodge the presupposed forces of social ordering that have long underwritten functionalist accounts of religion. The swarm as form calls into inverted relief the technological and sociological preconditions—the state, industry, the patriarchal family—that structured late nineteenth-century bourgeois relations of production and were therefore indigenous to the imperialist imaginary that enduringly constituted primitivist fantasies about religion. The tribe constituted in kinship relations through religion rightfully has an important place in contemporary sociological analysis. But as with the digital swarm paradigmatically, as often as not our tribes nowadays are irregulars. Online and in the streets, we convene situationally, we trade in solidarity and destruction for a time, and then we disperse, only later to be reconstituted once again for more togetherness, more fun, more combat, more grief, more time-wasting. Maybe, as a thing in the world to be scrutinized and assessed, the default shape of contemporary religious sociality is less a Church, and more something along the lines of a swarm.

THE PASSION OF KARL OVE KNAUSGAARD, A MAN WHO WOULD NOT SWARM

In its frustrating way, *Book Six* overcompensates for what had before been a conspicuous, borderline suspicious absence of politics in *My Struggle*. Is Knausgaard a reactionary? His hilarious contempt for Swedish gender egalitarianism in *Book Two* was but the most obvious indicator. Through *Book Five* I might have argued that Knausgaard's somewhat elitist suspicion of the masses may have indicated a hostility to democracy. At the very least, the relative paucity of documented happenings beyond Karl Ove's immediate orbit would suggest a disregard for the political. But that characterization would have proven false.

Karl Ove Knausgaard's sensibility belongs to a type I would characterize as independent. The self, nature, and art are paramount. Sensory perception, intensity of feeling, and drives to truth, beauty, and, in its way, goodness—these are what matter. This sensibility is suspicious of the social as the place where things are devalued, deadened, and made stupid and dangerous. Premodern precursors for this sensibility can be found in Euripides, in Plato, in the Prophets, and in Augustine. This tradition articulates a suspicion of the mass, of idolatry, and it is highly attentive to the cozy relationship between collective enthusiasm and grave sin. Secular iterations abound. In the nineteenth century, this impulse gives us Nietzsche's free spirit and Emerson's cult of individuality. A century later, at the nexus of German National Socialism and emergent media culture, this impulse yields the Frankfurt school. As postwar American consumer culture is infused with Black culture, it yields the notion of being *cool*. If constituted as a tradition, its cardinal edict could well be *Thou shalt not swarm*.

Swarm refusal places most standard forms of political engagement out of bounds, but in its way it also constitutes a politics. The principled politics of swarm refusal become clear in Knausgaard's account of the social mechanics of Nazi extermination. The dangerous animalization of the swarm is less about the dehumanized other rendered murderable than about the mobilized collectivity itself. For Knausgaard, the Nazis dehumanized the Jews as "they" into the Jew as "it," but it was in the first-person plural where the murderousness resided: "It was the 'we' who carried it out."[32] Without this human propensity to form this "we," which modern European nationalisms harness and foment, the Holocaust would have been impossible.

Knausgaard's will to refuse the swarm reaches its fullest articulation in what I take to be *Book Six*'s one moment of true transgression. The Hitler biography is full of pseudo-transgressions—of the sacred strictures that purportedly govern how "we" talk about the Holocaust but which Knausgaard in his independence refuses to abide—but the book's moment of real blasphemy happens later.[33]

"I have never felt myself to belong to any we," Knausgaard writes toward the very end of part 1. In his first-tier rationale, which is psychological, he paints himself as the excluded party: "I have never felt good enough, . . . never felt like I deserved it." Taken one way, this is simply a masochistic Lutheran spin on secular non-belonging as canonically named by that *other* Marx, Groucho: the condition of not wanting to belong to any club that would have you for a member. As an ethical matter, however, this is the hallmark of independence. Continuing in this vein, Knausgaard confesses

32. Knausgaard, *My Struggle, Book Six*, 826.

33. Needless to say, "we" here emphatically excludes anyone remotely proximate to the august tradition of secular Jewish comedy that includes Lenny Bruce, Mel Brooks, and too many others to mention.

"his feeling of being on the outside," which was most acute at *gymnas*.[34] His sense of non-belonging at graduation, his inability to have more than one friend at a time, and the salvation he discovered in the identity of *artist*, of being a *writer*, all follow from this animating disposition. It is at this point that the blasphemy arrives. Only in the preceding summer had Knausgaard "experienced something different for the first time." It was on the occasion of the Utøya massacre that Knausgaard first felt overcome by his Norwegianness. A sense of connection to his people overcame him, both with those with whom he was intimate and with those he didn't know at all. And he felt a need to be there, to witness, to experience, to feel his feelings not in solitude, but in communion with others.

For a reader reluctant to connect Norwegian rituals of civic mourning in the wake of the Utøya massacre to the social psychology of Nazism, Knausgaard ties a bow around the necessary conclusion:

> Only afterward did I realize that these must have been the same forces, the enormous forces that reside within the we, that came over the German people in the 1930s. That was how good it must have felt, how secure the identity that they were being offered must have appeared to them. The flags and banners, the torches, the demonstrations: that was what it must have been like.[35]

At its most confident, then, Knausgaard's swarm skepticism is anything but apolitical. Rather, in an after-Auschwitz kind of way that I reject but can appreciate, swarm skepticism takes itself to be the *only* acceptable political mode. Given "the basic mimetic structure of violence"—and in his analysis of Nazism, Knausgaard indeed makes extensive use of René Girard—one unfortunately has no better option than to categorically refuse imitation and social aggregation.[36] The price is loneliness. But what one surrenders in terms of solidarity is made up by ensuring that one is never a party to the mass hysterias from which genocide stems. In the face of a gathering "we," it is imperative to remain aloof.

But as with Durkheim's church, the politics of independence is a rather refined form. Before swarm skepticism can become a politics, it must first

34. Knausgaard, *My Struggle, Book Six*, 808.
35. Knausgaard, *My Struggle, Book Six*, 810. The point I'm making here about bona fide blasphemy versus kabuki blasphemy I would also make about the 9/11 bit at the tail end of Cartman's riff in *The Aristocrats*: https://www.youtube.com/watch?v=CyKGHVA6rbO.
36. Knausgaard, *My Struggle, Book Six*, 723. For the source text, see René Girard, *Violence and the Sacred* (Baltimore, MD: Johns Hopkins Press, 1977).

be constituted as an aesthetics. At lower temperatures swarm skepticism merely mandates abstention from stupidity and idolatry, which is why in *Book Three* taste in music and literature becomes so central to Karl Ove's self-fashioning. What begins with practices of discerning consumption, in young adulthood becomes something more ambitious, and, in fits and starts, disciplinary. As a young man in *Book Four* and *Book Five*, Karl Ove eschews swarming, but actively courts the heightened intensities and self-overcoming that swarming commonly affords. He swarms, that is to say, but he swarms *authentically*. That is, he swarms alone.

This too has a tradition. Mystical and sometimes chaotic, this tradition could group Whitman, Blake, Bataille, and de Sade. From a distance, one might mistake the discernment and drive of the solo swarmer for being *cool*, but as those who have access to his inner life can attest, Karl Ove is anything but. Rather, when swarming solo, Karl Ove is closer to a maniac or demon. We might well call the solitary mode of swarming *frenzy*.

Of the many paths to frenzy, the most important to young Karl Ove proves the most difficult: that is the frenzy of writing. *Book Four*'s lonely, ascetic retreat to the north is, in this regard, in sum, essentially a negative result. A single episode can perhaps stand in for the whole. Karl Ove "tried to write. It didn't go very well, and the evening's defeat cast a shadow over everything." Distraction gives way to frustration, which gives way to feelings of failure, which give way to distraction again, which gives way to sexual longing. Sublimation and its discontents. With the internet still years away, Karl Ove pines for the porn mags of yore, which had yet to be "replaced by anything else." In music played at high volume, Karl Ove finds a way into some sort of writing rhythm, albeit not one nearly powerful enough to overcome self-consciousness, the annihilation of which is one of the hallmarks of frenzy. At most, what Karl Ove is able to conjure is a semblance of a writer: "When darkness fell I let it enter the flat too, apart from on the desk, where a small lamp shone like an island in the night." With Led Zeppelin blaring, Karl Ove sticks to the task, but his image of his self remains in the way: "There was me and my writing, an island of light in the darkness, that was how I imagined it."[37] Despite his best efforts, frenzy does not come.

What exactly do we have here? Is this a solitary man alone with his eventual vocation, or is this an "'80s person" playing a man alone with his vocation in the private movie of his mind? According to Knausgaard's theory of the self as historical self, which I endorse, there is no fully disaggregating these two things, inasmuch as from where Karl Ove is positioned, the first is

37. Knausgaard, *My Struggle, Book Four*, 349–51.

swallowed up in the second. Whether in his failure Karl Ove is failing to be Goethe or failing to be Brett Easton Ellis, *Book Four* offers some assurance to those of us tormented by the internet that the problem of distraction is nothing for which new technology is uniquely responsible.[38]

The will to frenzy follows Karl Ove to Bergen in *Book Five*. Unable still to lose himself in writing, Karl Ove frenzies instead with alcohol, with stimulants, and, more elusively, via sex. Occasionally, and most dramatically, in touchstone episodes in *Book Two* and *Book Five*, he cuts himself.

Book Six represents a testament to overcoming. By *Book Six*, Karl Ove has put aside his childish incontinence of the will. From what we can observe, he barely drinks, and he no longer cuts himself. He does two things primarily: he writes maniacally, and he executes his obligations as a family man. In each sphere he is by now more or less machine-like. Writing times are blocked out, and barring an externally imposed obstacle, he writes, and writes lucidly, with a seeming unselfconsciousness that one can only envy. In contrast to the earlier books, descriptions of the writing process largely recede. As far as his long-embattled struggle to write is concerned, the doorstop we hold in our hands says everything that needs to be said. Nor does excessive passion get in his way in the sphere of love. Now, according to the scripts of maturity, the passions of youth have been supplanted with the duties of age: love is no longer about surges of feeling; love is a slate of things one must do and therefore does, even when tired or preoccupied. In each sphere, where once he struggled, he now moves freely. All grown up, Karl Ove has successfully routinized the will to frenzy into habit.

With the capacity to write (and write!) without distraction, Karl Ove's disciplined frenzy brings voluminous quantities of lucid prose and critical and popular acclaim to boot. All too easy to have predicted, therefore, is the agony of the independent soul who finds himself placed at the center of a swarm. The feelings are awful. At the cusp of publication, Karl Ove experiences being the object of familial hatred. He chokes on the immorality of having betrayed his family's secrets. And he is forced to confront his errors of recollection, which signal the failure of his literary endeavor. He remembers his teenage self, whose social discomfort and drive to authenticity launched him on the course he painstakingly took:

> And what I related to then only instinctively or emotionally, the social world, whose power I felt whenever my cheeks burned with shame or I was consumed with self-reproach because of something I had done that made me

38. Pascal's observation that "the unhappiness of men arises from one single fact that they cannot stay quietly in their own chamber" comes to mind here. On new technologies and their correlative anxieties see "Simple Answers," by xkcd, online at https://xkcd.com/1289/.

> feel so inadequate, so awkward, so indistinct, so totally stupid or foolish, but also unprincipled and dishonest and fraudulent, now I see more clearly, not least after having written these books, which in their every sentence have tried to transcend the social world by conveying the innermost thoughts and innermost feelings of my private self, my own internal life, but also by describing the private sphere of my family as it exists behind the façade all families set up against the social world, doing so in a public forum, a novel.[39]

As a young man Karl Ove sought to flee the shame of the social world by means of his writing. Repeatedly he failed. After monumental struggle, he triumphed. But in overwhelming success he comes to see the self-defeating character of his enterprise. By tilting against the windmills of the social world by means of a literary form that captures the private and true, he has succeeded not in escaping *from* the social world, but in betraying all that was sacred to him by sacrificing the personal and private *to* the social.

Having to show up and perform as himself at the novel's publicity stops is profoundly upsetting. Press junkets–readings, book signings–are invariably humiliating. At such events, so as "to create a 'we'"–which is to say, to enable his audience to experience the pleasures of the swarm–Karl Ove is repeatedly called on to betray his novel. Shamefully, he complies. The resulting adulation is thin gruel: "The smiles, the friendliness, the admiration I encounter when I sign books is unbearable, not because it isn't well meant or honest, but because it is on false premises." The rapturous applause he garners at his readings is in response to who he nominally *is*, to his famous name. This, Karl Ove understands, is the culture of celebrity, and as such, it is a textbook case of misrecognition. Ethically, psychologically, there is no taking such stuff at face value: "Deep down, I have to reject it."[40] And so, praise washes off like shower suds, whereas criticisms, most acutely of his betrayals and misrepresentations, sting and linger.

READING *MY STRUGGLE* AS A REQUIEM FOR A LOST ANALOG WORLD

This essay began as an attempt to make sense of the Knausgaard swarm and of my own place in it. As I first articulated to the collective in 2016, in Knausgaard's devotional attentiveness to the world as writer, in Karl Ove's compulsive attentiveness to the world as observer, and in the immersive reading experience fostered by each in tandem, the Knausgaard swarm

39. Knausgaard, *My Struggle, Book Six*, 824.
40. Knausgaard, *My Struggle, Book Six*, 971.

is, among other things, a requiem for a lost analog world. One of the ways these books pertain to religion is by offering an ethnography of the late-twentieth-century analog quotidian. Therein, *My Struggle* presents, in content, form, and in readerly practice, a portal to a place where once and recently enchantment reigned. I felt already confident in this encapsulation in 2016 and, having recently swarmed joyfully in the "internet novel" swarm of early 2021, my confidence level has only risen.[41] I know full well that such a lost world where devotion was easy is, and has always been, a fantasy, but that doesn't make the holy mode of being I encountered in the pages of *My Struggle* any less compelling.

Whether due to content or style, my will to historicize engendered productive and enduring tensions in our collective's deliberations, particularly between me and Winnifred Sullivan. As our transcript records Sullivan saying in that first meeting, "I understand the importance of historicization, the power of it. But it can also be diminishing." This tension: between seeing value as more or less inherent versus seeing value as more or less contingent (if I am characterizing our disputes accurately) called important, competing commitments to the surface.

Why was it important to me to approach the Knausgaard phenomenon as foremost a sociological one? One plausible reason is that I am an internet person. Another is that a disagreement with Sullivan is a thing to be avoided and courted in equal measure, and, at least when I get excitable—and the experience of our collective has been an exciting one for me—temptation tends to win out over aversion. More foundational orientations may also be relevant, such as my self-defining passage as a young man from Jewish orthopraxis to Jewish secularity, a process of heartbreaking and awakening that made me into a scholar of religion of a decidedly Durkheimian sort. Yes, the Torah is totemic, but not because it was given by God to Moses on Sinai. Rather, the Torah is totemic because for millennia Jewish people have built selves, communities, and worlds amid its mutually reinforcing laws and stories—with "Torah" indicating both.

Another set of reasons, arguably as foundational, for my stubborn insistence that there is nothing inherently swarm-inducingly special about Knausgaard's *My Struggle* is that, like Karl Ove, I too was an "'80s person." And that meant that, like Karl Ove, I was formatively conditioned in a middlebrow consumerist mode of evaluating myself and others on the basis of the sorts of things they swarmed on. As with *My Struggle* itself—which

41. The relevant swarm was around the back-to-back releases of Lauren Oyler's *Fake Accounts* (New York: Catapult Books, 2021) and Patricia Lockwood's *No One Is Talking About This* (New York: Riverhead Books, 2021). For what it's worth, I enjoyed disliking the former and loved the latter.

over the years has lost its patina of *cool*—"coolness" faded as the relevant criterion for assessment, but the template is not entirely gone. I find this cultural tendency interesting, and, as with other formative insights that we use to make sense of the world, I have a hard time not graphing it onto the things in the world I'm seeking to understand.

Like many other eighties people, Knausgaard included, in the nineties I became a theory person. In that strange interregnum of freedom and weightlessness between the Cold War and the War on Terror, I had world-reshaping encounters with Nietzsche's "Truth and Lies," Saussure's *Course on General Linguistics*, Jameson's *Postmodernism*, as well as with Durkheim's *Elementary Forms* and Girard's *Violence and the Sacred*. Through this disciplinary process, I came by an operating assumption that value (and values), good and bad, venerated and reviled, are assigned arbitrarily within a given cultural field. When the second, great American Walter Benjamin swarm kicked up at the turn of the century, and I had occasion to read "On Language as Such and on the Language of Man," I came to see the secularizing stance I had embraced—what Benjamin cuttingly calls the "bourgeois conception of language"—as itself historically and materially conditioned.[42]

In sum, I got caught up in the Knausgaard swarm, and I brought the concept of the swarm in with me. I am committed to the idea that the value of this collective's work has not been dependent on our choice of text. Provided that it was long enough to justify repeated, ritualized encounters, another text might just as well have served our purposes. But, as fortune would have it, it wasn't another text, it was this one. Thinking in dialogue with the other members of this collective, along the way I came to see the potential value of the swarm for the study of religion. Then, as brought into relief only in *Book Six*, the swarm also proved to be a valuable heuristic for thinking through the ethics of *My Struggle*, an ethics that one wouldn't be wrong to dub "religious." Karl Ove, Knausgaard, Karl Ove Knausgaard is a man/two men/a sequence of men, mulishly determined independent spirits who categorically refuse to swarm, and yet whose literary achievement kicks off a swarm transatlantic in reach. He learns to sublimate his more destructive impulses and masters his compulsion to frenzy to become a *writer*, though only—in ways both generic and parodically severe—at his own expense and at the expense of those who love him.

42. Walter Benjamin, *Selected Writings, 1: 1913-1926* (Cambridge, MA: Harvard University Press, 2004), 65.

13 JANUARY 2018 BLOOMINGTON, INDIANA

BENDER: I appreciate the way you think with the blues-gospel face-off here. How do we think about that in terms of the visual-cultural stakes of [*A Time for Everything*]?

HARRISS: . . . We have to recognize it as fiction, which I think is a question at the heart of reading *My Struggle*. . . . That's why I was so thrilled to see you turn to the form of the novel, . . . because that's what makes it fiction. And I am very willing to be loosey-goosey with truth, history, fiction, but once you get into multi-tons of pages, there becomes an exhaustiveness that is there, but the other thing about life is that that's not even remotely part of it. It's still stylized. Or a frame. Or maybe it's not the frame . . . but there is a way in which we circumscribe it. I don't take history as–I don't want to say that it's failure. But I think it is more useful to understand it for what it is because there is the assumption of the true or not true. There is the intellectual shorthand that I want to play with.

SULLIVAN: So how does that work in the music analogy?

HARRISS: In the gospel-blues dichotomy, it is not sacred-secular. It's more like sacred-profane. Both are participant in the same story or the same myth. That's what I find intriguing about the story of Anna . . . and why I think it's blues-like. It's a retelling of the myth from a different perspective.

SULLIVAN: Is this also the Saturday night, Sunday morning story?

DUBLER: What does that mean?

HARRISS: In Southern Black contexts at least, you have very much the same people going to social locations at which the music, movement, rhythms, harmonies are the same. The joke is that Saturday night you sing "I love you, baby." On Sunday morning you sing, "I love you,

Jesus." The rituals map onto one another, and yet they are understood to be fundamentally incommensurable.

SULLIVAN: But they are also fundamentally dependent. That's why sacred-profane as opposed to sacred-secular.

HARRISS: Yes. What I see here, in just the devastation, keep going up the mountain and keep going up the mountain. And they are sitting there with their effects around them, and this battleship comes out of the fog. Waiting around . . . to borrow a phrase from Townes van Zandt: "waiting around to die." I was drawing on that. It is tangible, material, and yet it is utterly inconceivable.

BENDER: If we imagine *A Time for Everything* and its materials as the sacred, what is the profane? What is the Saturday night to his Sunday morning?

HARRISS: I wouldn't say this is *the* profane, but I think an element of the profane would be the extra-canonical portions. The unofficial, the unsanctioned, the unregulated parts of the story.

BENDER: You mean the unsanctioned parts of the story of Noah?

HARRISS: Yes, in this case.

BENDER: Okay, but this is such a high culture thing. The whole thing is Sunday morning. There is Giotto, there is elaboration of seventeenth-century thinkers, the Bible . . .

SULLIVAN: But Sunday morning is not a high to the Saturday low.

BENDER: Okay, alright, you're right. But it seems like there is a line, there is an aesthetic line that keeps this in a world of sacredness . . .

SULLIVAN: This is church and chapel. If you want the high and the low . . .

HARRISS: One of the reasons I can toggle back and forth between Knausgaard and the blues is that I recognize that there can be practical distinctions of this kind of high and low, but I also think that–well someone like Albert Murray, who is writing about a blues idiom but he is talking about Shakespeare, Hemingway, Duke Ellington. These become all part of the piece for him. While the social contexts or the points of references for specific blues people may be specific texts and may be low culture, there is a way that much like the adaptability/malleability of Scripture, there is way that the blues is an ur-text. There is something inherent in its Western-ness. This is also [Murray's] argument for why American culture is black culture. The reason why I can be so cavalier about this is that I don't put any stock in that distinction.

BENDER: Yes, but I don't think that Knausgaard or the narrator feels the same. Or I guess that is a question . . .

[Later.]

HARRISS: It's also a question of the narrator here and the narrator in *My Struggle*. If we know anything, we know that pop music is the structural experience of Karl Ove, and so I think it's not untenable to think about the blues. In a way that he is able to organize life through music, there is a way we can think about the blues disposition of the people down in the flood versus the people on the ark. It is a workable principle . . .

CARLSON: Is part of the worry . . . it seems like you're worried, Courtney, about the high culture thing?

BENDER: I'm fascinated! I'm fascinated by the aesthetic charge of the text. Not only are they the beautiful things but they are the things that carry over into Knausgaard's argument about materiality. And everything else, all the other material aspects of angels that are flooding everywhere are out of the picture. And I'm not saying that you have to be down with those kitschy depictions of angels, because I hate those too, but I am curious because it seems to work against the . . .

CARLSON: . . . down-in-the-valley . . . right, because high culture is for a very exclusive set of people who know about the references to the angels and aren't thinking about the humble kitsch figurines when the content of the story is about the people who are drowning . . .

BENDER: This is not a critical point where I am saying he is excluding human experience. I'm just trying to . . .

CARLSON: . . . figure out how it fits together.

SULLIVAN: Can I try something out for you? One of the problems with the high and low thing . . . The high part here is the art. But we have low biblical culture and high art.

BENDER: Yes!

SULLIVAN: Right, which is weird. So, we have low-biblical Christianity and yet, the turning point for this whole story is the viewing of one of the iconic pieces of Western art . . .

/ 5 /

Angels

Winnifred Fallers Sullivan

PRELUDE

When I was in graduate school one of our teachers was murdered in a stall in the second-floor men's bathroom in the middle of one Tuesday afternoon during term time. He was killed with a single shot to the head apparently fired over the partition from the adjoining stall. It was a shocking event. We, students and faculty, stumbled out of Bond Chapel on the University of Chicago campus the next day into the pouring rain and a crowd of reporters and cameramen, unbelieving. The murder remains unsolved.[1]

There was talk of his writings on Romanian politics–of the secret societies he studied and maybe dabbled in–of a possible vengeful student or lover. Dangerous, prurient, and wanton stories circulated that distastefully suggested that it was his unwise intellectual habits that accounted for his death; we entertained these possibilities even while each of us had during his life experienced his unfailing and unusual personal kindness. A crack had opened onto something usually kept carefully cabined in our tidy academic world. As I have reflected on Karl Ove Knausgaard's propensity for vertiginous and telescoping shifts of scale and reference, I have found myself thinking about Ioan Culianu.

Culianu would stand in the front of the class and announce that "Life is a fractal in Hilbert space." Then silence. We had all been required, at the beginning of this course called "Religious Sects" (a course title easily misunderstood when spoken), to read a book by Rudy Rucker introducing

1. "The Cold Case of a University of Chicago Professor's Murder," https://www.chicagomag.com/Chicago-Magazine/September-2018/The-Cold-Case-of-a-University-of-Chicago-Professors-Murder/.

FIGURE 5: *The Angel Standing in the Sun*, exhibited 1846. J. M. W. Turner. Turner Bequest, 1856. Photo: Tate.

us to the basic math of fractals and multi-dimensional space.[2] Culianu's statement about life was taken from Rucker. We had, I think, most of us, only dimly understood Rucker's book. But we were mesmerized by Culianu and so struggled to discern his reading of religion.

Ioan Culianu studied medieval magic and esotericism. He was a young but vastly learned man. Our class was basically about the losers in the his-

2. Rudy Rucker, *Mind Tools: The Five Levels of Mathematical Reality* (Boston: Mariner Books, 1988).

tory of religions, those who did not make it into the received narratives of the normative traditions. It was about all of those in between—those left hanging in a sprawling panorama of human religious activity. Culianu had what seemed an inexhaustible interest in and knowledge of these forgotten byways, of the small sects which had only fleeting or largely hidden histories. He would periodically draw a vast and complex map on the blackboard illustrating all of the many, many logical possibilities pregnant in a particular religious event or doctrine and then retrieve from his mental archive a story of the tiny group—or sometimes single individual—that had taken up each possible crystallization of variation. In the end, the entire blackboard would be covered with a web of branching possibilities. We were drawn into a miasmic sea of human compulsion and creativity. The only limit on the fineness of the web was the ending of the class period. The lesson was that if a logical possibility existed—someone was bound to emerge to live it out—and that we should honor the losers as well as the winners.[3]

All of the variations appeared entirely equal and equivalent in his map. There was no hierarchy and no through line. Each iteration was both necessarily distinct, of course, and yet, also, in some sense the result of the same operation. Each attempt to live out what was taken to be the mandate of the gods, however far from the mainstream, was equally valid from a scholarly standpoint—and, I think, perhaps, for him, equally worthy as an ethical matter. We were enchanted. Well. I was enchanted. I wrote a paper about the Nation of Islam—which looked quite different to me under the influence of this fractal world.

Culianu was murdered almost twenty-five years ago. His death was frighteningly sudden and illegible. Almost by definition, no reason could be given for such an act. It would be obscene.

Like J. Z. Smith, I think, Culianu sought to describe "the messiness of the given world" without prejudice.[4] In contrast to the philosopher or the theologian, Smith says, "[t]here are no places, on which [the historian might stand]. . . . There is, for him, no real beginning, but only the plunge which he takes at some arbitrary point to avoid the unhappy alternatives of infinite regress or silence. His standpoint is not discovered; rather, it is fabricated with no claim beyond that of sheer survival."[5] I am not entirely

3. Ioan Culianu also wrote fiction. For a taste of his literary imagination, see, "The Language of Creation" in *Thus Spake the Corpse: An Exquisite Corpse Reader*, ed. Andrei Codrescu and Laura Rosenthal (Black Sparrow Press: 1999).
4. Jonathan Z. Smith, *Map Is Not Territory: Studies in the History of Religions* (Leiden: E. J. Brill, 1978), 129.
5. Smith, *Map Is Not Territory*, 129.

sure I know what Smith meant by this–and many who read him miss, I think, the glimpse of the abyss in his work–infinite regress is never wholly avoided–but I think that "sheer survival" is what Knausgaard is after too. We might call this religion as compulsion. Or, as work. Both Smith and Culianu understood religion and the study of religion to involve labor, serious labor. But the study of religion also demanded respect for what humans have done–what they have, in Knausgaard's words, longed for.[6]

There is much more to be said about what both Smith and Culianu have written about religion, their differences as well as what they shared. I enlist them here in an effort to triangulate on the passages our group read together from Knausgaard. Culianu's work, read here by way of Smith, understands religion to inhere in the very mass of material of the world, not apart from it. Reading for religion–and writing religion–depend on a radical openness to what we might learn from the encounter with what is there revealed. It also means coming to terms with the extent to which the way we do our work is determined by the fallout from the reformations of the sixteenth century. In other words, can the recursiveness of the immanent be revelatory?

One writes, Knausgaard says, in order to understand what one does not know–to discern what is prior to, or what conditions, one's knowing, that which is embedded in the language we use and in our experience of the material world. One writes, he says, in order "to see something foreign appear on the page in front of you."[7] What is tantalizing in his writing is his capacity to bring the reader's attention to that "something foreign." The foreignness is marked in various ways in *My Struggle*–including the use of the *mise en abyme* and the presence of angels. Their appearance could thus be considered revelation.

In *Givenness and Revelation*, his Gifford lectures, Jean-Luc Marion describes what he calls a phenomenological theology in response to the great standoff between reason and revelation. Confining himself there to the texts of the Christian bible, he reads them as revealing that Christ is what he calls "the icon of the invisibility of God"–of impossibility–of "the irreducible depth of field."[8] It is only by crossing over the epistemological break–by listening–by becoming the witness–that one puts oneself in a place that is "phenomenally operative."[9] By "phenomenally operative," I understand him to refer to the work that is done by opening oneself to the

6. See Karl Ove Knausgaard, *So Much Longing in So Little Space: The Art of Edvard Munch* (London: Penguin Books, 2019).

7. Karl Ove Knausgaard, *Inadvertent*, 81.

8. Jean Luc Marion, *Givenness and Revelation* (Oxford: Oxford University Press, 2016), 75.

9. Marion, *Givenness and Revelation*, 86.

givenness of the phenomenon–or the foreign, in Knausgaard's words–as epitomized for Marion in the phenomenon of the Christ.

I will endeavor in this short essay to attempt a theological reading of Knausgaard, inspired in part by a reading of Marion.[10]

REVELATION

Knausgaard's university degree was in art history. He returns often to paintings. Paintings too for Knausgaard seem to have a capacity to show us something foreign–something of the givenness of the world. The English painter, J. M. W. Turner, painted a number of works in which the viewer is given a head-on view of the sun. Some were scenes from the ancient world. Others depicted large landscapes set in contemporary Europe. *The Angel Standing in the Sun* (reproduced here, on the second page of the chapter) conjures the end of the world. The day of judgment is bathed in the light of a blinding sun and centered on the archangel Michael with raised sword, accompanied by a huge swirl of birds. He hovers above the tormented figures below, a scattering of biblical characters apparently standing in somehow for the totality of the human experience.

In the first exhibition of the painting, this passage was posted next to it, at Turner's request:

> And I saw an angel standing in the sun; and he cried with a loud voice, saying to all the fowls that fly in the midst of heaven, Come and gather yourselves together unto the supper of the great God; That ye may eat the flesh of kings, and the flesh of captains and the flesh of mighty men, and the flesh of horses, and of them that sit on them, both free and bond, both small and great. (Rev. 19:17-18)

In the catalog for the exhibit, "a couplet from Samuel Rogers's epic poem *The Voyage of Columbus* of 1810, also appeared: 'The morning march that flashes to the sun; The feast of vultures when the day is done.'"[11] In his essay on the painting, James Herbert explains that John Ruskin, otherwise a huge admirer of Turner's work, disliked this one painting in part because of the liberty it took with the biblical scenes. Herbert regards Turner's textual selections as curiously unilluminating–even contradictory and tangential–to the effect of the work–a work that in its power short circuits any mere

10. There is, interestingly, a considerable overlap of literary and artistic references between Knausgaard and Marion, including to the painting of J. M. W. Turner, as we will see.
11. See James D. Herbert, "Turner's Uncertain Angel," *Journal of Religion* 91, no. 4 (2011): 437-69.

biblical illustration or political reference.[12] Yet both Turner's license and his biblical appropriation seem curiously appropriate in the context of Knausgaard's work, the collapsing of time and space and literary genre, and the presence of angels, characteristic of his imagination as well.

Knausgaard's own discussion of Turner's paintings comes in the course of an astonishing riff on death and art and the sublime in the middle of the long section on Hitler in *Book Six* of *My Struggle*. The author/narrator, Karl Ove, has traveled with his family to an intergenerational gathering in the Norwegian countryside. They are there, in part, because Magne, the grandfather, is dying of cancer. Karl Ove comments that Magne will soon no longer see the sun: "And, oh, the sun. He would never see the sun again."[13] Knausgaard ranges his family on the hillside just as Noah's family is ranged in his biblical fan fiction, *A Time for Everything*, awaiting the deluge.[14] Interwoven among references to Broch, Joyce, Virgil, and a bicycle accident in Stockholm that he had witnessed, Knausgaard remembers his encounter with the sun of another Turner painting, *Dido Building Carthage*, in the Tate Gallery in London:

> The sun is the primary subject, suspended high above the scene, its rays pervading everything, illuminating all surfaces, either directly or indirectly, conjuring forth all colours, warming the air, making it thick and consuming all distinctions, in a way tying the various elements of the scene together, though without any of the people present even being aware of it. How can this be possible, I thought to myself as I stood there. How can they go about beneath something as mighty and immense, such an insanely creative principle, this enormous sphere of gas aflame in the sky, and yet ignore it so completely? They do not see the sun, but Turner did and, thanks to him, we do too. The sun in this painting is so predominant it is hard not to think of it as holy, and that Turner was worshipping it.[15]

Both Marion and Knausgaard discuss Turner's paintings in their work. For Marion, as for Knausgaard, I think, Turner's sun paintings come close to summoning the blinding experience of divine revelation.[16] As Knausgaard

12. Further undoing a narrowly biblical reading, according to Herbert, was the pairing by Turner of "The Angel" with his pseudo-mythological *Undine Giving the Ring to Masaniello, Fisherman of Naples*, also featuring brilliant light, the two exhibited together at the Royal Academy of 1846. Herbert, "Turner's Uncertain Angel," 440.
13. Knausgaard, *My Struggle Book Six*, 649.
14. Karl Ove Knausgaard, *A Time for Everything*, trans. James Anderson (Brooklyn, NY: Archipelago Books, 2008), 331-34.
15. Knausgaard, *My Struggle Book Six*, 651.
16. Marion's interest in Turner's sun paintings is referenced in the foreword to Marion's

says, "[I]n these sudden states of clearsightedness that everyone must know, . . . for a few seconds you catch sight of another world from the one you were in only a moment earlier, . . . the world seems to step forward and show itself for a brief glimpse before reverting and leaving everything as before."[17] Then "something in the world emerges before us, passes through our conception of it and for a brief moment reveals itself the way it is."[18] This is what Marion calls "givenness." Its structure is trinitarian.[19]

MORE ANGELS

In Knausgaard's second novel, *A Time for Everything*, the flat voice in which the narrator speaks of angels—as, for example, "The origin of angels is uncertain"[20]—forces the reader to accept their existence. One could refuse to read on, but if one does not refuse then one is complicit. The problem is no longer whether angels are real. The problem is what kind of beings they are and what they are up to. For the narrator of the novel, one question is, Why are they still here? Why do they persist in a world without God? He concludes that they are trapped here by God's death. No longer able to serve as intermediaries, they are pathologically dependent on us, constantly seeking our approval. And we keep them around because they still reveal something of what it means to be human.

It is not just in *A Time for Everything*. Angel-talk is also presented as the key to the writer-narrator Knausgaard's motivation and competence as a novelist—and a key to Knausgaard's struggle to find the proper distance from his father and his father's death. To death more broadly. And to writing.

As the narrator tells us in *Book Five* of *My Struggle*, it was the introduction of angels into the story that broke his writer's block. After recounting his habit of frequently recycling versions of stories of his family, particularly a recurring scene in which he and his father and brother find a dead seagull while they are out crabbing, he relates that

> in February 2002 something happened. I had started another short text, located in the nineteenth century but let everything that exists now, exist then, and the scene was Tromøya, yet it wasn't, a completely different story

---

Givenness and Revelation by Ramona Fotiade and David Jasper, entitled "Jean Luc Marion: A Reflection", xi.

17. Knausgaard, *My Struggle, Book One*, 218.
18. Knausgaard, *My Struggle, Book Six*, 664.
19. Marion, *Givenness and Revelation*, 89-115.
20. Knausgaard, *A Time for Everything*, 19.

> emerged, and in this parallel world, which resembled ours but wasn't, I had Yngve, Dad, and me taking a boat to Torungen one summer's night. I described the night as I remembered it with one exception: the seagull Dad shone his flashlight on had a pair of small, thin, armlike growths beneath its wings. They had once been angels, I had him say, and then I knew; this is a novel. Finally, a novel![21]

A version of this scene had also appeared in the coda to *A Time for Everything*. "[A]ngels, I had him say." Much is compressed into these five words. Perhaps most importantly, the appearance of the angels led to "I . . . *had* . . . him." Something foreign had appeared before him and then he was able to properly locate his father in the story, in *his* story.

Seagulls, the narrator of the coda to *A Time for Everything*, Henry Vankel tells us, pervaded his childhood memories:

> When I grew up in the 1980s, there were seagulls everywhere. . . . There was something loathsome about them, perhaps because of the nakedness and openness of their bodies, which sat so badly with the impression they otherwise gave: gluttonous, brutal, primitive . . . it was this lack of belonging that we shared with the gulls, for what were marine birds like them doing so far away from the open sea? The common assumption was that they were sponging off us, rather like rats. Nobody considered that they might be yearning for us. That was why they lived so close to our world.[22]

Describing the outing with his father and brother, Vankel recalls that, while gathering wood for a fire,

> I saw something white against the darkness of the rock in front of me, stopped and knelt down: it was a dead seagull. I put my wood down and felt it. Its body was still warm. . . . I saw the thickening at the joints of the thin legs, the reptile-like fold of skin between the claws, the empty eyes, and was filled with nausea . . .
>
> "What were you looking at just now?" he asked.
>
> "A dead seagull," I said.
>
> . . . .
>
> "Did you know that seagulls were angels once?" he said.[23]

Vankel then observes of his father,

21. Knausgaard, *My Struggle, Book Five*, 622.
22. Knausgaard, *A Time for Everything*, 455.
23. Knausgaard, *A Time for Everything*, 463–64.

He lied about everything, but his lies were various; this one fortunately was only meant to tease us.

"I didn't know that," I said, and laughed. I could hear how forced it sounded.[24]

Knausgaard tells us in *Book Five* of *My Struggle* that it was his sudden ability to put the words about seagulls having been angels into his father's mouth that had provided the motivating force for his becoming a real writer. It was perhaps his transformation of the memory of his father's macabre teasing into a moment of revelation. The final sentence "I could hear how forced it sounded" leaves open the incompleteness that always accompanies revelation. Yet, the persistence and repetition of such scenes seems to be for Knausgaard, in Marion's words, "phenomenologically operative." This scene presents an interesting parallel structure to the face in the sea incident in Book One, discussed in the introduction to this volume. In both there is the cross-examination by the father, followed by the father's mocking of his credulity. These scenes also evince what Liane Carlson calls the "aesthetics of the abused child" in the title of her essay in chapter 3 of this volume.

In other writing, Knausgaard gives other accounts of how he became a writer. In *Inadvertent*, a short book/essay in a series called *Why I Write*, published by Yale University Press, he retells the story of the seagull/angel, but he also gives a longer and more complex account of his current understanding of how he became a writer. In *Inadvertent* Knausgaard refers to many books that impressed him over the years. But first he talks of the consolation that reading brought to him as a child and how books were a connection to his mother, who often brought them to him on her return home after work or school. "[T]he essential thing about books, I think, was that they constituted a place in the world where I could be."[25] Many of those books, he says, he never thought about again. But the one book that he says never left him from his childhood reading was *A Wizard of Earthsea* by Ursula Le Guin.[26] In explaining the importance of that book to him,

24. Knausgaard, *A Time for Everything*, 464.
25. Knausgaard, *Inadvertent*, 17.
26. *A Wizard of Earthsea* (Berkley, CA: Parnassus Books, 1968) is the first in a series of novels by Ursula LeGuin collectively entitled *Earthsea*. LeGuin writes at the borderline of fantasy and science fiction—she would be considered by many a genre writer. She has a powerful capacity to draw the reader into the world of her writing. LeGuin's novels also presciently address profound issues of the ethics of human life. See, for example, *The Left Hand of Darkness* (New York, NY: Ace Books, 1969) and *The Word for World Is Forest* (New York, NY: Berkley Books, 1972).

Knausgaard says simply, "I wanted to enter that space again."[27] *A Wizard of Earthsea,* he says, "opened the way for a kind of unreflecting, emotion-driven thoughts, something I had never experienced before; they were new to me and shockingly powerful."[28] The introduction of the angel seems to mark that space for him—a space for "emotion-driven thoughts."

The introduction of the seagull as fallen angel not only encapsulates a change in Knausgaard's writing; it also helps us to think about what might be understood to be religious about his writing. How might we reconcile the fact that, on the one hand, Knausgaard is accused of writing so transparently and realistically, even brutally so, about his own family and friends as to have unforgivably exposed them and all their private faults to public scrutiny . . . with the fact that, on the other hand, angels seem to be in some way the key to understanding his work? These are two different worlds, are they not? The world of abusive alcoholic fathers, absent mothers, infidelity, the pervasiveness of electronic media, and the sordid everydayness of family life today, on the one hand, and a world, on the other, in which solar revelation and angelic visitation are possible—even to be expected?

THE *MISE EN ABYME*

A characteristic of Knausgaard's fiction writing is the deliberate marking of a character's experience of a larger reality through the use of the *mise en abyme,* an opening onto what might also be thought of as fractal—or hierophanic. Consider a scene that is reprised in various versions in Knausgaard's works, one in which the narrator describes cleaning the banister in his grandmother's house just after his father had died. The account is forensic in its detail but it is also heavy with latent dread—the stickiness of the banister, the general neglect, and the filthy evidence of his father's drunken decline mix with the pull the cleaning products themselves exert over him. Together they draw him back to the cupboard under the sink of his childhood:

> [T]here was a packet of washing powder with a picture of a child holding the identical packet, and on that, of course, there was a picture of the same boy holding the same packet, and so on, and so on. Was it called Blenda? Whatever it was called, I often racked my brains over *mise en abyme,* which in principle of course was endless and also existed elsewhere, such as in the bathroom mirror by holding a mirror behind your head so that images of the mirrors were projected to and fro while going farther and farther back

27. Knausgaard, *Inadvertent,* 20.
28. Knausgaard, *Inadvertent,* 23.

> and becoming smaller and smaller as far as the eye could see. But what happened behind what the eye could see? Did the images carry on getting smaller and smaller?[29]

Mise en abyme—the reproduction of the picture in the picture—has a long pedigree in visual and textual arts. Even a cursory search for a genealogy for *mise en abyme* carries the reader into an analogous recursive and regressive vertigo-inducing trip down the rabbit hole.

Many accounts begin with André Gide's reflections on writing in his diary.[30] The entry for August 1893 begins with George Eliot: "'Our deeds act upon us as much as we act on them,' said George Eliot." And it ends with this: "An angry man tells a story; there is the subject of a book. A man telling a story is not enough; it must be an angry man and there must be a constant connection between his anger and the story he tells." The constant connection is necessary, Gide says, in order to achieve "reciprocity, not in one's relations with others, but with oneself. The subject that acts is oneself, the object that retroacts is a literary subject arising in the imagination. This is consequently an indirect method of acting upon oneself that I have outlined, and it is also, more directly, a tale." Being a writer requires attending to this reciprocity between text and writer.

Between these two observations on how writing necessarily acts upon the writer is Gide's often quoted passage on the *mise en abyme*:

> In a work of art, I rather like to find transposed, on the scale of the characters, the very subject of that work. Nothing throws a clearer light upon it or more surely establishes the proportions of the whole. Thus, in certain paintings of Memling or Quentin Metzys a small convex and dark mirror reflects the interior of the room in which the scene of the painting is taking place. Likewise, in Velazquez's painting of the *Meninas* (but somewhat differently). Finally, in literature, in the play scene in *Hamlet*, and elsewhere in many other plays. In *Wilhelm Meister*, the scenes of the puppets or the celebration at the castle; in *The Fall of the House of Usher*, the story that is read to Roderick, etc. None of these examples is altogether exact. What would be much more so, and would explain much better what I strove for in my *Cahiers*, in my *Narcisse*, and in the *Tentative*, is a comparison with the device of heraldry that consists in setting in the escutcheon a smaller one "en abyme," at the heart-point.

29. Knausgaard, *My Struggle, Book One*, 352. This passage was selected for our first discussion by Liane Carlson.
30. André Gide, *Journals*, trans. Justin O'Brien, vol. 1, *1889–1924*, 17. This is the entry for August 1893.

Gide is usually taken to be describing a self-enclosed recursivity. Yet, as Gide's examples and his own explanation makes clear, the power of the *mise en abyme* is in its capacity to both establish the internal meaning of a work of art or literature and to open that work onto a larger reality–onto the abyss. The particular "on the scale of the characters" discloses the universal unknowable.

Gide recounts that he found the most precise analogy to what he was trying to achieve in his fiction in French heraldic practice, the "setting in the escutcheon a smaller one 'en abyme,' at the heart-point." He also mentions the play within the play in *Hamlet* and Velázquez's *Las Meninas*. As Karl Ove himself notes, the device is also ubiquitous in advertising, where it has its own special name, the Droste Effect, after the illustration on the Swiss cocoa powder box of a young woman holding a box of cocoa which itself has an image of a girl holding a box, and so on. Karl Ove is haunted by branding. We see this preoccupation with branding at other moments as well. These images draw him into the religious world of advertising, one in which reality is mediated by the product and the image within the image anchors us to an already always existing magical power.[31] Dismissed by some as a postmodern device, it seems for others to have always been there and to describe the structure of reality; as Karl Ove says, *mise en abyme*, "in principle of course was endless and also existed everywhere."[32]

Following his own rabbit hole from the bleach to the beach and soccer fields of his childhood, shifting into lyrical mode, Karl Ove suddenly announces, "All of this still existed," but it wasn't the same:

> The sole difference, which is the difference between a child's reality and an adult's, was that they were no longer laden with meaning. A pair of Le Coq soccer boots was just a pair of soccer boots. If I felt anything when I held a pair in my hands now it was only a hangover from my childhood, nothing else, nothing in itself. The same with the sea, the same with the rocks, the same with the taste of salt that could fill your summer days to saturation, now it was just salt, end of story. The world was the same, yet it wasn't, for its meaning had been displaced, and was still being displaced, approaching closer and closer to meaninglessness.[33]

31. See Kathryn Lofton, *Consuming Religion* (Chicago: University of Chicago Press, 2017), for an analysis of this desire. Also, William Gibson, *Pattern Recognition* (London: Penguin Books, 2003), a novel whose protagonist has a marketable sensitivity to corporate symbols.
32. Knausgaard, *My Struggle, Book One*, 352.
33. Knausgaard, *My Struggle, Book One*, 353.

"[N]ow it was just salt, end of story." The passage ends with the announcement: "It didn't matter, nothing mattered, I just walked around the garden cutting the grass that had grown too tall."[34] Is adulthood no longer enchanted for Knausgaard? Something rings false about this effort to draw a sharp line between the magic of childhood and the flatness of adult experience. Or perhaps the problem is our tendency to conflate author and character? Perhaps "nothing mattered" is his grief speaking, not his self as witness, in Marion's sense.

The experience of *mise en abyme* is not, I think, for Knausgaard, just a hangover from childhood. In the end Karl Ove is unable to reduce his father or his father's death to meaninglessness. As J. Z. Smith would say—and as Marion and Culianu show—in life and in death survival depends on the labor we do both to recognize and to refuse the knowledge that we are suspended a hair's breadth from the abyss. Karl Ove—the character—has just written a whole book about how saturated with meaning his own world remains. The yearning of the angels moves—and scares—him. Karl Ove the writer longs to do what Rembrandt's portrait of the old man does. "It sees for us," he says.[35] Something outside of us, something foreign, opens before us. It is a revelation. Knausgaard can do that too—see for us by revealing what he does not wholly understand.

Mise en abyme is dangerous business. While deceptively simple in its replication and multiplication, many who write about it caution about its power. In an article on *mise en abyme* and metalepsis, Dorrit Cohn discusses the way in which figures of speech can cause vertigo by making the metaphysical claim that the reader and the characters in the story inhabit the same narrative. In an extreme case—she uses the example of Julio Cortázar's story "Continuity of Parks," in which the reader of a story is murdered by a character in the story—the recursive intimacy of the setting of the scene—the green velvet chair in which the reader sits also appears in the story—leads to the death of the reader.[36]

There are other gothic aspects to Knausgaard's work as well, to which we will return, after a digression on birds and angels.

34. Knausgaard, *My Struggle, Book One*, 406.

35. Knausgaard, *Inadvertent*, 30.

36. Dorrit Cohn, "Metalepsis and Mise en Abyme," *Narrative* 20, no. 1 (2012): 105-14. (Oddly, the volume of Cortázar's short stories in the Regenstein Library at the University of Chicago is missing that story, which has been cut from the volume with a razor.) Charles Williams also explores this terrain in his novels. See, for example, *All Hallow's Eve* (NY: Pellegrini & Cudahy, 1948). A reviewer of detective fiction, Williams apparently frequently expressed the desire to read that ultimate mystery novel in which all clues point to the detective himself. *Times Literary Supplement*, April 2, 2004, 21.

THE WILD DUCK AND *THE SEAGULL* (AN INTERLUDE IN WHICH I BRIEFLY PRETEND TO BE A LITERARY CRITIC)

How serious is Knausgaard about the seagull/angel? He cannot help but invoke Chekhov and Ibsen with this gesture. Indeed, he cannot help but add to the series. In the two plays, the plight and careers of the birds might be said to encapsulate the story in just the way that Gide suggests. Each exists both at the scale of the characters in the play and refers back to and reflects the whole.

Ibsen's play, *The Wild Duck*, was first performed in 1884; Chekhov's *The Seagull*, in 1896.[37] Chekhov's play is sometimes read as a satirical take on Ibsen's, the dead and stuffed seagull of his play replacing the crippled and imprisoned wild duck of Ibsen and Nina–who gets away–for Hedwig–who doesn't. Both male protagonists, however, like Hamlet, are paralyzed by the perfidy of their uncles.[38]

One might read Knausgaard's explanation of the importance of his account of his father with the dead seagull as also satirical–showing once more the power his father continues to exert–and the effect it has on him. He perversely owes him everything, even his vocation. But the symbolic bird also places him in the company of Chekhov and Ibsen. And like Hamlet–and Trigorin and Hjalmar–he, too, is unable to withstand his uncle's power.[39] References proliferate to the now-trite image of a bird standing in for the inevitably fruitless effort of humans to project themselves onto the soaring freedom of the unknowable–even terrifying–winged creature.

What actual difference does the angel make in Knausgaard's work?

37. *The Wild Duck* tells the story of Hjalmar Ekdal (a photographer, son of old Ekdal who does odd copying jobs for Werle, his former partner who betrayed him and is now marrying his secretary) and his wife Gina (former housekeeper and former mistress of Werle) and daughter Hedvik, who is going blind and keeps a live, crippled wild duck in their storeroom. They are very poor. Gregers Werle, son of the former partner comes to live with the Ekdahls–and takes an interest in the duck, seeing its injury and confinement as a metaphor for Hjalmar's own predicament. Gregers is determined to reveal the lies that bind all of them. In the end, Hedwig shoots herself. *The Seagull* features another crew of unhappy lovers and families. Treplev, a suicidal failed writer, son of a successful narcissistic actress, is in love with Nina, an aspiring actress who herself is in love with a successful writer, Trigorin. Early in the play, Treplev comes onstage with a dead seagull that he has shot and lays it at Nina's feet. The event gives Trigorin an idea for a story of a man who deliberately destroys a young woman who, until meeting him, was free like the seagull. Nina says to Treplev: "I am a seagull." At the end of the play, Shamraev (the estate manager) presents the stuffed seagull to Trigorin just before Treplev kills himself.

38. Jacob H. Adler, "Two *Hamlet* Plays: *The Wild Duck* and *The Sea Gull*," *Journal of Modern Literature* 1, no. 2 (1970): 226-48, http://www.jstor.org/stable/3830871.

39. In *Book Five* Karl Ove increasingly suspects his uncle of being involved in his father's death, and his uncle threatens to block publication of his novel.

Knausgaard is in a way more ambitious than Chekhov or Ibsen—or perhaps he is just writing a hundred years later. The identification of seagulls with angels opens on to a more sweeping and epic story. Knausgaard's relationship to the seagulls is different from that of the modernists. His seagulls are real and deeply alien. Perhaps they really are angels?

The scene with the father and the seagull/angel not only provides a key, a mirror on the novel, a metalepsis for *My Struggle*, it also draws in his earlier novel *A Time for Everything*, and maybe all of literature, as back story—through a kind of hyperlink or *mise en abyme*.

THE BODY COUNT RISES; THE MYSTERY DEEPENS

In *A Time for Everything* Knausgaard creates three spaces—spaces that might be understood to attempt to perform the magic he remembers from LeGuin—the Norwegianized landscape in which he sets the stories of Cain and Abel and Noah; the Tuscany of his fictional renaissance angelologist, Antinous Bellori; and the island retreat of writer Henrik Vankel. In each of these places he replays the father's death.

Toward the end of Antinous's life of searching for and researching angels, he comes upon archangels Michael and Raphael in a clearing in the forest. He witnesses Michael's death and his abandonment by Raphael and then walks over to look at the body. "This was what he'd dreamed of. All his adult life he'd dreamed of this: a dead angel."[40] Antinous picks up the dead angel and takes the body home with him. "All the way home . . . he thought about the angel in his arms. But not about what it was. Only what it represented. It could get him everything he'd yearned for. Fame, respect, admiration; . . . they would worship him."[41] He makes plans to dissect the angel. "The angels had had eternal life, then they'd been trapped here and become mortal. But they hadn't become human; . . . he might be holding the very key to life."[42] This scene is uncannily similar to the one about the seagull. The dead angel, like the dead seagull, externalizes his predicament. Its body, like the body of the seagull, is both like and unlike a human body.

Sitting in his study that evening, with the dead angel on ice in the cellar, Antinous reflects on what he had seen:

> *It looked as if Raphael had done it before.* There was no grief there. Michael, God's general, the foremost amongst the archangels, immortal—shouldn't his death induce a little more than these simple hand gestures? That single glance?

40. Knausgaard, *A Time for Everything*, 443.
41. Knausgaard, *A Time for Everything*, 444.
42. Knausgaard, *A Time for Everything*, 445.

> Raphael had looked at him the way a mother looks at a sleeping child. She goes out, and then she comes back in the morning.
>
> But its brow was cold, Antinous wrote. And there was no pulse.
>
> What did he know about an angel's body temperature?
>
> What did he know about an angel's heart rhythms?
>
> He knew nothing about them, he realized, as he sat there writing. He'd always regarded his writing as a sort of friend, a friend who would always listen to him, and this time was no exception, for the very last thing Antinous Bellori wrote in his notebooks, was, triflingly enough, that unfortunately he'd have to stop there, he had to check up on something, and it couldn't wait.[43]

This scene, almost gothic in its mood (one can visualize the black-and-white film in which he is seen rising from his chair amid flickering lights and swelling music), shows us Antinous just before he abruptly vanishes from the novel.

In this scene, Knausgaard shows us how writing works on the writer, just as Gide claims. The italicized sentence in the excerpt above quotes an italicized sentence from the previous paragraph. In that previous paragraph, he had first narrated Antinous's sleeplessness after he had put the dead angel on ice; then he shows us Antinous recalling the earlier scene with Michael and Raphael, concluding with his realization, "*It was almost as if it had done the same thing before*." The italics call the reader's attention to the real time effect–underlining, perhaps, the appearance of a meta voice–the one in which Antinous (and Knausgaard?) then expound in slow motion: "*like a mother following her routines when she puts her children to bed*," the reference to the apparently indifferent mother adding to the chill. We see the same obsessive recursiveness when he shows us Noah writing in real time, working on categorizing everything, including angels.[44] These writers are noticing themselves being acted upon. That is what writing does. That is why writing is Antinous's/Knausgaard's friend. Our friend.

The stop-time effect also recalls the scenes in *Book One* and *Book Five* of *My Struggle* when Karl Ove sees the blood on his dead father's face and realizes that there had been no blood in the house. The narration of Antinous's last moments likewise suddenly takes on the mood of a crime thriller. Maybe the angel is not dead. He puts his pen down. It is like his father's missing blood. He realizes he knows nothing. He sees the gaps. And you feel the fear. If Michael is not dead . . .

We are first introduced to the missing blood in *My Struggle* at the end

43. Knausgaard, *A Time for Everything*, 446-47.
44. Knausgaard, *A Time for Everything*, 190-218.

of *Book One*. The undertaker warns them, "[T]here was a lot of blood, you see, so . . . well, we did what we could, but it's still visible."[45]

> *The blood?*
>
> He looked at us.
>
> I shivered.
>
> Are you ready?
>
> "Yes," Yngve said.
>
> He opened the door and we followed him into a larger room. Dad was lying on a bier in the middle. His eyes were closed, his features composed.
>
> "Oh God."
>
> I stood beside Yngve, in front of my father. His cheeks were crimson, saturated with blood. It must have gotten caught in the pores when they tried to wipe it away. And the nose, it was broken.[46]

In the coda to *A Time for Everything* where the mystery of the father's death also appears, Henrik Vankel tells us about it but also does not reveal what had happened:

> Fifteen years later he was dead. And so violent were the circumstances surrounding his death that it not only altered our future, but also our past . . . the wildness of what he finally did had retrospective force, and now in some strange way is present in the whole of our childhood.[47]

We still don't know what happened. We don't know exactly what happened to Henrik or to Karl Ove's father. Or to Antinous. "During the hunting season in the autumn of 1606," we are told in *A Time for Everything*, "an unknown man was found in the mountains some miles from Ardo with his body torn open and his skull smashed."[48] There are other mysterious violent deaths in *A Time for Everything*. Jared. Barak. How did Jared die? Did Abel kill Jared so he could take over from Jared and be close to the Garden? Or did the angels kill Jared? Or was it a bear? Suddenly the background violence crowds in.

Knausgaard gins up the story of Jared's death out of an apocryphal account of Abel's search for the tree of life. When Jared doesn't come down from the mountain one night, Cain and Abel are sent in search of him. Abel "finds" first some dead sheep and then Jared dead as well. "It looks like

45. Knausgaard, *My Struggle, Book One*, 408.
46. Knausgaard, *My Struggle, Book One*, 408.
47. Knausgaard, *A Time for Everything*, 466.
48. Knausgaard, *A Time for Everything*, 424.

the work of a bear," Abel says. Adam gives the flock to Abel, and he goes to live on the mountain. And presumably also tries to get into the Garden by a back way. He begins to act erratically. Faking drowning. Having fits. Then comes the sacrifice, when we learn just how good Abel is at killing. What about Barak and the man on the roof? Lamech brings Barak a knife from the fair. He goes outside and whittles on a bow. Then Lamech finds him on the ground bleeding from the mouth, having apparently fallen from the tree. Barak dies the next day. What was Lamech doing in the tree? We don't know.

And we don't know what terrible thing Henrik Jankel did to cause his exile to the island. The closer we look at the text, the more of these gaps appear, and the more we try to patch them over with our theories. Is it God or is it the angels? Are all angels angels of death? "They regard us," Knausgaard tells us, "with total apathy."[49] Like the sun. Their withdrawal from the Garden signals the onset of the Flood.

What did Antinous know about angels? Nothing, he says at the end of his life, after a lifetime of study. And the narrator in *A Time for Everything* keeps reminding us how elusive that knowledge is.[50] But angels are still somehow a key to Knausgaard's father's death. To death. And to his own writing–to the space to which he wanted to return:

> It was the yearning for the angels that drove Antinous to write, and this may seem ironic, maybe he even found it so himself. The most important revelation in *On the Nature of Angels* was that the worship of its immaterial aspects had distorted the divine and turned it into something else, something abstract and written, while in reality it was corporeal and concrete, as the angels he'd seen quite clearly showed. *That* was where he wanted to be. And to get there, he had to write.[51]

As the title of Knausgaard's book on Edvard Munch announces, . . . *So much longing* . . . and as he returns to time and again in *Inadvertent*, his writing is driven by yearning.

LOVE

Karl Ove tells us in *Book Six* of *My Struggle* that what he learned from writing the book was to understand simultaneity–that other people have real lives.

49. Knausgaard, *A Time for Everything*, 379.
50. See Susan E. Schreiner, *Are You Alone Wise? The Search for Certainty in the Early Modern Era* (New York: Oxford University Press, 2010) for one account of the world in which Antinous lived.
51. Knausgaard, *A Time for Everything*, 413.

> [P]erhaps the most surprising thing I discovered while writing this novel was that everyone who had appeared in my life, even my friends at nursery, my mother's coworkers at Kokkeplassen, the neighbour kids in Tybakken, the cleaning lady we had there, my old teachers, and everyone else who had been there in my vicinity from when I was six months old to when I was thirteen, existed simultaneously with me now, and had always done so.[52]

> Naturally, I didn't really think that to be true, had never even entertained the thought, but something inside me had certainly experienced things in that way, that the places I left, and the people who populated them, died away after I was gone. For that reason it had not been them I had written about, but my recollections of them. The fact that they still existed in their own right, at the same time as my writing about them, had not occurred to me.[53]

Other people not only exist in their own right but the various versions of them over time all exist simultaneously.

> The man reading about the man reading about the man reading. The line of faces which disappeared into the illusory depths of the mirror when, as a boy, I had stood in front of it holding another mirror to reflect the image. Smaller and smaller and smaller, deeper and deeper into the distance, into all eternity, for it was impossible to stop this movement, it could only become so small that it could not be distinguished from its surroundings . . . The fractal system, on which so much in our world is based, was like that: an image within an image within an image, ad infinitum.[54]

Writing *My Struggle* was in a sense an exercise in representing this reality. The simultaneity and equal value of lives. Writing about Hamlet and Jean Genet and Rembrandt, he concludes: "I am you . . . Genet said, Your neighbour is you. From this too there is no exception, not even in the case of someone such as Adolf Hitler."[55]

These novels exhibit charity of a kind that Karl Ove learns in part from being a father. But also that he learned as a writer. Marion would call it love. Because what is foreign is revealed to him through writing.

52. Knausgaard, *My Struggle, Book Six*, 259.
53. Knausgaard, *My Struggle, Book Six*, 259.
54. Knausgaard, *My Struggle, Book Five*, 853-54.
55. Knausgaard, *My Struggle, Book Five*, 831.

13 JANUARY 2017 NEW YORK CITY

HARRISS: I really appreciate the move to the quotidian you describe, Courtney, a related sense of secularity, "flat and secular time," that makes sure that unpredictability is never mis-recognized as otherworldly, sacred, meaningful. Human experience as ongoing misalignment of praxis/*doxa*. . . . Novels and funerals both rely on making an alignment, doing work, trial and error, mighty effort going into the need for alignment. . . . Meaning may always erupt in the secular flow. Courtney picks up on the drop of the gaze in the disco passage. This is also in the description of Hans Olaf's "Picasso" face. Monstrousness, misalignment of the face is rendered according to an artist who specialized in accenting form by fracturing form. Perhaps Jeremy can speak more to something about Picasso. This threat, this gaze from Hans Olaf is one of knowing, of intimacy. . . . It is also one threatening formalization that brings praxis/*doxa* into closer orbit. Menace, knowing, form–deliberate disruption of form to create some alignment of praxis/*doxa*. This brought mind to another moment from volume two of *My Struggle*, where Karl Ove cuts himself and disfigures his face. Thus, the communion scene finds new homes in volume five–things are coming back and then pushing together, cosmic forces at work. The face thing takes a real turn, finds new resonance in Hans Olaf–attempting to align interior with exterior by cutting the face. So, we might ask what happened to Karl Ove?

CARLSON [Reading from *My Struggle, Book Two*]: "I turned and crossed the square, aware that behind me she was walking in the opposite direction, back to the party. A crowd of people had gathered around the front door beneath the trees. Arve wasn't there, so I went back, found him, told him what Linda had said to me, that she was interested in him, now they could be together. 'But I'm not interested in her, you see,' he said. 'I've *got* a wonderful girlfriend. Shame for you, though,' he said. I said it wasn't a shame for me, and crossed the square again, as though in a tunnel where nothing existed except myself, passed the crowd standing outside the house, through the hallway and into my room, where the screen of my computer was lit. I pulled out the plug, switched it off, went into the bathroom, grabbed the glass on the sink, and hurled it at the wall with all the strength I could muster. I watched to hear if there was any reaction. Then I took the biggest shard I could find and started cutting my face. I did it methodically, making the cuts as deep as I could, and covered my whole face. The chin, cheeks, forehead, nose, underneath the chin. At regular intervals, I wiped away the blood with a towel. Kept cutting. Wiped the blood away. By the time I was satisfied with my handiwork there was hardly room for one more cut, and I went to bed. Long before I woke, I knew something terrible had taken place."

/ 6 /

Incidentals

(WHEN THE SLUGS COME) (IN THE CUT)

Jeremy Biles

Incidental

Noun. An incidental detail. Extras, contingencies. Odds and ends. From Latin, *falling upon, happening to.*

Adjective. Casual (happening by chance; fortuitous; careless or offhand), occurring casually in connection with something else; of minor importance. Happening or likely to happen in an unplanned or subordinate conjunction with something else; incurred casually and in addition to the regular amount.

From Latin *incidentem*, present participle of *incidere*, to fall in, fall, find the way, light upon, fall in with; fall upon, occur; happen, befall. From *in-* "on" + *-cidere*, combining form of *cadere* "to fall," from root *kad-* "to fall."

It forms all or part of: accident, cadaver, casual, casualty, chance, cheat, coincidence, decadence, decay, incident, occasion . . .

Latin *casus* "a chance, occasion, opportunity; accident, mishap," literally "a falling," from *cadere* "to fall, sink, settle down, decline, perish."[1]

/

Incidentals become incidents. Incidents become events. Events change everything.

1. Etymologies dervied from *etymonline.com*.

(The world in a grain of sand.)

The inadvertent is inescapable, and the contingent, strangely, is necessary, is *the* necessary–necessity itself: the chance occurrence that could not have been otherwise.

Incidentals happen, despite the odds. They make space to take place. Sometimes they sneak and crawl and creep, imperceptibly; you notice them, if at all, too late. Sometimes they pop out, as if they'd been waiting to happen–an ambush, sudden or slow. Sometimes they bubble up, emerging or erupting. Or they lie there, waiting for you to trip over them, or to squash them under your shoe, whether inadvertently or deliberately.

How do they move? How do they tend and trend? Always downward, in a slow or precipitous fall. When they erupt from below, this is an inverted fall. When they drift across surfaces, this is a lateral fall. And when they drop from above, it's as if they've always been there at your feet. If they seem to incline upward, this is by dint of accrual, accumulation–sliding down, they pile up.

Incidentals disrupt the incidental, which is to say: that which constitutes the everyday is an immanent rupture. Incision of the ubiquitous, a ubiquity of incisions. The thousand cuts of every little detail. And out it all comes.

The incidental, the everyday, is a zone of dis-contents. A zone of charges and discharges. Of tragic faults and hilarious falls. Of passages–passages of texts and times, where summer slips into a fall. A zone whose circumference is nowhere and whose center is all over the place.

Incidentals, accidentals, contingencies, chance occurrences, occasions that could never have been foreseen but could not have been otherwise: *the very stuff of the quotidian, the decomposing composition of everyday life.*

/

Detail

"Relate or narrate in particulars," from French *detailer* "cut up in pieces; narrate in particulars." Meaning "divide or set off."

To cut or slash (/) into parts and pieces.

/

Something incidental, a detail–something small can cut it all up, break it all open.

Break open what?

A world.

The world?

Gathering clues for a mystery with no possible solution: a provisional notion of joy.

/

Secret

From Latin *secretus*, "set apart, withdrawn, hidden, concealed, private"; "set apart, divide, exclude"; "separate"; "to discriminate, distinguish."

Secrete

Back-formation of *secretion* (to discharge), "a dividing, separation"; "to separate, set apart."

Analyze

"To dissect, take to pieces"; "examine critically to get the essence of."

Articulate

"To divide speech into distinct parts"; "to separate into joints"; "to join, to attach by joints." From *articulus* "a part, a member, a joint" (see *article*).

/

Karl Ove Knausgaard's seasons quartet: four books of incidentals. *Autumn, Winter,* and *Summer* each comprise a cluster of articles named by things plucked from everyday life: plastic bags, beds, vomit, buttons, chairs, stuffed animals, Q-tips, sexual desire, grass lawns, clothes, eggs. . . . The article clusters are preceded or followed by other kinds of incidental writing–letters to an unborn daughter, in the case of *Autumn* and *Winter*; and in the case of *Summer*, entries in a diary (that genre whose name derives from "daily"). *Spring* is different; the book is a long letter addressed to the author's young daughter.

/

What makes a detail—a something-or-other that might otherwise get overlooked, lost, or unnoticed in its surrounding milieu—become salient? What makes one among many stand out? What sets it apart? Why this thing and not that, as Knausgaard asks somewhere?

What is it to write (to read) *unsparingly*?

Why give one's attention to, say, a lime and not a bed? To coins and not fish? To a stunt show and not ice cream?

Why slugs and not . . . ?

/

Descriptive detail reveals the object of attention—the wasp, the lawn sprinkler, a childhood room, a moment of fear or sadness or joy. But might intensity of detail not only make salient, render more fully distinct and visible, the object being described, offering the reader a kind of revelatory portrait of the thing at hand, but also, sometimes—perhaps at the very same time—be used, consciously or unconsciously, deliberately or incidentally, to *cover something up*, whether it be some aspect of the object or some other seemingly unrelated matter entirely?

In some cases, perhaps, density of detail, thickness of description, elides vision; it obscures or distracts; it leads the eye astray or takes the reader off track. Descriptive density in such cases might function like rich foliage that provides a hiding place for a predator waiting to attack, a hunter wanting to blend into her environs. On the other hand, it might provide cover for potential prey, a place of safety for stalked quarry. Or it might come into play in a game of hide and seek.

/

Knausgaard's article "Slugs" consists of a single, long paragraph—about three pages. Though the text is in this sense unbroken—no paragraph breaks cut it up—careful scrutiny reveals a tripartite structure, or three-part movement, to the article, which may therefore be divided along the lines of the following subheadings in the present essay: *Names of the Slug*, in which Knausgaard analyzes the slug, describing its essential features; *Naked and Sovereign*, in which Knausgaard encrypts a parodic parable within his article; and *Denouement*, in which the tragicomic culmination of Knausgaard's miniature epic is brought to a violent climax.

Knausgaard writes about slugs in *Summer*; the article on slugs is one among many in this book and the wider seasons quartet. "Slugs" is an entry in the cluster under the first subheading of the book, *June*. "Slugs" follows an essay on birch trees and precedes an essay on redcurrants. All the articles are approximately the same length, lending them a kind of uniformity in their heterogeneity.

In some sense, then, "Slugs" is like the other entries. It treats an everyday object or phenomenon; it is a minute text; it is very much *in medias res*, in the midst of other things, one among a broader cluster of topics gathered under a shared subheading. With "Slugs," as with other articles, Knausgaard focuses upon a thing—usually an object—and in doing so sets it apart from its environs before placing it back amidst the other stuff of everyday life. He takes a detail of life, an incidental element of the everyday, and renders it in detail—details upon details.

Often articles begin with a simple, straightforward definition, comparison, or description of physical attributes. For example, he opens "Redcurrants" with "Redcurrants are small, round, smooth berries which hang in clusters from branches of currant bushes, usually between five and fifteen on each stem," and "Tears" with "The eyes, with their vitreous body and their membranes, are kept continually moist, a thin film of water always covers them so that they don't dry out, and so that dust and dirt don't stick to them."[2]

The articles usually move from these relatively straightforward descriptions toward conclusions—*finales*, one might call them—that in many cases carry a sense of epiphanic insight or existential moment—illuminations or unexpected perspectives, sometimes expressed in a parting shot that reads like an aphorism. Or they culminate through almost mythical or magical imagery, poetic images that capture and convey a particular sentiment or idea. Thus the article that sets out to examine a banal item like "electric hand mixers" leads to the startling final insight that "man" is "supreme among the animals" because he is "the creature who runs aimlessly."[3] The article treating "rosebay willowherb" concludes with a poignant simile: "Greed for the new is old, and history merely a series of flickering see-through images seen at a great distance like the red deer in the meadow; it lifts its head and stands perfectly still for a few seconds, then vanishes into the forest."[4]

2. Karl Ove Knausgaard, *Summer* (New York: Penguin Press, 2018), 49, 67.
3. Knausgaard, *Summer*, 73.
4. Knausgaard, *Summer*, 243.

The articles, in which examination of the tiny and incidental reveals, at least sometimes, the grand and momentous, are acts of miscroscopy with telescopic implications: the world in a grain of sand.

/

Perhaps Knausgaard's articles in the seasons quartet—as well as his wider corpus?—should be read after the manner in which he writes—with a focus on incidentals, on minute details of the text?

/

The text in hand, the text before me—Knausgaard's "Slugs"—is in English, a translation from the original Norwegian. The translation is an incidental matter and therefore one to be taken seriously.[5]

A translation is a transfer in which something is inevitably lost. Some things are carried over, while others fall away. And still others are picked up, often inadvertently. Details start clinging to the translated text like stains or scratches that get picked up on a suitcase in the course of travel. And these unforeseen and unintended accruals can take on lives of their own—details with their own stories to tell, but that are at the same time part of the very substance of the text. In the course of reading a translation, new details, details that didn't appear in the "original," come to life unexpectedly. Not merely a degraded copy, the translated text is both double and other to the original. In some respects, in its accidental accruals, it might

5. All quotes from "Slugs" in the discussion below refer to the article that appears in Knausgaard, *Summer*, 45-47. The copy of the book sent to me upon online purchase includes on its cover, in an orange sphere, this note: "ADVANCE UNCORRECTED PROOFS—NOT FOR SALE." The title page of the book contains this extended caveat: "THESE ARE UNCORRECTED ADVANCE PROOFS BOUND FOR YOUR REVIEWING CONVENIENCE. In quoting from this book for reviews or any other purpose, please refer to the final printed book, because the author may make changes on these proofs before the book goes to press." I contacted the vendor about this matter and was issued a refund. But in the spirit of incidentalism that animates the present essay, I am writing with reference to the uncorrected proofs of "Slugs" (and *Summer*) at hand, which may or may not be identical to the final version of the article (and book). In other words, I want to discern what this particular rendering of "Slugs" offers, regardless of whether it coincides with the correct/ed version of the article. Is it worth considering the etymology of "correct," from *com-* + *regere*, meaning "move in a straight line"? The formation of straight lines of writing-thinking is not a desideratum of this essay, nor, I believe, of Knausgaard's mode of creation. Here, writing is writhing—twisting, bending, tortuous. On a related note: the texts scrutinized in this essay have all been translated from Norwegian into English, and are treated as English-language texts. Whether, or to what extent, any insights deriving from the present study extend to the original Norwegian texts, I, who do not read or speak Norwegian, do not know.

even exceed the original. To switch to a different metaphoric register, in translation, the text multiplies by dividing, by scissiparity: one becomes two. Something new, and maybe more, is brought forth in the splitting.

/

Translating a text: carrying it, as its etymology suggests, moving it, to take it beyond–itself?

To read a text: to translate a text. Every detail is significant, excessively significant.

Attention to detail as a mode of *inadvertency* ("not properly attentive," "unintentional"): a paradoxical formulation of the imperative of writing: to let things fall as they may, as they shall. To get incised, to lose myself, amidst the details, between your lines. A self-inflicted death by a thousand cuts.

A text is always translated at a deficit: something's going to be off: "lost in translation" is the cliché.

But one may wish to get lost in translation.

Translation is a passage, a travel–moving. So things get moved. And when things get moved, they get lost, dropped. One thing or another falls off, falls away. And there are always expenses. They pile up fast when you travel, when you're on the move. Incidentals accrue, and they have to be paid off. (Have to be paid off? Must there always be a payoff?)

NAMES OF THE SLUG

> *All the names we have given the small, soft, slimy, dark animals that slither slowly around the ground wherever it is moist–molluscs, lung snails, bladder snails, forest snails, nude snails–themselves have something moist and soft about them, it occurs to me . . .*

Names: Knausgaard's entry opens by invoking a list, perhaps a partial list, intended to indicate–even if not explicitly pronouncing–"all the names" by which slugs are known. (What names go unnamed here?) The animal picked out by the title of Knausgaard's brief article is polyonymous. The many names of the slug, Knausgaard suggests, partake of the moist and soft, have "something moist and soft about them." For instance, the *M* of *mollusc* derives from the "water" ideogram of Egyptian writing: . The crests of the capital *M* are wavelike in appearance, a matter made more apparent when several *M*'s are strung together: *MMMMM*. In the lowercase *m*, such as appears in Knausgaard's "molluscs," the sharpness of the waves has been *softened*—there is something "soft" about the slugs—in other words, rounded, making the letter appear less like choppy water than something *softly* watery, verging on wet—"moist." The small *m* is an icon of the moist that links the property of moistness to the mollusc, one among the panoply of names for the slug.

Continuing to elaborate explicitly upon what remains implicit but connoted in Knausgaard, one might observe other features of the word *slug*. The *s* itself is slippery, slithery, sliding, curving like a slug's bending body or like a circuitous trail of mucous slime. And indeed the initial *sl* of *slug* is also present in *slime* (as well as *slithery, slippery* . . .), thus establishing, by repetition, a kind of intimacy between the name of the animal and its key traits: sliminess is essential to the slug; slugs partake of the slimy (and slitheriness, slipperiness . . .).

As for the *ug* that follows the *sl* in *slug*: the *ug* is a frequently vague but nonetheless significant guttural sound. It is, first of all, the sound often associated with prehistoric, prelinguistic humans, who in the popular imagination communicate through modulations of *ug*, a kind of ur-sound at the origins of articulate speech. But *ug* is also a gagging, retching, glottal sound proper to the repulsion that follows an encounter with the *sl*ippery, *sl*ithering, *sl*imy *sl*ug. If the very name of the slug conveys something of the essence of the slug, it also announces the human response to the encounter with the slug—an encounter with a slithery *sl* elicits, is immediately followed by, a disgusted *ug* sound (usually written with a silent *h*: *ugh*). The *ug* is the sound that issues from the depths of the body before language is available, or when the limits of articulation are exceeded. It is a sound that falls outside the boundaries of articulate language.

The *ug* "names" the origins and the end of language; it is before and beyond language.[6] To this observation we might add a further, related one: lacking a skeleton, the slug's body is soft, through and through—unarticulated. The slug's name not only contains the *ug* that is beyond articulate language; the slug concretely (but softly) *embodies* that which is before and beyond language.

Articulation: etymologically, "to divide speech into distinct parts" and "to separate into joints." To articulate is to link by division, to con-join by cutting, to cohere through incision, to separate according to joints.

Slugs, unarticulated and inarticulate, are, in this particular sense, formless. In their very presence, they announce, without pronouncing, an incoherence that haunts the human. This, anyway, is the beginning of the story, but certainly not its end.

6. One may compare this *ug* with the Sanskrit *pranava* and *om*.

For as we will see, *slugs embody the birth of language from the sentiment of disgust. They are the sacrificial victims that establish the very possibility of communication.*

In this way, slugs are the tragic heroes of a drama without end. And "Slugs," the article by Karl Ove Knausgaard, conveys, without containing, this drama.

So much in a name. *Slug*, the short, monosyllabic name for a small, mucus-secreting creature, evokes an epic tragedy.

Like the animal it names, the word *slug* is short. Young slugs, and some full-grown slugs, are about the length of the word *slug* when typed in 12-point font, as you see here: slug. The very largest slugs—the banana slug, the most prodigious of these little monsters—grow to about ten inches, and could thus stretch the length of a page of text on standard typing paper with one-inch margins. The black slugs of Knausgaard's childhood ("When I was growing up, all slugs were black") grow to three and a half inches—exactly the length of a typed line of text in my 2018 Penguin English translation of Knausgaard's book *Summer.*

Names and identity are interlinked notions in Knausgaard's thought. A name names a single and singular identity. In the case of the polyonymous creature that we, following Knausgaard, are referring to simply as a slug, the multiplicity of names corresponds to an ambiguity in its identity—an essential, constitutive ambiguity. It is as if a creature as malleable—or formless, from the human perspective, in the sense suggested above—as the slug cannot be apprehended with a single name; something so amorphous, at least as it exists in the human imagination, requires many names. The slug slides from name to name much as it oozes over the ferns and moss of the forest.

The opening phrase of the opening passage cited in italics above exhibits a density of *s* and *m* words—so many names for the slug and its key qualities. Thus we find: *slug, small, soft, slimy, slither, slowly, snails, moist, molluscs. Moist* and *soft* appear twice in the first sentence of the essay, suggesting that these qualities are of special importance; they are essential attributes of slugs. It might be said that slugs are *the* moist and *the* soft—embodiments of moistness and softness. We shall accordingly pay special attention to the moist and the soft.

> *. . . and every time I see a slug these days I am struck by how it inverts qualities that normally belong to the intimate human sphere and there express great beauty—nude is vulnerable, soft is arousing, lungs are the spirit of life, the forest is pure nature—for slugs' nakedness, the slugs' softness, the slugs' lungs and the slugs' forest are instead repulsive, deeply undesirable and loathsome.*

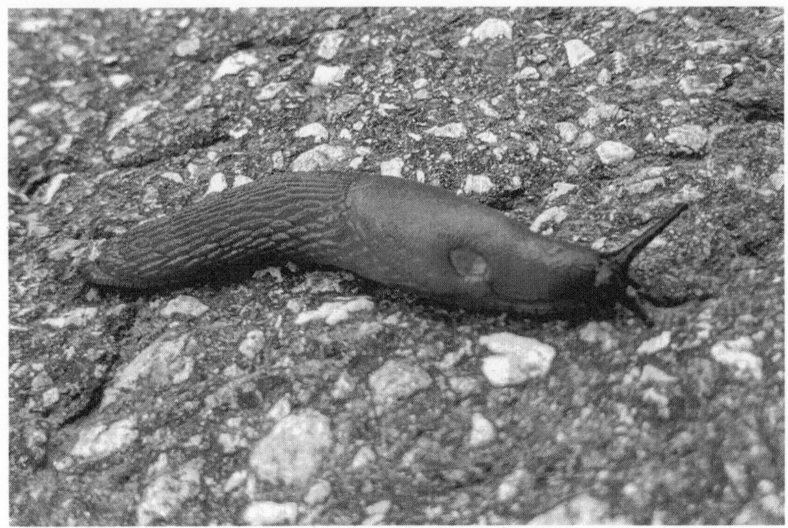

FIGURE 6: A Norwegian slug. Photo by the author.

Thus ends the lengthy, recursive first sentence of Knausgaard's tiny essay on slugs, a long sentence within a short text that joins other short essays in a cluster contained in a volume that is part of a larger set of books within a wider corpus.

What is the relationship of part to whole, of detail to the thing in its entirety? This question obsesses Knausgaard.

Related–how, exactly?–to the question of part/whole is another point of obsessive recurrence in Knausgaard's thought: repetition. Knausgaard, one might say, betrays a kind of repetition compulsion about repetition itself; repetition is an eternally recurring theme–sometimes explicit, sometimes ulterior–throughout his *oeuvre*.

Slugs exhibit a form of repetition: they proliferate in abundance. This animal's numerousness, as Knausgaard's descriptions suggest, makes individual slugs indistinguishable from one another (from the human perspective) and therefore anonymous ("they" are "everywhere," he says more than once in his essay). Thus the polyonymous slug is also anonymous: polyanonymous? Slugs are the many and the one, the any and the none.

To reiterate: the first sentence of "Slugs" is long and, if not precisely winding, it nonetheless circles–*almost*–back upon itself, thereby forming an imperfect loop, something akin to a *spiral*: an imprecise doubling not unlike a slug's trail . . .

. . . for we are first offered an array of sluggish attributes–small, soft, slimy–followed by an array of sluggish names–molluscs, etc.–that them-

FIGURE 7: "Snail trail" by Thomas Guest. Uploaded to Flickr in 2009 (CC BY 2.0, https://creativecommons.org/licenses/by/2.0/).

selves partake of sluggish attributes: a first instance of doubling. Then Knausgaard notes that these attributes "invert" those qualities belonging to the "intimate human sphere," expressing not human beauty but sluggish repulsiveness. Here he announces the human qualities that find their inverted counterparts in the slug; in the "intimate human sphere," nudity is equated with vulnerability, softness with arousal, lungs with life spirit, forest with "pure" nature, whereas these same attributes are, when exhibited by the slug, repulsive, undesirable, loathsome.[7] The human sphere is doubled in the gastropodosphere, the human being doubled in the slug. All this is conveyed in a linear but looping sentence: a written strand of human language, a string of words in a stack of straight lines that doubles back upon itself, thereby parodying, or parodied by, the slug's slimy, looping trail.

Thus, in the first sentence of this essay, Knausgaard begins a demonstration in the form of an act of human articulation that resembles a slug's curving mucous traces—a matter to which we will return (a matter that will return to us). But is the slug the parody of the human, or the human the parody of the slug?

7. On inversion, see Mikhail Bakhtin, *Rabelais and His World*, trans. Helene Iswolsky (Bloomington: Indiana University Press, 2009). See also Peter Stallybrass and Allon White, *The Politics and Poetics of Transgression* (Ithaca, NY: Cornell University Press, 1986).

Slugs are, by Knausgaard's estimation, the inverted other of the human; the *alien* world of the slug is the grotesque counterpart to the *intimate* human sphere. If the "intimate human sphere" is the world of human communication and community–which exhibits coherence through modes of *attraction* (modes of social binding, linking)–the slug appears from this perspective like an invasion of foreign bodies that disrupts and corrupts pure communication and community, disarticulating the human sense of coherence (the sense of being human as distinct from animals, as we will discuss), and stimulating loathing and *repulsion*.

Knausgaard inquires into this loathsomeness, this repulsion elicited by the slug. What makes slugs so disgusting and distressing to at least some humans? Why do traits that are the most beautiful in the intimate human sphere become repulsive when found in the slug?

Knausgaard observes that snails–slugs with shells–are "less repulsive than slugs," hypothesizing that "it is the nakedness in itself that puts us off," much as the nakedness of a rat's hairless tail is that rodent's most repulsive attribute. This is the comparison Knausgaard makes: the slug is like a rat's tail. But Knausgaard immediately disqualifies the hypothesis he has just hazarded, noting that "there are plenty of other animals that lack a clear distinction between their outer and inner body, for instance jellyfish and earthworms, which should therefore seem just as repulsive to us."

Worth noting here is that Knausgaard equates, without elucidating the underlying logic of his thinking, "nakedness" with "lack[ing] a clear distinction between outer and inner body." There has been no indication, no explicit account, of why *nakedness* is made to slide into a *lack of distinction* between *outer* and *inner* body. Perhaps Knausgaard finds the equation, the connection, so patent as to obviate comment: to be naked simply *is* to have elided the distinction between inner and outer body.

But what of this? Knausgaard's logic would seem to be that nakedness is a state of exposure of, or a matter of rendering exposed (making "outer"), what should have remained covered up, namely the "inner" body. What, then, is this inner body that is on display when naked? The answer is not simple or obvious, despite the examples of the "inner" body that Knausgaard will eventually offer: lungs, heart, liver–the "interior organs." Because for Knausgaard, as we will soon expose in further detail, it would seem that what really counts as the "inner" body is not (or not only) the interior organs–the organs concealed beneath skin–but those parts of the body that *should be covered by clothing*–namely the genitals. *This* "inner" body–the genitals–is what the slug exteriorizes, makes explicit, and this, we will see, is part of the basis of the slugs' ability to repulse. In short, Knausgaard slides between two poles in his double notion of nudity, one explicit—exposure of *that which lies under the skin* (i.e., the interior organs)—and the other unannounced—*that which is hidden behind clothing* (i.e., the genitals).

We should note that it is at the very point of discussing nudity as a "lack of a clear distinction" that Knausgaard's own text fails to maintain a clear distinction between two notions of nudity; the boundary between them is indistinct. This discrepancy, and the implicit switching between these two notions of nudity or nakedness—one pronounced and one implied, one exposed and one hidden—calls for scrutiny.

So let us return to Knausgaard's example of the hairless tail of the rat. The rat's tail, Knausgaard suggests, is "the most repulsive thing about a rat" because it is naked. But nakedness alone does not explain the disgust elicited by the rat, as "there are plenty of other animals that lack a clear distinction between their outer and inner body." Jellyfish and earthworms are "naked," but do not inspire a comparable revulsion. Therefore, Knausgaard concludes, nakedness cannot (fully) account for the disgust elicited by rats nor, by extension, that of slugs. But here Knausgaard seems not (fully) to recognize the notion of nudity operative in the rat's repulsiveness. The text at once suggests and fails to perceive that the nudity of the rat is of the genital sort. The hairless tail is repulsive because it is *phallic*; it corresponds to a part of the human body that should be covered by clothing. This fact would explain why the rat's tail disturbs while the naked jellyfish does not.

But why, one may ask, does an earthworm's nudity not disturb? Is the worm not phallic? It is. But unlike the rat, the earthworm has no "clothes," no fur at all—and therefore its nakedness is not *obscene*. By contrast, the rat's hairless tail appears to emerge from the furry body of the rat like a penis slithering out from the trousers. According to the underlying logic of Knausgaard's text, it is precisely the clothing—the covering—that makes something capable of being *rendered naked*, and thus prone to eliciting a disturbance that registers as repulsion. (To this idea, we will discover, Knausgaard's text contains a pendant notion: it is by keeping a certain something [or things] covered up that humans are afforded their sense of dignity, for it is this covering-up that maintains a boundary between human and animal.)

To understand the disgust elicited by slugs, we must analyze the text further. Inquiring into the slugs' repulsiveness, Knausgaard formulates another hypothesis in the form of a question: Does not the repulsion elicited by the nakedness of the slug devolve upon *resemblance*? "Could it be," he asks, that slugs disgust us "because slugs resemble us more, are closer to us than jellyfish?"

Slugs are, Knausgaard suggests, more *like* humans than jellyfish, and it is on account of this *likeness* to humans that slugs in their nakedness are repulsive. Knausgaard supports his conjecture with a further question: "Is it precisely that they have lungs, that they have a heart, that they have eyes which makes their nakedness seem so repulsive?" Note here that he names two internal organs that will appear later–lungs and heart–along with the eyes. But, curiously, Knausgaard immediately–in the very next sentence–mitigates the resemblance he has just proposed, noting that slugs' "eyes are of a very different and alien construction, placed as they are at the end of tentacles, one of two pairs, the upper pair being for the eyes, the lower pair for smells, like a kind of nose extension."

At this point, we should pause briefly to summarize the almost rhythmic peripeties, the dramatic *alternations*, already evident in this text, for Knausgaard slides back and forth, or slips around in circles, reversing things he has asserted, even as he slips between dual notions of nakedness: Slugs are *other*; they *invert* the human. They are repulsive, perhaps, in their nakedness. But other animals are naked, so what makes slugs particularly repulsive? Their very resemblance to humans. But in fact the points of resemblance to humans are yet further instances of otherness, of their "alien" constitution.

Knausgaard is uncertain, and his text in a sense confused–articulate but not quite coherent. This confusion, combined with the emerging litany of questions through which Knausgaard's account edges forward, lend the text a conjectural, subjunctive mood. Much has been observed about slugs–their physiognomy; their mode of movement; their slimy exudations; the ways in which they "invert" the human sphere; the affective, visceral responses of disgust they inspire in human beings. . . . But nothing yet accounts for the repulsion and loathsomeness that the text seeks not only to describe but to explain, to *apprehend*. Instead, in the space of just a page, it has already devolved into a state of lucid, and even beautiful, confusion.

Indeed, having just asked why slugs are repulsive and then going on to note the (non-)resemblance of slugs to humans, Knausgaard now slides into a different question. "What is it we see when [slugs] come slithering out after a rainy night, slowly and with heads raised?" The transition to this question is curious, as it follows immediately upon the description of the two pairs of tentacles borne by the slug. The emergence of this particular question reaches the reader as a surprise, for it does not follow directly *from*, even though it follows immediately *upon*, the description of the tentacles. These tentacles, Knausgaard has noted, bear the slugs' sensory organs–one pair "for the eyes" and one "for smells." This observation about the slugs' dual mechanisms of perception might logically open onto to the question: "What is it that the *slugs* see and smell when they come slithering out?" (And to be sure, elsewhere Knausgaard does not hesitate to speculate about animal perceptions, about what it's like to perceive the world as a given animal; see, for instance, his essay "Bats" or his writings on photographs of birds.)[8]

But this question is not the one Knausgaard asks. Rather, he asks the *inverse* question–not, What do slugs perceive? but, What is it we *humans* see when slugs come slithering out after a rainy night, slowly and with heads raised? The question reiterates, with a difference, the question already presented in his article–What accounts for the disgust elicited by slugs?–thus constituting a looping line of inquiry. And yet this detail of the text, this seemingly incidental feature–the placement of this particular question after this particular sentence in so inconspicuous a manner, this subtle, almost imperceptible subversion of readerly expectation–produces a tiny shock of reversal. Countering the expectation set up by the sentence that has immediately preceded it–the sentence that includes the description of the tentacles–this question takes the reader by surprise. It is both *anticipated* (already announced) and *unexpected*, giving it the quality of something at once *slow* and *sudden*: a quiet disruption, a soft explosion. (In this way, to anticipate upcoming descriptions in Knausgaard's article, the question *resembles a slug*: it emerges quietly but unexpectedly, slowly and suddenly.)

Keeping in mind the still unanswered question of what constitutes the "inner body," we now ask, with Knausgaard, What *do* we see when the slugs come? His reply marks a turning point in the text.

NAKED AND SOVEREIGN

> *What is it we see when they come slithering out after a rainy night, slowly and with heads raised? They resemble aged majesties, the rulers of the forest floor, emperors of rotted leaves and moist soil. But this striking dignity, which should make us venerate them, rather like the Egyptians venerated cats and Indians venerate cows, is entirely lost sight of due to the repulsiveness their nudity and slimy smoothness exude. Isn't there something almost provocative about them? Something counter to nature? They seem to belong to the interior organs in a body, lungs, livers, hearts, which are all smooth and rounded and naked, without any distinction between inner and outer. Is that why they disgust us, because they look like little lungs creeping around by themselves, with antenna-like eyes,*

8. "Bats" is found in *Summer*, 55–57. Knausgaard writes on birds in "To Be a Bird," in the *New Yorker*, May 2, 2019; https://www.newyorker.com/culture/photo-booth/karl-ove-knausgaard-on-stephen-gills-bird-images-in-the-pillar.

> *like little livers, like little hearts? Is this why they seem almost provocative, because they are counter to nature, and then the go creeping around like it was the most natural thing in the world, eating and reproducing, and everything has to happen so damned slowly, everything has to be so damned dignified–who the hell do slugs think they are? Millimeter after millimeter they slide along between the moist blades of grass, the wet ferns, across the soft moss, and live their lives in harmony with their abilities and limitations, as all living things do.*

What we see when the slugs come is, first of all, described, again, in terms of simile, similitude, *resemblance*: slugs "resemble" kings, emperors. They are *like* humans, specifically sovereign humans, in their "dignified" bearing. Though Knausgaard does not mention this detail, the fleshy respiratory cavity atop a slug's body is called a "mantle"–another kingly association. But what grants them their dignity, according to Knausgaard, is their slowness–they rush to please no one–and their raised heads. Together, these traits afford slugs their air of superiority, their regal bearing. Upon first reading, one may wonder why these specific traits, unlike nudity, softness, and so on, make slugs proximal to the intimate human sphere. Why are these features not inverted, causing disgust? Why do they convey dignity and regal repose rather than stimulate loathing?

But indeed, much as the slugs' nudity, softness, and other qualities are "inverted," making them not desirable but loathsome, here, too, the slugs' noble comportment is "lost sight of," and in a similarly inversive manner; the sovereign air is undermined by the "repulsiveness" that attends the slugs' "nudity and slimy smoothness." The repulsion that is fomented by the slugs' nudity thus makes of their would-be dignity something "provocative" and "counter to nature."

Knausgaard mentions these characteristics–provocative, counter to nature–twice in this passage. First they are mentioned in questions that sit alongside each other: slugs are provocative; slugs are counter to nature. The progression of the two questions seems to suggest that slugs are provocative and *therefore* counter to nature. Or perhaps "counter to nature" is intended to gloss "provocative"? Whatever the case, their second mention comes in the context of yet another pair of questions: "Is this why they seem almost provocative, because they are counter to nature . . . ?" Now a different, perhaps inverse, relation between provocativeness and contrariness to nature is suggested: Knausgaard here considers slugs to be provocative *because* they are counter to nature.

Like so many other aspects of Knausgaard's essay (and his writings more broadly), the switch here is seemingly a merely incidental detail, but it should provoke sustained inquiry. How exactly are the slugs counter to nature, and what about being counter to nature is provocative—or vice versa? So let us cut into the text and focus upon the details, marking out a new line of inquiry.

Counter to nature: in other words, monstrous. A monster, as many scholars of teratology have observed, is that which falls outside the categories by which we organize natural (and social) phenomena; a monster is a prodigy that exists in excess of the taxonomic conceptual systems intended to produce and maintain the "natural" order. Manifoldly ambiguous—in ways we have only begun to unpack—slugs, as imagined by Knausgaard, are tiny monsters. No less than kings and emperors, whose auratic authority sets them apart from ordinary people, slugs seem to exceed the order of the ordinary and the bounds of the natural, even and especially in their everydayness and their resemblance to the human. Indeed, by Knausgaard's reckoning, it is, in part, their very *proximity* to the human that lends slugs their air of monstrosity; it is because they "resemble" humans, broaching and even breaching the boundary separating us from them, human from naked animal, that they are monstrous. This "disgusting" aspect of slugs corresponds to the repulsion inspired by monsters: in various ways, through various modes, monsters tend to be at once *like* humans and *inversions* of the human. This proximity of that which is alien or other, the threat of a breakdown of borders of distinction between human and not-human, is one facet of the *horror* elicited by monsters.[9]

Monsters invert the human in a variety of ways. For instance, monsters exteriorize interiors, or discombobulate the proper organization of bodily organs. Thus the Cambodian *krasue* spirit-monster consists of a floating head with internal organs dangling from the neck in a manner that resembles a jellyfish. Monsters also disorganize through hybridity, combining human and animal or alien attributes, such as seen in John Carpenter's classic horror movie *The Thing* (1982), in which alien monsters, at first indistinguishable from humans, also manifest as horrible hybrids and creatures in which the boundary between exterior and interior is dissolved, with inner organs in plain sight. Or consider the more recent (2017) British horror movie *The Ritual*, which features Moder, a gigantic, moose-like beast with a head that incorporates parts of a human body. Monsters counter nature

9. On monsters as "counter to nature," see Arnold Davidson, "The Horror of Monsters," in *The Boundaries of Humanity: Humans, Animals, Machines*, ed. James S. Sheehan and Morton Sosna (Berkley: University of California Press, 1991). For a discussion of monstrosity, abjection, and horror movies, see Barbara Creed, *The Monstrous-Feminine: Film, Feminism, and Psychoanalysis* (New York: Routledge, 1993).

FIGURE 8: The monstrous human-alien hybrid from John Carpenter's movie The Thing (Universal Pictures, 1982).

FIGURE 9: Human and animal mingle in the body of the monstrous Moder from The Ritual, directed by David Bruckner (Netflix, 2017).

by challenging the classifications by which we conceptually organize nature; they undermine (or overcome) the taxonomies through which order—natural, social, political, organic—is established and maintained.

Slugs accede to the monstrous in Knausgaard's imagination, both in their likeness to humans—they share organs with humans, they embody human traits of dignity, and so forth—and in being alien to the human sphere, repulsively inverting the human in their very proximity to the human.

At the same time, to return to one of the lines of inquiry set out above, Knausgaard takes slugs to exteriorize interiors, turning bodies inside out, thereby eliding the "distinction between inner and outer." We have already observed that the nakedness that Knausgaard links with loss of distinction between inner and outer has to do with a revelation of a certain *exterior* part of the body, namely the part that, according to the prevailing social order of which Knausgaard is a part, must remain covered with clothing: the genitals.

But here Knausgaard is explicit about what he intends by "interior organs": slugs "seem to belong to the interior organs in a body, lungs, livers, hearts, which are all smooth and rounded and naked." That slugs resemble interior organs–and that they *embody disembodied* organs–helps account for the loathing, the fearful disgust, they arouse. As Freud notes in his essay "The Uncanny," the ambivalent species of fright that goes by the name "uncanny" may be stimulated by the sight of organs cut off, set apart, from their corporeal context, and taking on a life of their own.[10] Slugs partake of this dramatically uncanny aspect; by Knausgaard's account, they present themselves as sentient, disembodied organs, independently animated.

Slugs, to repeat, appear to be "without any distinction between inner and outer." And is this "why they disgust us," Knausgaard asks again? "Is this why they seem almost provocative?" Here one must note the incremental nearness, perhaps even the simultaneity or identification, that Knausgaard assumes between the sentiment of disgust and the sentiment of provocation (sexual titillation). Knausgaard is not alone in positing a close affiliation of disgust and sexual excitement. To be sure, numerous literary, philosophical, and psychoanalytic texts affirm the closeness, or simultaneity, of attraction and repulsion in erotic arousal. In fact, this simultaneity is often taken to be the very essence of *fascination*.[11]

How to account for the curiously arousing effect of this simultaneity, this coincidence of opposites? Why and how are provocation and disgust related?

Some recent studies of disgust suggest that the peculiarly human sentiment of disgust is stimulated by phenomena that challenge boundary distinctions, particularly the distinction between inside and outside, and between life and death. And as Julia Kristeva argues in her famous study *Powers of Horror*, abject materials–vomit, excrement, mucus, and the like–breach the boundaries of the body, revealing its vulnerable porosity,

10. See Sigmund Freud, *The Uncanny*, translated by David McLintock (New York: Penguin, 2003).
11. See, for example, Georges Bataille, *Erotism: Death and Sensuality*, translated by Mary Dalwood (San Francisco: City Lights Books, 1986).

thereby calling into question the secure integrality of our bodies in a manner that prompts corresponding existential uncertainty and an anxious sense of repulsion.[12]

Boundary dissolution, particularly between life and death, is also central to the account of disgust articulated by philosopher Colin McGinn, who argues that disgust is elicited by the creeping presence of death within life, as found, for instance, in decaying flesh:

> What is disgusting is death *as presented in the form of living tissue*. It is death in the context of life that disgusts—the death or dying of the living. Not death *tout court*, but death in the *midst* of life, surrounded by it. Or again, it is the living *becoming dead*, making that dreadful transition. . . . Disgust occurs in that ambiguous territory between life and death, when both conditions are present in some form: it is not life per se or death per se that disgusts, but their uneasy juxtaposition. . . . What disgusts is the *interpenetration* of life and death.[13]

Taking up McGinn's insights, perhaps the (or one) loss of distinction signified by slugs in their oozing ambiguity is the distinction between life and death. Perhaps slugs—whose soft, mucus-exuding bodies betoken putrescence; whose malleable, capsule-like forms resemble mobile coagulations; whose uncanny slowness creeps like decay; whose likeness to interior organs gives them the aspect of a body coming undone—perhaps slugs stimulate disgust because they seem to exist in a "zone of indistinction," where life and death interpenetrate.

If the loss of distinction between life and death arouses disgust, disgust is nonetheless linked with sexual arousal. Scholars of disgust note that, as organs of both sexual pleasure and excretion, the genitals are fascinating sites of simultaneous attraction and repulsion. Psychoanalytic thinkers as well as literary writers in the lineage of the Marquis de Sade suggest that disgust in fact *stimulates*, heightens, sexual arousal.

In light of these observations, one may be given to wonder if Knausgaard, citing the loss of distinction between inner and outer as an elicitor of disgust, is more right than he knows. The repulsion and provocation of slugs lies, indeed, in the breakdown of distinctions, but the full implicative amplitude of this boundary dissolution is greater than Knausgaard

12. See Julia Kristeva, *Powers of Horror* (New York: Columbia University Press, 1982). On related matters pertaining to dirt, see also Mary Douglas, *Purity and Danger* (New York: Routledge, 2002), especially the chapters "Powers and Dangers" and "The System Shattered and Renewed."

13. Colin McGinn, *The Meaning of Disgust* (Oxford: Oxford University Press, 2011), 90.

recognizes in his short essay. In addition to the uncanny exteriorization of interior organs, and in addition to their stimulating "nakedness," slugs fascinate according to the breakdown of the distinction between life and death that they embody, and thereby mingle sexual arousal and repulsion.

Much has now been said of the disgusting aspect of slugs. What more may be observed about their specifically *provocative* aspect?

We may begin by noting that slugs are hermaphroditic, possessing both male and female sexual organs. This anatomical fact bolsters Knausgaard's observations concerning the resemblance of slugs to humans, which for him has to do in part with the matter of slugs having organs that humans also possess. But I suspect that the peculiar ambivalence aroused by slugs has little to do with the fact that these creatures physically possess both male and female sexual organs (however much this fact might challenge conceptual binarism pertaining to human gender and sexual anatomy). Moving beyond the realm of anatomy and into the psychological-symbolic associations that Knausgaard gestures toward, we will find that the more potently hermaphroditic aspect of slugs is at once more hidden and more manifest than the slugs' dual genitalia.

Slugs are patently–one might say *obscenely*–phallic. Slugs may indeed resemble, as Knausgaard would have it, creeping livers, hearts, and lungs. But just as surely as they resemble these organs, they resemble penises. That said, if phallicism is generally linked with hardness and dryness, one may wonder at the touted *softness* and *moistness* of slugs. It is these qualities that afford slugs the other side of the customary sexual binary; in their softness and moistness, as well as their labial delicacy, slugs resemble aspects of female genitalia. Slugs are, then, doubly hermaphroditic.

The simultaneously phallic and labial aspect of slugs–this characteristic can be named with an aptly hybridic portmanteau word: *phallabial*–may seem to stand in tension with Knausgaard's contention that slugs are like *internal* organs exteriorized. But in fact, to return again and always to the matter of nudity, the phallabialism of slugs bears out Knausgaard's observation even more acutely than Knausgaard's own comparison of slugs with the internal organs he names; he is more right than he knows. For the organs that go unnamed, unpronounced, in Knausgaard's text–despite the author's sensitivity to the slugs' "provocative" aspect–are of special significance. In their phallic obscenity and labial moistness, slugs are roving emblems of humans *denuded*, stripped of their clothing. This observation requires explanation.

The most pertinent "lack" of "any clear distinction" between inner and outer, as embodied in the slug, is more accurately a *loss* of distinction–not a simple absence, in other words, but a *subtractive experience*. It is not so much in the exteriorization of interior organs (heart, liver, etc.) that the arousing provocation of slugs takes hold, but in the sense they give of one being *rendered naked*–stripped, unclothed. To be clear, it is not that slugs are denuded; they are always already naked. Rather, unlike the nudity of a jellyfish, but like the nudity of the rat's tail, beholding the slug stimulates an experience akin to disrobing. Slugs solicit the stimulating, exciting sense of shame and embarrassment that comes with the act of taking off one's clothing in the presence of another.

The rat's naked tail is obscene because it seems to emerge from its "clothed" body. Similarly, slugs, though hairless, are obscene because, as Knausgaard suggests, they resemble humans in their socially "dignified"–that is, clothed–state. But this dignity is "lost sight of" precisely because the slug appears exposed: an exteriorization of what should have remained hidden from sight, behind clothing. Slugs thus resemble us not precisely as naked, but in our denudation. If they have a noble bearing, something befitting the most elevated image of the human being, the sovereign, then the egregious genital nudity they simultaneously embody is all the more obscene for the contrast it presents with our "dignity." Further, slugs confront us with our basest *animality*–our genitals. This reminder of our proximity to animality by virtue of distinction from which our dignity, our humanity itself, is established, is a further source of disgust.

The disturbingly provocative nature of the slug has to do, then, with a sense of rendering available to sight what should have remained hidden by clothes, and what is furthest from human "dignity": genital animality. Beholding the slug is tantamount to the simultaneously socially anxious and sexually arousing act of taking off one's clothes in the presence of the other. Extrapolating from Knausgaard, then, one might suggest that *to gaze upon the "naked" slug is to have an experience at the level of denudation*. It is to disclose, to dis-clothe, a *secret*.

To support this point, we should grant further attention to what might seem incidental details of Knausgaard's text–which describes slugs as both "nude" and as "emperors," but which leaves unspoken the significance of this pairing–thereby revealing a *parabolic* aspect to the text–parabolic in a double sense.

First, the text is manifestly parabolic in the etymological sense that it *juxtaposes* the slug and the human, and thus makes a comparison between the two: slugs "resemble us." In this way, now borrowing from Pythagorean geometry, the text places "human" and "slug" in a relation of similitude. A parabola is a curve exhibiting *mirror symmetry*. Knausgaard, we have already observed, places human and slug in a relation of mirror symmetry–a point-by-point inversion (the slug "inverts qualities that normally belong to the human sphere; . . . nude is vulnerable," etc.)–along an "axis of symmetry." Slugs and humans are mutually parabolic.

But Knausgaard's text also carries out a mirroring operation on a preexisting parable; "Slugs" encrypts an inverted parable, a counter-parable, or perhaps the parody of a parable, in a manner that complicates the play of inner and outer, hidden and revealed, already under discussion. Observing that the "naked" slug also resembles an "emperor" in its "striking dignity" cannot but call to mind Hans Christian Anderson's parable of "The Emperor's New Clothes." The tale is well known and need not be rehearsed here. But we may ask what it means to retell that story *in miniature*–embedded within the essay "Slugs"–and *in disguise*–with the slug in the place of the human emperor. Like the emperor of Anderson's story, who by the tale's end suspects that the child who had proclaimed the emperor's nudity–*But he hasn't got anything on!*–is indeed right but nonetheless persists in his pompous parade, the slug "slides along," naked and haughty–"so damned dignified," in Knausgaard's words.

But of course, the slug lacks the pretense of the emperor. The slug's nakedness, along with its other disgust-inducing attributes, appears "counter to nature," but only from the human's point of view–which is itself counter to nature. That is to say, nudity is "natural"; clothing is cultural; and for a human to declare a slug's nudity–*He hasn't got anything on!*–and attribute to this nudity something "counter to nature" is itself already an inversion of the natural, the naked.

The crypto-parabolic aspect of Knausgaard's essay "Slugs," its unannounced retelling of "The Emperor's New Clothes," makes of this portion of the essay, excerpted in italics above, a mirror inversion of Anderson's parable. "Who the hell do slugs think they are?" parading around unembarrassedly, Knausgaard asks on behalf of the reader. In Anderson's tale, the emperor, at once sensing and disavowing the truth of the situation, doubles down on his haughtiness, when he, naked before the eyes of all, *should be* embarrassed. In Knausgaard's tale, we find an inversion. The slug, sovereignly indifferent to its nudity, stimulates embarrassment in the human who beholds it, and by extension, in the reader whose eyes gaze upon the text of "Slugs."

The townspeople have been duped, and the emperor as well. The emperor persists in his error, in bad faith. The slug, by contrast, *is what it is*; it "lives in harmony" with itself and its environment. Much as Anderson's tale ends with a reversal in the form of a revelation–the townspeople, echoing the little girl, cry out, "He hasn't got anything on!"–Knausgaard's retelling of the parable ends with a reversal, a contradiction, an inversion of his earlier assertion, twice repeated, that slugs are "counter to nature." For, of course, they are not counter to nature; on the contrary, as Knausgaard now acknowledges, they "live their lives in harmony" with themselves and their environment, with the "moist blades of grass, the wet ferns," within their "abilities and limitations." There is a switching, an alternation. Slugs are counter to nature; slugs are in harmony with nature. Slugs are set apart from nature, and they are *not* set apart from nature, not counter to nature, but are *of a piece with nature, part of the "whole" which is "nature."* Given this inversion, this passage of Knausgaard's text may thus be seen as doubly parabolic: a parabola (inverted mirror symmetry) of a parable.

Knausgaard's text is a play of doubles, an uncanny mirror, a *mise en abyme* of inverted reflections, of dual and dueling nudes. And with this observation, we loop back yet again to the intertwining questions of disgust, provocation, and the dissolution of boundaries. We now turn to the third and final portion of the text, the third act of the drama—the downfall, the tragicomic denouement.

/

But first, to cut in. This could have happened elsewhere; it's a bit arbitrary, but this is as good a place as any—here, anterior to the end, at the outset of the denouement (the unbinding, the untying, the unknotting of the knot)—to insert another cut, another connection—cutting in to set things unraveling, to solve the mystery by dissolving, further breaking up, the texts (Knausgaard's text—and the text you're reading now?), to disclose something else that has been hidden, unspoken—something that speaks, in fact, to an unspoken something in speech itself: the obscene underside of speech, of language, at its very origins. There's something nauseating about this thing, something disgusting.

The slug's loathsomeness, the obscenity that inspires disgust, by Knausgaard's account, has to do with its "nudity and slimy smoothness." Slippery but sticky, naked and exposed, the slug also exposes what should have remained hidden. In doing so, we have seen, it denudes those who behold it; it's "provocative" that way.

In reading, in beholding, "Slugs," perhaps a similar exposure, and a similar provocation, takes place. Something hidden—implicit, secret and secretive—lies in wait, wanting to show itself—but it tends to be a bit ashamed by the prospect of appearing nakedly. So it comes out in ways and at times we don't always expect. It's slippery, and it slips. It lives in a grotto, so it partakes of the grotesque. It emerges, sometimes slowly, sometimes in flashes, from the damp cavern that is its uncanny home. It is lubricious with secretions. It is a creature of shadow and depth, but it lurks at the edges, at the border between inner and outer. It is glimpsed but rarely gazed upon in the open. When it really rears its head, it's obscene. It insults, but it also seduces. To feel its caress can inspire repulsion or it can render one liquidic with pleasure: you melt at its touch. It's strangely soft but curiously strong. Blunt, it nevertheless cuts. Like a slug, it is unarticulated, lacking joints. But it has the power to cut and to conjoin, to rend and to bind. In fact, it combines by dividing. It articulates, in other words. It is an organ–inner? outer? yes–it is *the* organ of articulation.

Of all the human organs, perhaps the *tongue*–though it goes unmentioned by Knausgaard, whether intentionally suppressed or unconsciously repressed or merely unnoticed–perhaps the tongue is the organ that the slug most resembles. Whatever the case, in all the ways suggested above–and there are more–the slug and the tongue are akin. And like the slug, the tongue is both familiar and not, both banal and other. It dwells in the cavity from which words, medium of human communication, issue, and yet, as you will have already observed, it "inverts qualities that normally belong to the intimate human sphere." The tongue, taken as a detail, separated out for examination, becomes monstrous. It is a mucus-exuding, writhing little beast, its shifting shape indefinite, contracting and relaxing in the salivary depression of your buccal cavity. It's not classed as an interior organ, but it's not exterior, either–it partakes of both the inner and outer. It gets exposed, it is in contact with the outer world, even taking it in. At the same time, like the interior organs, it is "round and naked," and exhibits the quality that Knausgaard attributes to the heart, liver, and lungs: it is "without any distinction between inner and outer."

(To cut into this cut with a *paren-thesis* provoked by Knausgaard's assertion that interior organs exhibit no "distinction between inner and outer": What could this possibly mean? How is it that interior organs are "without distinction between inner and outer"? With the liver, as with the jellyfish, for example, perhaps Knausgaard means that it appears *all of a piece*, somehow undifferentiated, a homogenous entity whose surface is no different from its inner substance? But of course the liver has divisions and differences; it has lobes and ligaments, veins and chambers. As much as any other organ, it can be said to have an inner and an outer, surface and interior. It contains depths. The same can of course be said of the heart and lungs. Or the jellyfish. So what sense can be made of Knausgaard's curious characterization, his assertion that interior organs lack distinction between inner and outer? It is almost as if he is conflating the externalization of the interior organs–a breaching of a bodily boundary–with an indistinction of inner and outer pertaining to the organ itself. As if, that is to say, he is losing the distinction between two kinds of distinction, as if in crossing one boundary—externalizing the inner organs—he dissolves another: the distinction between inner and outer in a given organ. Knausgaard reiterates boundary distinctions at various levels—organ, body—but also reproduces the loss of distinction in discussion of those distinctions. His writing in this sense breaks down; grammatically correct and eloquent, it is nevertheless incoherent: it again moves into incoherence.

This is not the only place in which an uncanny slippage or switching occurs. When, for instance, Knausgaard addresses the "sublime," not only does he note that the sublime centrally involves the dissolution of boundaries (a loss of self in the face of something overwhelming); in doing so, the conceptual distinctions that have governed his commentary begin to switch and slip. In his discussion of an experience of the sublime undergone when beholding a massive ship, the very characteristics that he begins by attributing to "life" come to be affiliated, in an unannounced and by all indications unintentional manner, with its opposite, "death." Life and death slip into each other, or switch, almost unnoticeably.[14] This interpenetration of life and death, we recall from above, is a, or the, source of disgust. By a curious syllogism, then, perhaps disgust, such as stimulated by the slug, and the sense of the sublime are intimately linked? Perhaps the massive marine vessel and the relatively minuscule slug are, in this sense, identical?

The ship and the slug, the sublime and the loathsome: each is internally ambivalent, mingling attraction and repulsion, and each is the double of the other: identical and inverted. They are parodic doubles in which opposites slip and slide—they switch or alternate as distinctions break down, boundaries dissolve.

Secret identities: sublime and slug.

On the basis of these observations, the *paren-thesis* I wish to proffer here is this: irreducible ambivalence, the dissolution of boundaries—the rapid, unintentional, and apparently incidental switching of registers: these are indicators of *the sacred*; they characterize contact with the fundament of the sacred, the sense of the sacred in its fundamentally ambivalent amplitude, where distinctions break down and everything is its other. The sacred is, and is lived in, this zone of indistinction. To put the matter in properly paradoxical terms, *the sacred is (an experience of) the fundamental incoherence of being.*

Everything becomes something, becomes everything, else: *divine inconsistency.*

Knausgaard writes: *I am you.*[15] This is a concise formulation of the sacred

14. See Knausgaard, *My Struggle, Book Six*, 621-49. Knausgaard discusses the sublimity of the sight of the massive cruise ship beginning on 636. A careful reading of this section reveals the switching, the confusion of life and death, I refer to above.
15. Knausgaard, *My Struggle, Book Six*, 830.

secret, the secreted sacred: distinctions between inner and outer dissolve, and one slips into the other. A slippery sense of the sacred, a lubricious secretion, a secret that seeps through everything–*everything*–even if it doesn't make sense.)

/

Disembodying the organs, setting them off and apart, separating them out of their usual milieu, rendering them as distinct *details*, removed from their corporeal context and imagined as autonomous, "creeping around by themselves," separate and animated . . .

The slug, too, can be rendered into parts: the length of its underside is its "foot" and the secretive respiratory lobe (covering up genitals and anus) is its "mantle." Thus analyzed in detail, one finds the low and high, base and regal, are embodied in the slug.

A disgusting thought: your tongue is a naked animal, a slug in your buccal orifice–a naked, wet organ; an alien entity; a stranger in your mouth, a monster in your head.

Slug/tongue: intimates and others to each other. The tongue, like the slug, can inspire repulsion; it, too, is slimy, for it, too, secretes mucus.

But the repulsion that Knausgaard seeks to comprehend in relation to the slug betrays a deep and simultaneous attraction: one detects the fascinated desire stimulated by, and the seductiveness that coincides with, the "deeply undesirable" aspect of the slug. The slug is ambivalence embodied: it turns a switch, again and again.

The slug is repulsion seeping desire; the tongue is allure tainted by disgust.

The tongue lives in the cut, in the salivary cavern of the mouth. And the mouth–to pronounce a secret that everyone knows–is the upper end of a tube that terminates, after much twisting, in a puckered knot that likes to open: the anus.

Mouth and anus: two open ends of a single tube: each the double of the other: conjoined opposites–open loop.

(((Anilingus: the supremely intimate act: orifice to orifice / mouth to anus / the slug's double, embedding itself in the fundament of the other–deep in the cut, source of *the gift*: whispering a secret beyond articulation . . .)))

Everything breaks down. The boundaries don't stand. All is inconsistency.

A zone of indistinction in which repulsion and attraction coincide in fascinated desire.

A mystical compulsion.

(Your tongue is a slug, and more.)

Death and life, attraction and repulsion, interpenetrating: disgust (sacred horror).

Rendering everything in detail, cutting it all up, Knausgaard writes into the space of in-consistency, the space of in-coherence, where all unravels and all is connected.

A denouement deep in the cut, where everything intimately conjoins, where each thing is another, where nothing holds itself together: this is the zone of the sacred, the zone of indistinction: birth of language from the spirit of disgust.

DENOUEMENT

> *When I was growing up all slugs were black, and they appeared after a downpour, as if from the bowels of the earth, suddenly they were everywhere, in the middle of the lawn, on the paths, even on the black asphalt roads of the housing development. It was said that it would start to rain if you stepped on a slug, so we took great care to avoid that. Still, sometimes it happened, sometimes inadvertently, other times deliberately: all children must have stepped on a slug at one time and seen its soft innards ooze out on the asphalt and the black blend with orange and white. Since then a new species of slug has invaded Scandinavia, so-called killer slugs, big brown slugs from Portugal or Spain which reproduce with amazing speed and cause great damage to gardens, since they gobble up everything they can find. One year the garden here was full of them, they were everywhere, as if they had rained from the sky.*

Here things really begin to unravel, even as they get more knotted up. To mix metaphors, things get harder to see, even and especially as they proliferate. What things? *Everything*–details, slugs, metaphors, meanings. . . . It all threatens to get lost in incoherent superfluity, in an inconsistent plethoric overflow–a garden choking on its own fructificative effervescence–fodder for a tide of voracious little gastropods devouring the environment of which they are a part . . .

The beginning of the ending of "Slugs," the opening of its final movement, the denouement, in the terms I've set out here, returns to the start–a kind of temporal looping back, in other words–with Knausgaard recalling the wildly propagating slugs of his childhood: slugs multiplying across the pavement, on paths, amidst lawns–ominously omnipresent, "everywhere"–having emerged, he writes, from the "bowels of the earth."

This little, latter detail, this short and familiar phrase, this nigh incidental intestinal cliché—"the bowels of the earth"—is something like the oft-dinky titular molluscs themselves, which reproduce with an intensity, an "amazing speed," that increases their perceived sense of indistinguishability and ubiquity, such that they are both seen and easily overlooked, to the point of being crushed "sometimes *inadvertently*."[16] The phrase *the bowels of such-and-such* is so familiar as to go almost unheard, apt to be passed over without serious consideration. But subtly—one could say *subliminally*—its meanings emanate, seeping into the surrounding text. The familiar phrase "bowels of the earth" is nonetheless, or all the more, richly associative, spreading its connotative substance trickling (down) through the remainder of the text. To take a preliminary example—for the effects of the phrase, whether or not announced, will suffuse not just what is most proximate, but *all that remains*—the telluric tones in which Knausgaard describes the slugs—brown, black, orange darkened as they blend into the asphalt—are now further imbued with an excremental aura; the slugs are sliding fecal dabs issuing from the netherworld, emanating from the depths—of childhood, of the earth, of the body.

The bowels of the earth: the deepest depths, the realm of decay and rot, of chaos, of unformed matter—and thus the most fertile site of creative expulsion. Slugs: birthed from the mucous-lined bowels, discharged from the fundament. Knausgaard's cliché marks, infects, inflects a generative passage. It makes excreta of its subjects—slug, reader, writer . . . The bowels are a space of transformation, where what was becomes something other. It is the passage of the formless, whence forms—still provisional, in flux, underdetermined—issue. The bowels enclose and disclose what shall be unbounded, open. The bowels relinquish and give: ceaseless passage, endless movement, forever opening.

/

Forms emerge and forms merge.

It happens as if by accident. Unplanned. Unintended. Inadvertent. A thing takes shape. The shape makes the thing. The thing is what I seek, but I barely notice it, even when it's at my feet. And then—too late.

The thing gets squashed, its bodily boundary burst—another expulsion of the interior. What was a slug becomes what it always was: something else.

16. Emphasis added.

To make the insides come out. Knausgaard is obsessed with the passage from interior to exterior. It defines his writing, which is to say that what defines his writing is a loss of self-definition, a loss of self. It happens incidentally, unintentionally–inadvertently.[17]

Writing falls. It befalls you, or you fall into a zone in which it takes place. A zone of indistinction, the passage from the inner to outer: opening up, spilling your guts, confessing, apparently, without reserve (but there's always a secret, always something beyond articulation, a detail that can't yet be exposed–so maybe it gets hidden in other details . . .). For Knausgaard, writing is a convulsive compulsion. It twists him up, turns him out, but he can't help but do it. It's "merciless." (He says, without saying it: *I am the slug that wants to be crushed, lacerated, cut open–sacrificed.* A disgusting thought.)

/

In the passage presently under discussion ("When I was growing up" . . .) everything changes. Nothing is just itself. Switches and inversions prevail. It is as if this passage, and perhaps "Slugs" as a whole, has emerged from the bowels, for the bowels are a zone of indistinction as well as an indistinct zone, an in-the-stink zone. Expulsed progeny of the bowels, expelled from the depths of the earth, slugs are themselves part of and counter to nature. They are shifting and liminal ("lacking clear distinction," they "slide along between"), they are "naked," they are, to the human imagination, filthy (fecal, slimy, denizens of the dirt). They are animated mud; the sentient slug is immersed within and emerges from sludge.

And they're "everywhere," they get into everything–they bear the marks and leave the traces of the bowels whence they came; their soft, secretive bodies bespeak an ambivalent, indistinct zone of flux and influx that solicits endless interpretation: labile and labial, fecal and phallic, repulsive and infiltrative, evasive and invasive, male and female, everywhere and invisible, counter to and in harmony with nature. . . . In slugs ambiguity and ambivalence converge. They are reproductively hermaphroditic and hermeneutically seductive, at once excreted from and pervading the penetralia, moving out of and back into the bowels of the text, of the earth, of the reader, of this writer.

/

17. See Knausgaard, *Inadvertent.*

The slug (your tongue): at the origin of language. The slug leaving its looping trail, the material trace of writing. The slug's soft body secreting the substance that introduces a mark, a soft cut into the world–the world of "nature"–of which it is a part: *language as an act of incoherence.*

/

Slugs conjugate and proliferate. To repeat: Knausgaard observes (even if he doesn't always recognize) that slugs are always *this and that*–hermaphroditic, polyonymous, polyvalent, slow and sudden, liquid and solid, against and within nature, human and monster, everywhere and nowhere, visible and invisible, banal and curious, lowly and royal, emerging from below and falling from above. They are ambivalence in slow motion.

Slow and *strange* motion. They locomote by excreting mucus as they contract-relax, contract-relax, contract-relax: rhythms of convulsive propulsion. In this way, too, *slugs are of the bowels*, the anal zone (excretory, fecal), and they are embodiments of the anal zone: that zone of indistinction, fraught with ambivalence, retentive and expulsive, contractive and expansive–dilating and dilatory, slow.[18] They seem never to get anywhere, but then suddenly, they're everywhere, you're surrounded, and they have devoured everything. They take over your world.

Sluggish writing: slow and sudden accretion: adding to the world by cutting it up into details.

Slugs emerge: upsurge from the depths. They erupt out from below, and irrupt into your world, to devour it.

/

From and of the zone of indistinction, slugs are liquidic forms, like semi-solids, soft matter. Slugs are *quasi*.

/

The bowels of the earth: expulsive, producing repulsive slugs. Expulsion–repulsion. Expelled from the bowels, naked and stained–repulsive. Expelled–*not from the Garden* but irrupting *into the garden*: the origins of another parable, the beginning of another parody that will play out slowly,

18. See Sigmund Freud, *Three Essays on the Theory of Sexuality*, trans. James Strachey (New York: Basic Books, 2000).

a fall that befalls with incidental inevitability. In this parable, one finds not a single serpent, but a slew of slugs, a plethoric plague in the garden: a mythic admixture–with more to come.

How to apprehend this excremental-erotic fomentation? Where to begin?

/

We return again to the beginning of the article, and we ask again, with Knausgaard, Why are slugs repulsive? The slugs, he says, are repulsive in their *nudity*, in their *inversion* of human qualities, in the *lack of distinction* between outer and inner bodies–but now these characteristics of the slug must be retrospectively (retroactively?) reread in the visceral register of the bowels; they are inflected by the loamy odor of the underworld from which they emerge.

The slugs are excremental, fecal–they appear like turds. Beholding the fecality of the slugs–and who could deny that they appear like sliding excremental forms, such that, were a cluster to be glimpsed in the basin of a public toilet, like the leavings of a stranger, they would be flushed, eyes quickly averted, with nothing but a shiver?–reinforces and extends the qualities of nudity, inversion, lack of distinction that constitute the essence of repulsion. "Bowels of the earth" now encourages acknowledgment of a further valence of repulsiveness seemingly *not recognized* by Knausgaard, in a way that both exceeds and redoubles the elements of repulsion *named* by Knausgaard. The slugs are repulsive in their nudity, in their inversion of human qualities, in the lack of distinction between outer and inner bodies: this Knausgaard tells us. But what has he left unsaid, unobserved? What is spoken only *in passing*, by way of a rote metaphor like *bowels of the earth*. . . . ?

/

Knausgaard is not scatophobic, at least not exceptionally so; he delves into the shit. In one particularly salient passage, he describes the strange wonder of shitting outdoors, in the woods. The confusion–doing outside what should happen inside–is dramatically reproduced in the act of defecation itself. The bowels, the rectum, the anal aperture dilating and contracting in sphincteral dynamism: in their expansive metaphoric range, the "bowels" are the very space of passage, of simultaneity of inside and out, where the most private and intimate shows itself, compulsively, expulsively.

Strange *mise en abyme*: bowels, bathroom, forest. . . .

/

So, slugs emerge from the bowels. But at the same time, as Knausgaard tells the tale, the slugs *fall.* They fall all over the place; and the timing of the fall is strange. Their fall is an uncanny timespace. For the slugs that emerge from *below* and *after* a downpour seem also to fall from *above* and *with* the downpour; they *are the downpour itself*; it is "as if they had rained from the sky," Knausgaard writes. The downpour of the slugs, their identification with the rain, reinforces their position in the metaphorical register of the moist, the watery, the wet.

Slugs, it might be said, are a quasi-rain. Something like rain ("*as if* they had rained" . . .). And like a biblical plague, Knausgaard's slugs rain down and destroy; they "gobble up everything they can find"–scourge of the moist, the hungry, the repulsive.

But the verb *rain* is substantialized in the slug itself, which is to say that slugs are the substance of the rain, they rain down, they are what the rain is. The etymological meaning of rain–"moist," "wet"–returns us to Knausgaard's meditations on the name of the slug–names of the moist that are themselves moist.

A confusion of directions–above/below–and of time: after the rain, in the raining–and of substance: water/feces/earth/sky. They all converge in the slug: in-coherence in which nothing is itself, and everything is bound up with its other.

Details proliferate. Details upon details. Excrement upon incident. A dense growth from the fertile fundament.

Falling apart, it all comes together.

Issuing from above and welling up from below–as if rain itself, merging with earth in its very bowels, shaped itself into the form of slugs, to emerge from the fundament, reproducing minutely but voluminously, . . . slugs are at once elemental and excremental, doubly evoking their essential moistness and softness–now at once genital and rectal, seed and germ, stomach and foot (pod, -ped, poo . . .), the universal childhood myth of anal birth finding expression in the living reality of the proliferative slug.[19]

To mark a preliminary passage with an open terminus: _slug_rain_feces_sodden earth_moist channels_slippery passages_ . . . : lowly links in an earthbound parade . . .

. . . that may never yet conclude. Because also flowing through this leaky metaphorical channel of the moist are the mucous secretions of the slug,

19. See Freud, *Three Essays on the Theory of Sexuality.*

which recall the mucous membranes of the secretive bowels. Slugs, feces–secretions of the earth's and the body's bowels, ever birthed again, a fund that keeps on giving back what it receives, with change.

/

And then superstition steps in–and on. It says, Watch where your foot falls; take care not to crush the slugs, for stepping on one will bring rain (will bring slugs raining down in nauseating superabundance). But in a single *faux pas*, chance and necessity inevitably merge: the incidental incident always happens: *all children must have stepped on a slug at one time*. At one time (or another), at some time (in other words), the child's crushing step makes the times of the slug strangely simultaneous: slugs come before the rain (a slug is crushed, the rain will come); they follow the rain ("appear[ing] after a downpour"); they are coextensive with the rain ("as if they had rained from the sky").

/

Details: look long enough at a detail, and you set it off. It multiplies. It takes on a strange aspect, each and every time. Each thing, cut apart from the rest, is liable to become something else, until it becomes everything else. The world in a grain of sand, a droplet of water. The world in a garden. The slug, a world unto itself, in the world of the garden. And "Slugs," a world within a world.

The text, *any* text: a zone of indistinction in which each thing is like another, but–somehow–*different*.

Blended and luridly differentiated: the child crushes the slug and "soft innards ooze out onto the asphalt and the black blend[s] with orange and white." The black of the innards blends with the orange and white of the pavement? Or the orange and white innards blend with the black asphalt? What's what? The bowels expelled from the body expulsed by the bowels of the earth: a carnal play-within-a-play, a *mise en abyme* of disembowelment.

Killed, but also "killer," the slugs, too, are wanton. They "gobble up everything." They invade and consume their milieu: they extend the zone of indistinction, devouring and excreting the garden space around them. They expel the garden into which they were expelled. An inverted fall.

They are–again–"everywhere." All over, beneath one's feet.

The slug's body–a "foot" (a foot with a "mantle" and eyeballs at the ends of protruding stems)–underfoot.

Thus does fate befall the slug that falls beneath the foot of the child. As flies, so are slugs killed by wanton boys and girls—and mothers.

/

My mother-in-law used to gather the children around her and go slug-hunting. Armed with a bucket and sharp scissors they would walk across the grass, and when they found a slug they cut it into two and tossed the parts into the bucket. I couldn't watch, much less participate, it was too gruesome. But a raid like that, during which maybe twenty slugs were eliminated, was of no avail, a few days later there were just as many. At last, some time after my mother-in-law had gone home, I myself went out with a bucket and garden scissors. I knelt down in front of one of the brown slugs. It was as long as my long finger, thick as a sausage, with some sort of lengthwise grooves in its skin, and its broad foot, which reminded me of a belt, was beige. As I lifted it up it squirmed slowly in my grasp, and when I placed it between the blades of the sharp scissors its tentacles moved. I pushed the handles of the scissors together [. . .]

Whose drama is this? Who's doing the cutting? Mother. Child. Children of children. Will the writer take up the blades? Shall the reader? Scissors are at hand. Gleefully or dreadfully, the killing spree—bound to be gruesome—gets under way.

So much cutting to be done; the slugs always outpace the cutter.

Cut the infinite in two and you haven't halved anything—you've doubled it: two infinites. The slugs are already endless, propagating, profligate. Cut them, and words and worlds multiply. Uncountable names for the one that is already many.

/

This text—even a brief, incidental text ("Slugs"?)—contains everything: a world. A text that remains open to the end, open in the end, loose-ended. An end that is an opening unto another whole that can only ever be a part of that which endlessly exceeds it: the boundless—the world.

A text-world that is part of a whole. The world in a grain of sand.

/

My mother-in-law used to gather the children around her and go slug-hunting. Mother-in-law. The mother of my spouse. My mother and not exactly, or not just, my mother–a quasi-mother, but still every bit my mother. She gathers children–my children. Together they will hunt.

/

Armed with a bucket and sharp scissors they would walk across the grass . . . A bucket: the quarry is small; carrying a bucket, the hunters must expect to slaughter many slugs, one after another, and of a sudden: serial killing unto mass death.

Scissors, from the Latin *caedere* "to cut." Incidentally, if you cut away the interior "e" you're left with this remainder: *cadere*, which, to return to the outset of this essay, means *fall, decay, die*. Significantly, it's the root of "accident" and "chance."

/

. . . and when they found a slug they cut it into two and tossed the parts into the bucket. A slug: need we announce that the slug–small but monstrous; everywhere but easily overlooked; falling from above but emerging, accruing, from below; cutting into life–into a garden, into time, a day–and consuming it; a mass of particulars, standing apart from the whole (contrary to nature, the garden, the forest) and yet of a piece with it, a part of the whole (in harmony with nature); and now literally divided, cut to pieces–need we reiterate what has implicitly been announced all along–that the slug is an incidental, a detail–an incidental detail?

Details–incidents accruing in increments–falling to pieces, leaving deposits, depositing traces–parts and particles and particulars: this is nothing other than *everyday life* itself. Constitutive details: life is nothing but the experience of the comprisal-without-containment of details, infinitely decomposable, infinitely flourishing.

Gathering details in a bucket: tragedy and–possibly, inevitably–comedy (cut into by occasional farce).

The quasi-mother with her scissors: one can hardly avoid the associations that have been teeming just below the surface, the subliminal mythic associations of the final act of this production: for the slug, naked and indecent, is not only labial and anal-fecal; it is also *phallic* (and kingly, paternal) . . . and the mother-in-law, armed with scissors for slicing up slugs, is a castrating mother. This story now verges on, tends toward, an Oedipal drama; it is a quasi-Oedipal drama.

/

I couldn't watch, much less participate, it was too gruesome. The author averts his eyes (blinds himself), turning away from the action of slicing up and disposing of the very thing he finds loathsome. Splitting the detestable creatures in two only doubles his disgust. Some monsters multiply when divided.

/

But a raid like that, during which maybe twenty slugs were eliminated, was of no avail, a few days later there were just as many. The labor of killing is–in vain! Cleaving into infinity leaves two infinities remaining. Details cut into further details. Division that multiplies, endlessly. The realization that it's *all for nothing*: no payoff, no return on one's efforts. *Horror vacui*: all is lost, *all is loss* in the movement of translation: zone of indistinction: perpetual peripety in the garden . . .

/

At last, some time after my mother-in-law had gone home, I myself went out with a bucket and garden scissors. A surprising turn: the disgust has turned to desire–to kill. After some time (a conspicuously ambiguous phrase; time is out of joint here; the man becomes a child again), the son takes up the weapon that the mother had wielded. I hold the bucket to gather the pieces.

/

I knelt down in front of one of the brown slugs. The gesture of kneeling: a stance of humility, parodic or not, before the sovereign slug, the emperor, the father, the phallus. Regicide–patricide–is imminent, on a darkening horizon. Bending and lowering of the formerly erect body–a compromise of the phallic disposition–already the body, bending, lowering, is becoming more slug-like in identification with that from which it wishes to distinguish itself. A tragicomic posture of supplication–not just kneeling, but kneeling *in front of*, kneeling *before* the other, to open up the other: father, king, tongue, phallus–a mere slug.

/

It was as long as my long finger, thick as a sausage, with some sort of lengthwise grooves in its skin, and its broad foot, which reminded me of a belt, was beige. The slug is here compared in length to the "long finger"–that is, a middle finger, the finger most routinely associated with the penis, the most phallic finger, the fucking finger. The slug is made akin to the penis, which is furthermore thick as a sausage–tumescing the phallic association. Phalluses are multiplying–a sure sign that defense against castration anxiety is in effect. I see that the slug's *foot* is grooved, again calling to mind Oedipus, whose name means "swollen foot"–so called for the scars he bore from being abandoned in the wilderness as a child.

/

As I lifted it up it squirmed slowly in my grasp, and when I placed it between the blades of the sharp scissors its tentacles moved. Kneeling, I lift the slug, as if raising the eucharistic elements, as if presenting the sacrifice. I place the slug (and all that it signifies) where the blades cross, on a cross. (Wasn't Oedipus at the crossroads when he killed his father? And what of the cross on which the Son of the Father died? Abandoned, his body screams *I AM YOU*: lapsing into a divine comedy.) Now the author, anxious unto ecstasy, becomes agent of his own castrative sacrifice.

Between two blades that will divide and double the slug.

(Reading between the lines, hoping to get cut.)

/

I pushed the handles of the scissors together. The reader imagines the author, provoked, taking up a pen, to write–a pen as duplicitous as a pair of scissors poised to render the final detail.

/

and as the blades sliced into its body I heard it screaming, low and shrill.

the blades. Double blades of the scissors. The body of the text, the world, the writer, the reader sliced open. Interiors exposed; that which was inside comes out.

sliced into its body. The slug is sacrificed, the author is castrated, the father slain, the king is dead. . . . almost–

I heard it screaming, low and shrill. Does the slug scream? Sacrificed, cut, death penetrating its still-writhing body, does the slug still live? The writer hears the slug screaming–a scream of birth from the fundament, a scream of fundamental ambivalence, at once low and its opposite–high-pitched, shrill.[20] High and low, a single duplicitous utterance: an eruption of the author's disgust coinciding with an irruption of the cut of language into the pre- and post-articulate *all*: origin and end of language in a scream, an inarticulate scream proclaiming the birth of articulation. Writing and writhing. The primal act of sacrifice–the incision that divides and multiplies, that distinguishes and renders incoherent. Death penetrating life in a sacrificial cut, a final fall at the start of the all, a detail that is the origin of speech, of writing: sacred horror: the birth of language from the spirit of disgust . . .

/

_slug_king_father_high_low_foot_penis_belt_labia_tongue_feces_inside_
outside_writer_reader_death_life_

(_self_other_)

/

I am you.

20. In the cleft of the fundament, from which only a back- or underside of the divine is glimpsed: an inverted echo of Exodus 33: 21-23: "When my glory passes by, I will put you in a cleft in the rock and cover you with my hand until I have passed by. Then I will remove my hand and you will see my back; but my face must not be seen."

12 JANUARY 2018 BLOOMINGTON, INDIANA

DUBLER: My intuition is . . . inevitably we are doing the theology of these books. And this is going to prioritize these issues of transcendence and meaning more than those moments that define my experience as a reader.

HARRISS: This meaning versus significance–meaning has some systematic sensibility. Where significance is the section breaks, it's the signs and it is not necessarily depth but its meaning without system of depth. It is connections and pointing. I don't quite know where to go with that, but I hear significance versus meaning as a distinction between depth or flatness.

BILES: I'm going to say, this *mise en abyme* is great. I think it is super helpful and interesting. I visualize it standing between two mirrors. There's nothing flatter than mirrors, and nothing deeper than two mirrors reflecting each other. That seems to describe part of what's going on with flatness of description and meaning/significance. You have to insert yourself between the two mirrors and then you can never see everything from that position, which is incredibly frustrating. Also, Cooper, you were thinking about this text as an act of writing. I hear Derrida in terms of spacing and writing. Related to spacing and difference versus meaning and this relates to the issue of flatness. You create these breaks in light of all of this.

[Later.]

CARLSON: . . . The flood part of the story [in *A Time for Everything*] is the part of the book you remember. I wonder how much of that is writing/reading all of this in the wake of [Hurricanes] Irma and Harvey and the irreducibility of the fact that floods are a reality and present and an encroaching reality. How much of our experience is being refracted through the fact that this is a reality that is no longer allegorical? I live in Manhattan . . . this city is not going to make it . . . versus how much it is genuinely the heart of the book . . . or the best realized part.

HARRISS: I cannot imagine a situation in which this wouldn't absolutely lay me out. Yes, reality but . . .

CARLSON: I think this for me is like providing a myth instead of images for something that I was already thinking about and that there is a fortuitous contingency. This is the text that I want to be reading in the moment that we are in.

DUBLER: I am with Cooper. The story of the flood is the story of . . . the dove and the olive branch, and the promise. This marginalizes that stuff correctly by making the story of the flood, the story of the flood.

CARLSON: Yes, but it is the story that we need for this moment.

HARRISS: It is around you in a circle because you are in the highest point of the known world and that is somehow going to stop this thing from consuming you . . . that is the story of . . . it is the story! If I can put this into the blues, this is the story of the blues. It doesn't matter what you do. This is why the flood is so . . . well, the experience of the 1927 flood, for example. But this is the reality: get your effects around you and maybe it will give you some extra time, but this is what you dwell in, make it mean something.

BENDER: When we read the Noah story before, everything disappears but some still remain. We are all the post-story of that. Our story in fact must be the story of the promise. To say that the real story is . . . is in fact . . . it pushes us to think: when is the moment where we now say that our story is not the one where we make a historical connection to this [story]. We are the remnants of that but instead . . . that claim that you made . . . it's not the real . . . you didn't say real . . . what'd you say?

DUBLER: The story of the flood is the story of the flood.

HARRISS: It's not the olive branch and the dove, it's the flood.

BENDER: Right, it's the flood. The other one is not unimportant.

DUBLER: No, the other one is the one we learn as a child. The one we abide in. The primary story. The animals.

BENDER: Yes, you abide in that!

DUBLER: And turn a blind eye. I'm not trying to excise it. It just becomes horror.

HARRISS: An alternate emphasis.

CARLSON: The horror that it always was.

/ 7 /

Shaping Our Ends

M. Cooper Harriss

Book Five of *My Struggle* ends with a punch line: Having detailed his painful abandonment of Tonje, their failing marriage, and their life together in Bergen, Karl Ove boards a night train seeking solace in distraction (to "keep . . . from thinking"), and rides off to a new beginning with Linda in Stockholm. "That was how I left Bergen" he says, almost flippantly, in sum.[1] This "last word," coming on the heels of the climax of Karl Ove's formative education and misadventures in Bergen, renders the volume a shaggy dog story, an origin myth that (in the end) steps away from–dodges, even–the brunt of this moment's emotional gravitas. In fact, I laughed out loud on first reading–not in the gauche manner of the viral 'LOL,' but out of uneasy surprise at Knausgaard's peripeteia, his final audacity. Does this quip represent a rare flinch for this most disclosive novelist, a mitigating gesture like a wink that keeps the novel from revealing too much? Or does it strive to shape this end in some other way as we depart with him from *Book Five*'s predominant setting, moving implicitly into the known-unknown of a future already explored at length in *Book Two*?

This chapter considers Knausgaard's endings across the six books of *My Struggle*, theorizing "the end" as it emerges from the nexus of time and narrative to generate Knausgaard's uniquely immersive style. In the first section, careful attention to the respective endings of the first five volumes distills the author's patterns according to Paul Ricoeur's *Time and Narrative* and Frank Kermode's *The Sense of an Ending*. In the process we shall explore the temporal functions of *My Struggle* as a novel that critics have claimed to "merge" reader and narrative voice into an ever-present unity

1. Knausgaard, *My Struggle, Book Five,* 624.

that emerges from the phenomenon of reading it.[2] Careful attention to Knausgaard's ends, then, reveals how–contrary to "abandoning every literary feint"–he generates the illusion of such merger through fiction's characteristic (and "untrue") manipulations of "realty."[3] The second, and final, section applies the implications of these earlier readings to *Book Six*–also known as *The End*. How does the way that Knausgaard charts his escape from this large and all-consuming work–indeed, his achievement of such an eschaton–recast the novel both in *Book Six* itself and across *My Struggle* writ large?

THE JACKET SLIPS

"That was how I left Bergen"–especially in the way that line lands–bears important implications for how we understand Knausgaard's six-volume, autobiographical narrative to work. Critics point to a quality of immediacy in *My Struggle,* the feeling of unmediated access to Knausgaard's (or is it Karl Ove's?) mind. We marvel at his ability to collapse the distance between reader and narrative. Zadie Smith, to take one example, claims that *My Struggle* works "not by synecdoche or metaphor, beauty or drama, or even storytelling. What's notable is Karl Ove's ability . . . to be fully present in and mindful of his own existence. Every detail is put down without apparent vanity or decoration, as if the writing and the living are happening simultaneously. . . . [It] immerses you totally. You live his life with him."[4] In this way the narrative's power derives from its ability to collapse, or *apparently* to collapse, the difficult distinction between the literary mechanism (words crafted in significant order) and a compelling experience of human life. Note that Smith dismisses literary devices (synecdoche, metaphor, and so forth) and aesthetics ("decoration") to render reading and living as simultaneous acts, as functions of one another. Still, doing so must also prove impossible, which Smith (who knows a thing or two about fiction) rhetorically concedes: "Apparent," "as if"–these qualifiers preserve the

2. Nina McLaughlin writes that "I have not wanted his books to end because I have not wanted to unmerge with him." See "Recapturing the World with Karl Ove Knausgaard," *LA Review of Books* (24 May 2013); https://lareviewofbooks.org/article/recapturing-the-world-with-karl-ove-knausgaard.

3. Jonathan Letham calls Knausgaard "a living hero who landed on greatness by abandoning every typical literary feint, an emperor whose nakedness surpasses royal finery." See "My Hero: Karl Ove Knausgaard," *Guardian* (31 January 2014): https://www.theguardian.com/books/2014/jan/31/my-hero-karl-ove-knausgaard-jonathan-lethem.

4. Zadie Smith, "Man vs. Corpse," *New York Review of Books* (5 December 2013): https://www.nybooks.com/articles/2013/12/05/zadie-smith-man-vs-corpse/.

sleight of hand even as they acknowledge it. Whatever the narrative may reveal, it also necessarily conceals plenty as well.

Readers recognize this limitation, too. We don't mow the entirety of the lawn with Karl Ove. Nor do we clean the whole house (even in narrative representation). Real-time recreation of doing these and the other activities of quotidian life would prove interminable and ultimately unreadable. It would never feel "real" in ways that readers claim the novel to achieve reality. In this way *My Struggle*, devoting hundreds of pages to the minutia of housecleaning, getting drunk, or gazing at a single painting, also deploys (in one representative example) three pages out of well more than six hundred in *Book Five* to make exponential leaps across time and narrative. From near the volume's end: "Tonje went to a seminar in Kristiansand, I had the whole day and night to write in, she came home three days later, wanted to go straight to a party . . .";[5] "After an hour I regretted my decision . . .";[6] "We went to bed, early the next morning I packed a suitcase and traveled up to Yngve's. . . . I was there for two days, talked to him, he thought I should stay with her . . .";[7] "I caught the train back to Tonje, we talked all night. . . ."[8] Knausgaard breathlessly forsakes sentences, opting instead for comma splices to provide urgency and hasten us along. These passages represent a novelistic sleight of hand through which Knausgaard manipulates narrative time into a representation of 'real time'—which is, itself, whatever its veracity, also and equally a fabrication. Our experience "under Karl Ove's skin" (another of Smith's metaphors) seems immersive and even "real" because of Knausgaard's successful and evocative fragmentation of time into a narrative fiction that succeeds, paradoxically, in refiguring fictional time as something more than true (*more than this / there is nothing more than this*) precisely because it is fiction. A narrative's ending shakes the reader from the grip of this illusion. It punctuates one's awareness of this artifice because it necessitates stepping out from under Karl Ove's skin. Removed from narrative time, one plays with the children, pets the dog, or prepares for the next day's class—whatever it is that one does in one's own ordinary time.

The first volume of Paul Ricoeur's *Time and Narrative* (1984) argues that "time becomes human time to the extent that it is organized after the manner of narrative; narrative, in turn, is meaningful to the extent that it portrays the features of temporal experience."[9] This mutual amplification

5. Knausgaard, *My Struggle, Book Five*, 622.
6. Knausgaard, *My Struggle, Book Five*, 623.
7. Knausgaard, *My Struggle, Book Five*, 624.
8. Knausgaard, *My Struggle, Book Five*, 624.
9. Paul Ricoeur, *Time and Narrative*, vol. 1, trans. K. McLaughlin and D. Pellauer (Chicago: University of Chicago Press, 1984), 3.

draws on Augustinian conceptions of time as they illuminate (and are illuminated by) Aristotelian emplotment. Augustinian time emerges from the recognition that human beings exist in an eternal present. Past and future can never constitute first-hand knowledge—even as we recognize that the world we inhabit extends beyond the present into unknowable past and future—both short-term (we no longer know even the recent past first-hand, for instance, only that it is past) and long-term (the world began long before we were born and shall likely continue long after our individual demise).[10] When Smith and other readers speak of Karl Ove's immediacy in *My Struggle*, they describe Knausgaard's effectiveness in rendering recognizable a representation of this monologically eternal present.

Significantly, *My Struggle* does not inhabit this eternal present. It is retrospective, a *memoir* of sorts that time-travels across different benchmarks of Karl Ove's life and experiences. Knausgaard does indeed represent the temporal experience of this present, but he does so through recourse to narrative. To account for this seeming paradox of time, Ricoeur inflects Augustinian time with the relationship that Aristotle describes "between lived experience and discourse" in his *Poetics*.[11] For Ricoeur, the paradox concerns mimesis: How might one represent the inherent fragmentation, heterogeneity, and, indeed, the surplus of a human experience in such a way that permits recognition and comprehensibility between subjects across space and time? His answer lies in Aristotelian *muthos*—emplotment, or the composition and construction of plots. Given the impossibility of knowing time and representing the particular and unmediated human experience of an eternal present, narrative subordinates such experience to digestible plots that mirror human experience. Even as Knausgaard does not narrate in full Karl Ove's activity and perspective in washing dishes or cooking meatballs, he does convey through this paradox of time and narrative—of phenomenon and emplotment, of truth and its even truer fabrication—the illusion of the eternal present of doing so. All of which brings us to endings and, by extension, to leaving Bergen.

We find echoes of Ricoeur in Frank Kermode's *The Sense of an Ending* (1967) because, in contradistinction to the eternally present quality of Augustinian time, plots themselves are terminal. They mirror an experience of time but, by necessity, they also simultaneously contain a beginning, a middle, and an end. Kermode argues that because human beings enter the world *in medias res* and depart it *in mediis rebus*, in order "to make sense of their span they need fictive concords with origins and ends, such as

10. See book 10 of Augustine's *Confessions*.
11. Ricoeur, *Time and Narrative*, 1:31.

give meaning to lives and poems. The end they imagine will reflect their irreducibly intermediary preoccupations. They fear it, and as far as we can see have always done so; the End is a figure for their own deaths."[12] Fictive endings permit one to observe final consequences, imposing the specter of death upon the eternal-present of narrative experience. In the process they control and alter how a reader perceives what has come before.

Consider two virtuosic footballers (to draw on Karl Ove's favorite sport). They are equally magnificent and a joy to watch play the game. Now imagine that one of these players suffered a catastrophic injury at or before her prime and could no longer play football. The other enjoys a long career, except perhaps she sticks around too long–past her prime and prowess. The end of the former's career signifies something different from the end of the latter player's that cannot be discerned while both remain active. Endings, like catastrophic injury or Kermode's death, seal the text, which becomes no longer an open and emerging system but a discrete one revised throughout by its last word, its culminating gesture. Beginning and middle become beholden to the significance of this end. "That was how I left Bergen"–the "punchline" of *Book Five*–effects such a change. "That was how I left Bergen," transforms what, for several-hundred pages, has behaved as a bildungsroman into a fool's errand at the last conceivable moment.

Consider other notable endings from *My Struggle*'s first five books. *Book One* presents a corpse–the body of Karl Ove's father, still unnamed–as Karl Ove stands before it, recognizing, in the end, the change (both physiological and ontological) wrought by his father's death. Whereas the sight of the corpse had distressed him when he first saw it on the day before, a function no doubt of the psychological abuse meted out by his father that Karl Ove tracks throughout the first book and elsewhere, he finds his perspective transformed: "There I saw his lifeless state. And that there was no longer any difference between what once had been my father and the table he was lying on, or the floor on which the table stood. . . . And death, which I have always regarded as the greatest dimension of life . . . was no more than a pipe that springs a leak, a branch that cracks in the wind, a jacket that slips off a clothes hanger and falls to the floor."[13] As this curtain falls, figuratively, and the book achieves literal closure, the corpse reframes and,

12. Frank Kermode, *The Sense of an Ending: Studies in the Theory of Fiction* (New York: Oxford University Press, 2000 [1967]), 7.

13. Knausgaard, *My Struggle, Book One*, 430. As Liane Carlson noted during our January 17, 2017, meeting: "Re-reading the last sentence of *Book One*, he's definitely glossing over things, but you also realize only later that he's leaving things out, that he's avoided things of great significance."

in the process, illuminates a reader's first glimpse of the father at the beginning of the narrative as he stands beside a hole he has dug in the garden—suggestive of a grave.[14] Death bookends *Book One,* yet Karl Ove's father's transition from imposing, abusive, stormy force of nature (our first vision of him "caus[es] the twilight to deepen")[15] into, essentially, an inanimate object, fundamentally alters the way that a reader, through Karl Ove's eyes, experiences him in any assessment of the novel.[16] By closing the hermeneutic circle as he does, Knausgaard alters the father's narrative significance in a way that a reader in the eternal present of narrative can never know in the midst of things.

The second book, the earlier account that details Karl Ove's courtship of and marriage to Linda and, likewise, reveals the bathos of his parents—especially his father—in separation and divorce, ends with an unexpected reflection from Karl Ove's mother on the beginning of her own marriage to his father. "I did love him," she affirms, narrating the story of how they first met—one of mistaken identity and misplaced affection. "I didn't quite catch his name. And for a long time I thought it was Knudsen." At first she preferred his friend, "But then I fell for your father . . . it's such a good memory. The sun, the grass in the park, the trees, the shade, all the people there. . . . We were so young, you know. . . . Yes, it was an adventure. The beginning of an adventure. That was how it felt."[17] One sees in this vignette a pithy and self-deprecating commentary on Knausgaard's egoistic account of himself in *Book Two* as a "man in love"—the English subtitle given to the volume. Perhaps in this way it registers another ironic flinch or reversal: Everyone has a version of such a story. Most people don't expend nearly six hundred pages in telling it.

During our 2017 meeting in New York, expanding on Knausgaard's sense of an ending, Josh Dubler shifted focus from my example of leaving Bergen to the conclusion of another volume—one that veers into the carnivalesque: The overeager Karl Ove, who has spent the course of *Book Four* in an increasingly desperate attempt to have sex with a woman, some woman,

14. The opening cadences of this book's introduction delve more deeply in this hermeneutic circle of death in *Book One*. The likeness to a grave was first noted in our collective conversations by Liane Carlson.

15. Knausgaard, *My Struggle, Book One*, 12.

16. A fascinating complication here derives from the fact that we encounter Karl Ove's father again—and again—in future books. He appears again as living man and corpse. As the section on *Book Six* discusses below, this is the unique function of the multivolume novel, wherein later details—including a major point of information—alter and close the book on this character.

17. Knausgaard, *My Struggle, Book Two*, 576.

(indeed, any woman!), "finally gets laid" (as Dubler would have it) by a woman named Vilde in a tent at a Roskilde music festival. The long road to this moment of triumph with Vilde is strewn with near misses and frustration brought on by Karl Ove's propensity for premature ejaculation. All the more telling is how Knausgaard sets up this conclusion—a long game deployed across the book. Specifically, whenever Karl Ove finds himself in a situation of escalating intimacy, Knausgaard expands time, amplifying the foreplay with incremental details, offering no mere play-by-play call but a florid and urgent disposition of the action at hand. Consider this passage, where Karl Ove hosts Irene in his apartment in Hafjord. We enter familiar territory as they sit together drinking and sharing awkward conversation:

> I put on a Chris Isaak record. I had worked all this out in advance, the muted, melancholic, yet slightly wild mood fit perfectly.
>
> She sat down on the sofa. I sat beside her, but not so close. She was wearing the same blouse she'd had on the first time she had been here. I couldn't see her full breasts underneath, but I sensed their presence as indeed I sensed her thighs under the tight blue jeans.[18]

Following more than two pages of chit-chat, Irene moves across the room where Karl Ove, at long last, makes his move: "I . . . gently wrapped my arms around her. It was as though she had been waiting because she immediately leaned back. I rested my cheek against hers and stroked her stomach, she turned to me, I kissed her." Knausgaard details incremental movement as Karl Ove's kisses move from neck to cheeks to "naked arm." Karl Ove suggests that they go to his bedroom where he climbs atop Irene and undresses her (if inelegantly so). Knausgaard details her breasts, Karl Ove's difficulty with her "trouser buttons," more details until right before the triumph of consummation: "Oh no, for Christ's sake, it can't be true, not now! Not now!" He has climaxed short of the starting gun.[19]

The several passages like this one contained in *Book Four* set up Karl Ove's ultimate success with Vilde in the tent at Roskilde (which ends the book). After four hundred pages of trying to "get laid," describing the sex can't be done. Again, Karl Ove details their foreplay. This time it works out. Barely so—"I was inside her and I managed to thrust twice before everything constricted and I held her tight." Twenty individual lines—each its own paragraph and most of them declarative—follow:

18. Knausgaard, *My Struggle, Book Five*, 344.
19. Knausgaard, *My Struggle, Book Five*, 346.

> Oh, it was brief, and it was embarrassing.
> She stroked my hair a few times.
> I lay on my back beside her.
> At least it had gone inside.
> That was the first time.
> I smiled.[20]

Description fails, yet it also becomes unnecessary. In the half page that remains they have sex "again, and then again" and again–including the notable final image of Karl Ove "pumping away" as Vilde, on all fours, vomits out the door of the tent.[21] The length of *Book Four* anticipates this moment and then can scarcely contain its erotic excess.

These narrative distinctions reflect something physiological, of course, marking the distinction between eros and its expenditure. But in these instances we recognize something else, too–the falling away of detail and lyrical cadence necessary to express eros. In some sense this should surprise no one. This is what writers do, after all. At the same time, it reflects Knausgaard's sleight of hand, his literary "feint" that obscures the extras and omissions to which readers are never privy without some critical effort. It also is worth noting that Karl Ove's hard-won sexual success changes something about our understanding of him as a protagonist. He is no longer the pathetic figure he has been made out to be all along. At the same time, the final image of him entering her as she vomits far exceeds a jocular cheer for one long deprived. There is something sinister in this detail that also casts our previous sympathies as problematic, at best.

Finally, consider the end of *Book Three*, the book that focuses almost exclusively on Karl Ove's childhood:

> After the moving van had left and we got into the car, Mom, Dad, and I, and we drove down the hill and over the bridge, it struck me with a huge sense of relief that I would never be returning, that everything I saw I was seeing for the final time. That the houses and the places that disappeared behind me were also disappearing out of my life, for good. Little did I know then that every detail of this landscape, and every single person living in it, would forever be lodged in my memory with a ring as true as perfect pitch.[22]

In this concluding observation Knausgaard beckons the reader out of Karl Ove's skin by affirming the long-term finality of his departure from Kris-

20. Knausgaard, *My Struggle, Book Five*, 484.
21. Knausgaard, *My Struggle, Book Five*, 485.
22. Knausgaard, *My Struggle, Book Three*, 464.

tiansand. At the same time, he casts the narrative experience–the eternal present that the phenomenon of reading the third book entails–as a function of retrospection, of "memory." The mode of engagement shifts. While closing the hermeneutic circle, Karl Ove acknowledges the extent to which the entire narrative has always been closed. The experience of reading has fabricated an illusion of presence that the phenomenon of the ending, in turn, exposes and reshapes.

Thus far we have established that Knausgaard's individual endings matter in the first five volumes (as it shall, of course, for *Book Six–The End*) for this very quality of drawing the reader out of the novel's spell. It ceases the immersive experience that Knausgaard crafts through the nexus of time and narrative and does so in a way that reframes what has come before. The novel ceases, it dies, and yet life goes on. At the core of these final shifts resides the opportunity for recognition or insight into the fabrication of this immersive experience. The illusion of reality that Knausgaard conjures, blending a reader's experience with what Karl Ove tells us (and, significantly, *does not* tell us) about his life, derives not from unmediated authorial openness, but stems from a sophisticated literary sensibility that distills emplotted, recognizable truths from fiction's fabrications. *My Struggle* becomes true (and all the more so) because it is fiction. While one may understand or presume this to be the case as a point of preliminary faith, the degree to which this maxim holds does not become fully evident until *Book Six* enacts its own sense of an ending.

THE END AS THE END

The End pulls a remarkable double duty, serving, in effect, as a double eschaton. In one sense the book qualifies as a discrete novel, containing, to wit, its own beginning, middle, and end. At the same time, *The End* represents the ending of *My Struggle*, the culmination of Knausgaard's broader system erected in the first five volumes and the closure of its hermeneutic circle.[23] Within these two primary senses of ending, however, we may locate a number of smaller moments that signal and enact such culmination. This immersive narrative, for instance, catches up to and enters itself, rendering a unique sense of self-authorship or even autoscription that appears to collapse the already compromised distinction between reader and nar-

23. One also might claim that, rather than beginning with the opening of *Book One*, *My Struggle* has its inception in the *end* of Knausgaard's second novel, *A Time for Everything*, where the voice of *My Struggle* and the narrator's contention with his father and brother emerge in their familiarity from that novel's "Coda." See Karl Ove Knausgaard, *A Time for Everything*, trans. James Anderson (Brooklyn, NY: Archipelago Books, 2009 [2004]), 453–99.

rative or narrator. It also offers the disclosure (or even the revelation) of a stunning accusation that alters how we understand the narrative that came before, shedding new light along the way on questions of *My Struggle*'s narrative genre, ranging, as it does, the borderlands of memoir and the novel. Finally, we witness the narrative voice's own resignation, invoking in the process a version of the death of the author (or of the narrative) while also reflecting the on-going-ness of life that endings emphasize outside of the narrative frame. In what follows we consider these curious senses of ending and how they contribute to *Book Six*'s double-eschaton as both a volume with an ending and an ending unto itself.

A distinctive component of *The End* resides in the particular way it breaks out of the temporal and narrative frame of the first five books. With a couple of exceptions (Karl Ove in the apartment he uses as an office in *Book Two*, for instance), *My Struggle* is almost entirely retrospective through the end of *Book Five*, when Karl Ove leaves Bergen. It tacks across timeframes, to be sure, but in spite of its characteristic sense of immersive immediacy, the narrative almost always concerns what *has* happened–not what *is* happening. Yet, from *The End*'s opening scenes, one becomes aware that *Book One* is on the horizon. While he is being photographed for his "forthcoming books," we also learn offhandedly that Karl Ove's uncle is upset and threatening to sue over the content of these books.[24] As he drives home, he gazes across the strait into Denmark and ponders the missing nightingales that Thomas has just described: "It was the perfect beginning for the novel I was going to write when *My Struggle* was finished."[25] *My Struggle* has come into range.

The anxieties surrounding the publication of *My Struggle–Book One*, certainly, but also the other volumes that are queuing up for release in the near future–occupy a significant place in *Book Six*. Karl Ove seeks name clearances, contacting people from his life whom the reader recognizes as characters featured in earlier installments of the novel. The texts gain readers and, as their popularity grows, Karl Ove suffers through publicity interviews for *My Struggle*. More distressingly, we witness the toll that this exposure takes on his family–particularly Linda, in whom it triggers a psychotic episode that renders her all the more exposed by its inclusion in *Book Six*. In this way she suffers, we might say, a double exposure. The risk of libel and Karl Ove's crippling anxiety cause him to fret over what Gunnar (whose name is not Gunnar, it turns out) will say about the depiction of his brother and parents, who are Karl Ove's father and grandparents. Through

24. Knausgaard, *My Struggle, Book Six*, 9, 17.
25. Knausgaard, *My Struggle, Book Six*, 18-19.

The End, *My Struggle* circles back upon itself. In this way it generates closure of the first hermeneutic circle (ranging from *Book One* to *Book Six*) while simultaneously enacting a new hermeneutic circle—the possibility of re-reading—that is informed by the emergence of the text from within itself.

Later in *Time and Narrative*, Ricoeur fleshes out his earlier conjunction of Augustinian time and Aristotelian emplotment through what he calls the "threefold mimesis." The threefold mimesis represents a hermeneutic circle that traces "a prefigured time that becomes a refigured time through the mediation of a configured time."[26] While one could say a great deal about this system, I want to dwell on the categories of configuration and refiguration. Configuration, for present purposes, represents the phenomenon of reading, of engaging with, a narrative. It remains ever in flux, mutable, evolving, susceptible to foreshadowing and obfuscation as well as literary conventions such as stock characters or peripeteia. As a narrative property, configuration remains open and evolving until the narrative ends. This ending inaugurates refiguration. Kermode's work on endings dwells within this instance of transition from configuration to refiguration. Closure codifies the narrative. Knowing how it ends, one can assess it in full as a closed text, opening it again in the process.

"That was how I left Bergen" represents one such transitional moment. Understanding it to alter what a reader has understood the narrative thread to be all along, it also forecloses further narrative possibilities (at least in the realm of configuration). The text is refigured by this closure, no longer in "the middest" of things (as Kermode puts it).[27] Recall the two football virtuosi discussed above. The configuration of the player struck down in or before her prime becomes refigured as tragic. The one who held on too long, whose diminished skills may grow painful to watch, may be refigured as pathetic. Only in retrospect can that refiguration take place. Furthermore, the experience of watching a magnificent goal scored by the one in or before her prime (and who later suffers a debilitating injury) proves to be a different experience when that narrative is closed than it is to witness this goal in the midst of things, while still being configured. The end ordinarily dictates (and even re-inscribes) what that experience means.

What proves fascinating in this context is that *The End* inaugurates the refiguration of *My Struggle* even as it continues to configure it. Consider this stunning reversal when the entire volume (and project) of the novel comes into view: Mired in acrimony with his Uncle Gunnar concerning the depiction of his father's alcoholic final days, his grandmother's dementia, and

26. Ricoeur, *Time and Narrative*, 50–51.
27. Kermode, *Sense of an Ending*, 8.

the implied lack of care that it casts upon Gunnar himself, Karl Ove begins to suspect a further reason why his uncle would not welcome the publicity. Surfacing from a discussion of *Hamlet*, Karl Ove asks himself: "What would I have done if my father died and I suspected someone of killing him? Would I have gone to the person I thought had killed him, who it turns out was my uncle, and avenge my father's death by killing him?"[28] This instance simultaneously represents both configuration and refiguration. It configures because it emplots the emerging and ongoing saga surrounding Karl Ove's father's death. This new wrinkle, cast recognizably in Hamlet's dilemma, builds toward the completion of what began, essentially, in the opening pages of *Book One*.

At the same time, this moment of peripeteia refigures as it configures. By entering its own narrative, the novel begins to alter that narrative even before it closes—even before the end of *The End.* The configuration of his struggle comes into view even as it deconstructs itself. Consider the climactic moment where he names his father, heretofore nameless. One would certainly be justified to understand this nameless antagonist to emerge from the ranks of other nameless characters who remained undenominated according to literary technique or convention. Instead, the reader learns that doing so was not a literary decision for Knausgaard, but a legal compromise intended to appease Gunnar. Karl Ove claims, "The story about him, Kai Åge Knausgaard, is the story about me, Karl Ove Knausgaard." Continuing, he owns up to no small measure of infidelity to historical accuracy, collapsing the generic distinction between fiction and memoir: "I have told [the story]. I have exaggerated, I have embellished, I have omitted, and there is a lot I haven't understood. But it isn't him I have described; it is my image of him. It is finished now."[29] It proves telling that such a confession, annihilating as it does the very pretense to "truth" that is alleged to characterize the broader project of *My Struggle*, is "finished" upon the recognition—the confession—of its artificiality. "What is art?" Knausgaard asks elsewhere. It is, among other things, the cultivated illusion of reality.

And, yet—despite this doubling of configuration and refiguration, this declaration of the end that deploys (at least in its English translation) the last words of Jesus on the cross ("It is finished," from John 19:30 [KJV])—*My Struggle* is, in fact, not finished. Indeed, *The End* continues for more than 110 pages—some ten percent of its running length. The novel's final paragraph offers a remarkable view of the mechanics involved in the shift orchestrated here as the end occurs, this transition from configuration to refiguration:

28. Knausgaard, *My Struggle, Book Six*, 829.
29. Knausgaard, *My Struggle, Book Six*, 1039.

"Now it is 7:07, and the novel is finally finished," Karl Ove says. We shift hard from the retrospective past into the narrative present, from past to present tense, as the novel—now "finished"—recedes into the past; into refiguration. Immediately he transitions to the future tense: "In two hours Linda will be coming here, I will hug her and tell her I've finished, and I will never do anything like this to her and our children again." He acknowledges an upcoming publicity interview and Linda's new book before announcing plans to return by train with her from Louisiana to Malmo, where they'll drive to their house: "[A]nd the whole way I will revel in, truly revel in, the thought that I am no longer a writer."[30] Here ends *My Struggle*.

The narrative "I" of *My Struggle* effectively resigns here. He (or it) is no longer (a writer)—though careful reading reveals that he merely commits to reveling in that thought, not to maintaining it. This final paragraph exists in a space both within and beyond the novel. More precisely put, this coda ends *My Struggle*, but it is not the only ending present on the page. Pushing above the hard break and even back onto the previous page, Karl Ove narrates a shift from the past to present tense that the "7:07" moment in the final paragraph later refigures through the tense shift it instigates from present to future: "I got up at four every morning and worked until the children had to be picked up, and I have been doing that until now, as I sit here writing this."[31] He turns next to Linda, moving her from past to present as well, and then into the future—shifting from "it resided in what she was" to "It resides in what she is," and from there to "I will never forgive myself for what I've exposed [Linda and the children] to, but I did it, and I will have to live with it."[32] These two endings, taking place across the break, mirror one another precisely as configuration. The first signals the conclusion of *The End*; the second closes *My Struggle* writ large. This double eschaton closes the hermeneutic circle, ceasing Karl Ove's configuration. A reader who arrives at this point can only ever encounter the narrative as a refigured one.

Significantly, and for this reason, the novels bear rereading. Endings may refigure narratives, but in doing so they also establish a new precondition for their configuration that builds on this new insight. The hermeneutic circle, when completed, permits the refigured text always to be configured anew, informed by prior knowledge and aiming toward refurbished ends from which they'll reconfigure again. This culmination of the narrative draws to its eschatological close, yet it inaugurates a new age, one refigured by the fullness of narrative time. And so: to these ends, in paraphrase of John the Revelator: Surely Karl Ove comes quickly.

30. Knausgaard, *My Struggle, Book Six*, 1152.
31. Knausgaard, *My Struggle, Book Six*, 1151–52.
32. Knausgaard, *My Struggle, Book Six*, 1152.

27 SEPTEMBER 2020 ZOOM

DUBLER: I've fallen in love . . . with Liane's first nugget [from our transcripts]. Where I'm chasing my tail and then Winni delivers the blow. I love this, so much.

BENDER: "There are all the other paragraphs!"

DUBLER: That could be a good first one?

BILES: Yeah, I love that line.

DUBLER: Yeah, that could go before your [nugget], Courtney, and you could put the *A Time for Everything*–this is again thinking about . . .

BENDER: . . . *Everything* can go elsewhere. I mean, think that some of our conversations–I agree–about *A Time for Everything* were really cool, and I don't know, but . . . That would be fine with me, to lead off with "there are all the other paragraphs . . ."

CARLSON: Yeah, I agree.

BENDER: Also, the "bad faith" there.

SULLIVAN: I don't think that was a blow, Josh. I think that was a realization that we were all in this fix.

CARLSON: But it is also a pretty great summary of everything that follows: "And then there are all the other paragraphs . . ."

[Laughter.]

BENDER: That could also be *the end* to our book. It's also like: we just gave you a hundred pages of this and we only talked about seven paragraphs.

CARLSON: That's totally true.

BILES: That could appear twice. I mean, we've got all the stuff about bookending and stuff. That *could* work as a line for both the beginning and the end that both closes and opens up at the same time.

CARLSON: True!

HARRISS: There's the hermeneutic circle.

BILES: Yeah . . ."and then there are all the other paragraphs" could appear on its own gray page at the very end again in the middle of a gray page that is otherwise blank, and that would be it.

THORSTENSEN: It could even be the title.

DUBLER: Although, hold it! But what about . . . or alternatively, including *this* statement, we could lead with this nugget, and then, the nugget that we're currently producing could go at the end.

BILES: That we're producing live, right now, as we speak?

DUBLER: Correct.

BILES: That's interesting. Especially inasmuch as that's kind of the gesture that Knausgaard makes.

BENDER: Volume Six!

DUBLER: Right? I think that would work really well.

HARRISS: So, should someone say, "We are no longer a collective?" Or something like that?

[Laughter.]

Outro

Hannah C. Garvey

When they talked Knausgaard, I listened.

In the winter of 2018, I was asked to serve as rapporteur and transcriptionist for what was then known to me only as a group of scholars who were reading books by a Norwegian author. Of the seven members, I knew two. That year, the publication of the final book of Knausgaard's *My Struggle* was delayed in the process of translation and as a result, the group was venturing into a different world–of seagulls and angels–in Knausgaard's *A Time for Everything*. The morning of their first meeting, I came prepared to scribe, but unclear on what I would be scribing. What exactly are they doing?

When they began to talk, I wrote, denoting their conversations over two days across hundreds of lines. At the conclusion of that 2018 meeting, I had a notebook filled with my contemporaneous capture of declarations, glosses of questions, and cues of the room's atmosphere. I also left with more than fifteen hours of raw audio recording, waiting to be transcribed.

Transcription is a curious process. We do not often speak in sentences we would write. But I could weave their threads together. I had been there. I knew what they were saying. And as I listened to them talk–again–I felt myself working to recreate what had happened in that room between them. I was in the act of recording the recording. Rendering into type what had happened: what they had said, what I had heard.

This was also a curious process because I said nothing. My voice was inconspicuously absent from the recordings. True, this is the role of a rapporteur: to listen, not talk. And writing that first transcript was a project in listening to them talk Knausgaard, for hours. Unfamiliar voices became familiar as I worked to relay their vocal personalities, crafting their spoken words into readable ones. When I finished that transcript, I remember pausing over what to title the document. Knausgaard Reading Group? Workshop? Collective?

What is happening here? What are they up to?

I was intrigued by them. Their commitment to reading, and to thinking, and to writing collectively felt good and even rare. When they met next in 2019 and in 2020, I again served as rapporteur, but these next two meetings felt different. Is it right to feel like I now knew them? I felt like I knew their voices, their cadences, their tics and themes. I found myself pausing more on the questions they were asking of the text and of themselves. Here is one example:

SULLIVAN: I worry about anything I say about this book would be so dumb . . .

BILES: I certainly share that anxiety.

DUBLER: Would be so dumb that . . . what?

SULLIVAN: That I would just be excruciatingly embarrassed.

BENDER: But as we said yesterday, he said all this dumb stuff . . .

SULLIVAN: . . . that was reassuring, you know!

BILES: . . . self-exposure, let it all hang out a bit. I think we should edit some of it but also show some of the . . .

SULLIVAN: We have made a safe space here.

BENDER: Yes, a safe space. Whenever I do one of these things I . . . Well, you think that our product as scholars is an edited volume as a representation of thinking. And I have always said that so much energy goes into that volume that other things that may have been possible are excluded: people exchanging ideas about how they write, or teach, or engage in other types of publics. I have always argued that there should be a product that we can talk about and describe and show but it does not necessarily have to be a document that is the encapsulation of something . . .

CARLSON: . . . people are like: *we don't want to read your anthology either!*

[Laughter.]

BENDER: Exactly! But this broader thing of what the product is . . .

SULLIVAN: It is us being changed.

BENDER: It is us being changed . . . and us changing the things that are out there . . . and that is all missionary and conversionary . . .

[Later.]

SULLIVAN: It would be good if whatever we make shows some of the ways in which we do *not* fit together, as well as the ways that we do.

DUBLER: I do not think that it is narcissistic to say that this group is interesting.

CARLSON: Do I not care about narcissism? Your interiority is your interiority . . .

SULLIVAN: I think that is the wrong reading of this book: narcissism.

CARLSON: Right, I just mean that all interiority is narcissistic.

BILES: There is narcissism and then there is narcissism.

DUBLER: Right. There is being a shitty parent because you are preoccupied about writing and there is being a shitty parent because you are preoccupied about writing about yourself. Those are all variations.

SULLIVAN: And there is being a shitty parent because everyone is a shitty parent . . .

BENDER: . . . I was thinking about why people do not read this [book] and sometimes it is because it comes across as narcissistic, or [a reviewer] says: well, I liked the rest of them, but this one, [*Book Six*], has too much of the religion and philosophy stuff . . . and then I think about the book itself, with a title that is super off-putting. The first thing it says is: "don't read this." Right? *My Struggle*. Or maybe it makes you curious? There are these ways that the book is so open, in the Bilesian openness, but also this apparatus of the closure around it that makes it so impenetrable. And the review world has a lot to do with that. It would be cool, if we could also, if we are talking about "the book" in any kind of way, if one of us could [write] on the way that . . .

SULLIVAN: . . . on it being misunderstood? Or misread as an object?

BENDER: Or even more than that—there is a certain performance that the book does that makes itself difficult to move into. And I think that that, and the reviews, are part and parcel of the book.

SULLIVAN: And I think that our decision to do this over four years has been really brilliant. I am glad that we did not decide to do it in one marathon week or something like that. It was so fortunate that we had the *A Time for Everything* hiatus—even though that was improvised. I feel like it has been a way for me to live with the books a little more.

DUBLER: There is something about religion there too, right?

SULLIVAN: Yes.

CARLSON: I think what has been nice for me about this . . . one of my favorite aspects of reading as a teenager was a sense of privacy—nobody reads the things that you read. And this feels like privacy in a group. There is solidarity, here . . .

[Quiet.]

SULLIVAN: There is something frivolous and self-indulgent about what we are doing.

DUBLER: More than anything else? Like AAR [American Academy of Religion]? [Laughter.] . . . but seriously. More than anything like that?

SULLIVAN: . . . We are having fun.

[Laughter.]

CARLSON: I think it is [the fun] and also, loving your object of study. That is a question–are you supposed to love your object of study? But also, I think it is bad for academics to have too much specialization–and that too much specialization makes you more inhuman.

DUBLER: Is that going to be your contribution? Writing that sentence?

[Laughter.]

CARLSON: This is the way the world ends . . .

[Laughter.]

There is intimacy here. And a negotiation of what that intimacy is exactly and where it is headed. I read tenuousness and uncertainty. Do they fit together? How? And how much of this should they show? I also read love, fun, and solidarity. The transcripts perform what I take to be fundamental curiosities of this collective: what does it mean to be a collective? To read collectively? And to write collectively? This is not your typical volume.

Bender, Biles, Carlson, Dubler, Harriss, Sullivan, and Thorstensen are, throughout the previous pages, talking to one another across and, quite literally, between their written prose. While Garvey is not in those above lines, nor anywhere in the three years and over three hundred pages of transcripts created, she was not absent. And as the introduction to this volume invites us to read and to write about Knausgaard and about religion, may this Outro also remind us to listen to ourselves and to each other.

And then there are all the other paragraphs . . .

Acknowledgments

This book came together over meetings across more than five years, during which time we were supported in countless ways by the institutions at which we worked, as well as by families, friends, and colleagues. We are particularly grateful for the generous support we received from the Department of Religion and the Institute for Religion, Culture and Public Life at Columbia University, as well as the Department of Religious Studies, the Center for Religion & the Human, and the College Arts and Humanities Institute at Indiana University Bloomington. At our first meetings, Kevin Witkow and Andrew McLaren served as exceedingly able rapporteurs. As we came to a conclusion, we were graciously hosted by Professor Sissel Undheim and the University of Bergen for a workshop on reading Karl Ove Knausgaard's *My Struggle*. We thank our editor, Kyle Wagner, and the anonymous reviewers at the University of Chicago Press for their encouragement and their critical engagement with our work.

Index

The Abyss (page numbers refer to this volume)

abjection/shame, 59-61, 88-97, 145, 148-50
angel(s), 30-31, 35, 105-23. *See also* seagulls
attention, 14, 40, 57-74, 130-33

Bible/biblical, 8, 9, 14, 30-31, 69-70, 79, 108-10, 159
blood, 28, 90, 120-21, 126
boundaries, 1-19, 33-34, 47, 139-55

childhood, 1-3, 30, 41, 47-48, 57-74, 83, 87, 112-21, 154-59
Christ, 12-14
Christian(ity), 2, 6, 27-28, 43-45
cleaning, 3-4, 15, 24, 62-70, 114, 171
cuts/gaps/openings, 96, 125-26, 133, 151-52

death, 1-5, 46-47, 52, 57, 105-7, 110-11, 117-22, 152-65, 173-80
details, 39, 61-71, 114, 127-65, 170, 175-76
divine/divinity, 5, 13, 30-31, 44-45, 90, 110, 152, 164-65
drinking/intoxication, 32, 64, 96, 171, 175

ecstasy/ecstatic, 7, 12-13, 164
end/ends/the end, 47, 52, 153, 161, 169-81
excess, 17-18, 32, 60-66, 117, 136, 143-44, 156-57, 161

face(s), 1-3, 57-59, 73, 120, 125-26
freedom, 4, 10-12, 66-67

Hamlet, 116, 118, 118n39, 120-23, 179-80
Hitler, 85, 89, 91, 93-94, 123

inadvertent, 10-12, 53, 65-66, 128, 133, 154-56

kitsch, 77-78, 84, 103

laughter, 19, 49, 112-13, 183-84, 186-88
longing/yearning, 12, 95, 108, 112, 117, 119, 122
love, 39-53, 72, 96, 99, 122-23, 174, 183, 188

mise en abyme, 3-5, 108, 114-23, 150, 158, 159-60, 167

outdoors, 12-13, 84, 154, 158

reading, 6-10, 15, 19, 77, 79, 97, 101, 108-10, 113, 123, 130-33, 142, 150, 152, 164, 167-68, 169-70, 177, 179, 181, 185-87

seagulls, 35, 111-19, 185
sex, 12-14, 86-87, 95-96, 135-38, 145-48, 158, 174-76
shit, 12-13, 62-70, 84, 145, 155-60, 158
sublime, 14, 70, 110, 152,
swarm, 10, 14, 77-99, 156, 160

tears/crying, 39-53, 60, 131

uncanny, 5-6, 16-17, 31-35, 107, 119-22, 145-52, 159

violence, 29-30, 60, 105

worlds, 6-7, 11, 13, 14, 18, 19, 22, 25-36, 43, 52, 56, 71, 80-99, 102, 105-23, 128-29, 132, 138, 157, 160-61, 164, 172, 185

writing, 5-19, 21, 31, 35, 39, 46, 53, 59, 84, 95-97, 108, 111-15, 120-23, 129, 132n5, 133, 152, 156-57, 165, 167, 169-81, 185-88

or

Life Is Simple (selected references; page numbers refer to Knausgaard's works. Abbreviations: MS I = *My Struggle, Book One*, MS II = *My Struggle, Book Two*, MS III = *My Struggle, Book Three*, MS IV = *My Struggle, Book Four*, MS V = *My Struggle, Book Five*, MS VI = *My Struggle, Book Six*, ATFE = *A Time for Everything*, Inadv. = *Inadvertent*, SML = *So Much Longing*, S = *Summer*)

abjection/shame, MS I, 27-28, 286, 335-36, 381-96; MS II, 38-39, 194-96, 245-46, 417, 435-37; MS III, 199-202, 407-10; MS IV, 251-58; MS V, 194, 261, 372, 403, 447-48, 561, 597-603, 610-24; MS VI, 54-55, 63, 111, 115, 170, 392, 448, 545, 756, 804, 921-22, 1019; ATFE, 479-99
angel(s), MS I, 220; MS II, 320, 436, 440-61; MS III, 235; MS V, 160-61, 622; MS VI, 46, 390, 409, 624; ATFE, 7-452; Inadv., 87. *See also* seagulls
attention, MS I, 351-53; MS II, 141; MS VI, 1052-54, 1086-89

Bible/biblical, MS I, 233; MS II, 336; MS III, 418; MS V, 160-61; MS VI, 433-34, 667-68, 679-97, 709-11, 855; ATFE, 40-334
blood, MS I, 408, 420-21; MS V, 359-62, 411, 518-19, 580; MS VI 682-85, 696-97, 702, 784-85, 1037; ATFE, 65-67, 118-19, 128-29
boundaries, MS I, 72, 162-64; MS III, 402; MS V, 107-8; MS VI, 834-35, 843; Inadv., 25; SML, 221

childhood, MS I, 7-184, 279-368; MS II, 21, 185, 394-95, 446, 500, 527; MS III, 12-14, 136-46, 247-48; MS IV, 159, 205-8, 253-54; MS V, 103-4, 115; MS VI, 1051-52
Christ, MS I, 13, 188-89; MS II, 439-41; MS V, 559; MS VI, 679-80; ATFE, 417-21
Christian(ity), MS I, 13, 155-57, 345; MS II, 96-100, 436-41, 458-64; MS III, 265-73; MS IV, 25-26, 71, 122, 203-25, 244-47; MS VI, 390, 560-63, 584, 604, 611, 622-25; ATFE, 25-27
cleaning, MS I, 54, 288, 300, 302, 306-7, 309-12, 339-40, 351-54, 361-65, 371-73; MS II, 257, 388-90; MS VI, 106-7, 165-73, 865-66, 936-37, 1151
cuts/gaps/openings, MS II, 194-96; MS V, 518-19; MS VI, 668-69; ATFE, 494-99; SML, 73, 116-19, 221

death, MS I, 7-13, 192-93, 222-24, 291-383, 425-30; MS II, 71, 99, 368, 376, 572-73; MS III, 25, 210-11, 295-96, 422; MS V, 184-85, 197-205, 394-95, 483, 590; MS VI, 9-1152; ATFE, 66-73; Inadv., 1
details, MS I, 33-35, 55; MS II, 542; MS IV, 121, 466; Inadv., 10
divine/divinity, MS I, 220, 233; MS II, 74, 98, 276; MS V, 604-7; ATFE, 34-35, 345-47, 413
drinking/intoxication, MS I, 28-29, 69-74, 114-40, 235-37, 372; MS II, 188-95, 250-65, 406-9, 485-88; MS IV, 35, 120-21, 251-58, 318-22, 403-8, 426, 450-51; MS V, 39-40, 89-94, 130-44, 210-11, 272-73, 355-56, 513-14, 590-99; MS VI, 929-31; ATFE, 83-85

ecstasy/ecstatic, MS II, 203; MS V, 227; MS VI, 451-52, 456-57, 463-64, 477-78, 633-44, 721, 802, 805
end/ends/the end, MS I, 430; MS II, 573; MS III, 345, 427; MS IV, 485; MS V, 624; MS VI, 9-1152
excess, MS I, 96-99; MS III, 327-29; MS VI, 637, 677-79, 682

face(s), MS I, 29-30, 187-89, 223; MS II, 165; MS V, 517-20; MS VI, 415, 684-87; ATFE, 69, 188-91, 496
freedom, MS I, 20-21, 100, 112, 163, 195, 205-6, 224, 281, 363; MS II, 231, 233, 362, 392-93, 417-18, 503; MS III, 280, 404-5; MS IV, 9, 84, 118, 251-52, 359-60, 408, 425-26; MS V, 214-16, 546-47, 567; MS VI, 20, 26, 203, 232, 248-50, 365, 490-91, 672, 884, 1053, 1141

Hamlet, MS II, 160; MS V, 199-200; MS VI, 20-22, 32, 372, 379, 419-23, 457, 828-30, 842, 1036-39; ATFE, 30
Hitler, MS II, 281, 481; MS VI, 479-634, 713-846

inadvertent, MS VI, 403; Inadv., 1-92

kitsch, ATFE, 421

laughter, MS I, 27, 30-31, 42, 202-3, 244-46, 393; MS VI, 17, 158-60, 875-76, 922, 1018
longing/yearning, MS I, 39, 158, 189, 218; MS II, 367-68, 460, 479; MS III, 49; MS IV, 9-10; MS VI, 633; ATFE, 413; Inadv., 18, 43-45, 57, 81; SML, 1-233
love, MS I, 39, 96, 150-69; MS II, 1-573; MS IV, 192, 424; MS VI, 883, 1005

mise en abyme, MS I, 351-53; MS V, 622; MS VI, 18-20, 177-83, 830-31, 853, 913-15, 957, 971-84, 1109-10; ATFE, 453-65; Inadv., 4

outdoors, MS I, 104-6, 405-6; MS III, 105-6, 280, 329; MS IV, 424; MS V, 198; MS VI, 946-48, 1107-9; ATFE, 305-7

reading, MS II, 96, 126, 267, 356-57, 421; MS III, 265-71, 391; MS V, 79-82; MS VI, 441-88

seagulls, MS I, 278, 309; MS II, 171-72, 233-34, 367, 383; MS III, 100, 400; MS IV, 476; MS V, 19, 622; MS VI, 362; ATFE, 453-66, 475; Inadv., 17, 87
sex, MS IV, 428-41; MS V, 191, 610; ATFE, 255-57; S, 45-47
shit, MS I, 307, 312; MS III, 104-6, 156; MS IV, 451; MS VI, 1055-56
sublime, MS I, 220; MS II, 405, 435, 565; MS III, 186, 282-82, 291, 426-27; MS IV, 115, 210, 304, 319-23; MS VI, 636, 665-66
swarm, MS VI, 465-66, 808-10, 834-35, 1006

tears/crying, MS I, 19, 224-25, 243-48, 285, 337, 346, 392, 399, 405, 422-23; MS II, 195-96, 239, 263-64, 315-16, 329-32, 335, 519; MS III, 40, 44-48, 109-10, 116-17, 125, 131-34, 147, 154-56, 183-85, 188-91, 214-17, 246, 273, 294, 295-96, 315, 321, 331, 336, 357, 361, 386-90, 397-98, 413-14, 419; MS IV, 142, 149, 159, 204, 239, 249-50, 256, 277, 296; MS V, 192-93, 243-44, 256, 272-73, 430, 476, 543-44, 586-87, 591, 593, 619; MS VI, 984, 989, 1150

uncanny, MS I, 385; MS III, 107-8; MS IV, 418-19; MS VI, 1072; ATFE, 7-499

violence, MS II, 239, 262; MS III, 184, 188-91, 252, 272-73, 300, 314, 423-24; MS IV, 116; MS VI, 821, 823-84, 840; ATFE, 128-30

worlds, MS I, 78, 176, 202-3, 216-22, 319-26, 352-53, 368-69, 428-29; MS II, 39, 53, 70-71, 94-100, 126-28, 135-40, 222-77, 384, 543-46; MS III, 87-96, 186-242, 280-82, 326-29; MS IV, 61-63, 120-21, 162-63, 226-27, 456; MS V, 118, 308-13, 380, 622; MS VI, 937, 959-60; ATFE, 345; SML, 161
writing, MS I, 39, 190-95, 218, 234, 422-23; MS II, 71-72, 320-21, 368, 543-45; MS IV, 18-36; MS V, 529-35, 622; MS VI, 181-83, 239-40, 758-59, 913-14, 975, 1152; ATFE, 446-47; Inadv., 1-92